young@heart
COMPUTING FOR SENIORS

Mary Furlong • **Stefan B. Lipson**

Osborne **McGraw-Hill**

Berkeley New York St. Louis San Francisco
Auckland Bogotá Hamburg London Madrid
Mexico City Milan Montreal New Delhi Panama City
Paris São Paulo Singapore Sydney
Tokyo Toronto

Osborne **McGraw-Hill**
2600 Tenth Street
Berkeley, California 94710
U.S.A.

For information on translations or book distributors outside the U.S.A., or to arrange bulk purchase discounts for sales promotions, premiums, or fundraisers, please contact Osborne McGraw-Hill at the above address.

Young@Heart: Computing for Seniors

1234567890 DOC 99876

ISBN 0-07-882178-9

Acquisitions Editor	Joanne Cuthbertson
Project Editor	Mark Karmendy
Proofreader	Stefany Otis
Director, Manufacturing and Production	Deborah Wilson
Interior Design	Emil Ihrig, VersaTech Associates
Page Composition	Sybil Ihrig, VersaTech Associates
Illustrator	Loretta Au
Cover Designer	California Design International

Photo Credits

Cover and Author Photographs: Bill Knowland, Direct Images
Cover photo models: Doris and Rhys Miller; Michael Furlong
Chapter Opening Photographs: Peter Hendricks /Emil Ihrig /MetaTools, Inc.
Text Photographs:

Advanced Gravis Computer Technology, Ltd. (Figure 8-14)
Chris Borton (Figures 8-4, -5)
Hewlett-Packard Co. (Figures 8-1, -2)
IBM (International Business Machines) (Illustrations 4-1, -2, -3)
Intel Corporation (Intel logo--Illustration 4-5)
Jr. Hansen Jr. Designs (DTP and graphics anatomy lessons)
Kidtech, Inc (Figure 8-17)
NEC Corporation/Advanced PC Design Center (Figure 4-1)
Quark, Inc. (Figure 10-5)
Specular International, Ltd.(Figure 15-12)
Wacom Technology Corporation (Figure 8-13)

Apple Computer, Inc. (Figure 8-15, Illustration 4-4)
Fractal Design Corporation (Figure 15-9)
MetaTools, Inc. (Figure 15-11)
Infogrip, Inc.(Figure 8-16)
Iomega Corporation (Figure 8-3)
Kensington Microware, Ltd. (Figure 8-12)
Mustek Inc.(Figures 8-10, -11)
Peter Gould (Figure 8-8)
Sony Elecronics, Inc. (Figure 8-7)
Supra Corporation (Figure 8-6)

As older people are demonstrating in great numbers that they can develop computer skills (in large measure because of Mary Furlong's work) and computers themselves become more user friendly, this timely book is a guide to a world of interactive enlightenment and usefulness. It certainly demolishes the myth about learning in later years.

—Hugh Downs
ABC News 20/20

As the new information technologies continue to have an increasing impact on our lives, any older adult who is not computer-literate will be prevented from enjoying the fullest participation in today's society. **young@heart** goes a long way toward resolving this inequity. The basic information about computers is all there—it is clear, written in understandable English and refreshingly free of the usual "technobabble." If you are an older adult and want to take a first, confident step toward computer literacy, there's no better place to start than **young@heart**.

—William D. Berkeley
President, Elderhostel

While hardware and software companies have focused on younger markets, Mary Furlong and SeniorNet have been making growing older in the computer age a rich and productive experience for thousands of seniors. For the increasing number of older adults who want to be part of the technology revolution, **young@heart** is a mature drivers' road map to the information superhighway.

—Gloria Cavanaugh
Executive Director,
American Society on Aging

If you think you are too old to be digital, you're just chicken. You'll love it. Try it. Get a kid to help you. Absent the kid, read this book.

—Nicholas Negroponte
MIT Media Lab
Author, *Being Digital*

About the Authors

Mary Furlong, Ed.D., is the founder and president of SeniorNet. She is the coauthor of *We Teach with Technology* and *Computers for Kids Over 60*. She is a professor of education at the University of San Francisco and holds a White House Appointment as a National Commissioner of Library and Information Science.

Stefan B. Lipson is an author, consultant, and software developer living in the San Francisco Bay Area. He has written for numerous magazines and has worked on multimedia projects for Apple Computer, The Fashion Institute Of Technology, and the Berklee College of Music. He holds a degree in electrical and computer engineering.

To my parents, Dan and Cele, who taught me about the values of learning and making ideas become reality.

To my family: my husband Fred, my children Dan and Mike (on cover), and my sister Diane. It is all of you who keep me young at heart.

To our SeniorNet community, members, volunteers, staff, and supporters; your ideas and experiences are reflected throughout this book.

And to Steve—my wonderful coauthor, thank you—you made it happen.

—Mary Furlong, February 1996

To Greta and Bill, my parents, who have taught me so much about computing by not knowing so much about computing—and who have taught me just about everything else.

To my wonderful wife, Jane, who delivered our beautiful new baby (in Chapter 10!) and whose support and patience delivered this book as well. And to our beautiful kids, Alexander and Madeleine.

To Mary Furlong, the SeniorNet staff, SeniorNet members, and the Learning Center participants and instructors: Thanks for opening my eyes to your wonderful and supportive community.

—Stefan B. Lipson, February 1996

CONTENTS

PART I

Learning the Lay of the Land 1

7   Be Prepared!-First Aid and Precautionary Tips **73**

8   Peripherals and Add-Ons: A Hardware Tour **83**

PART II

Applications   **115**

ACKNOWLEDGMENTS

Our names appear on the cover of this book but that never would have happened without the support, assistance, and guidance of a lot of people whose names couldn't fit on the cover! There are lots of people to thank in this book.

First, to the editorial staff at Osborne: special thanks to our friend and "relentless" acquisitions editor, Joanne Cuthbertson (the person responsible for introducing us!), whose support, perseverance, and unrelenting harassment(!), prevented numerous crashes and ensured the delivery of this book. It never could have happened without her. To Heidi Steele, our technical editor, who gently pointed out problems, both big and small; Mark Karmendy for making the unruly ruly and for mocking those of us with midwestern accents, Heidi Poulin for holding the reins with patience and good humor, and Anne Ellingsen and Kendal Andersen for marketing guidance. Special thanks to Sybil and Emil Ihrig at VersaTech Associates for their professionalism, tolerance, speed, and great design sense.

We would also like to thank the numerous vendors and their public relations firms for providing images, information, and support when we really needed it.

Thanks also to Lloyd Morrisett, President of The Markle Foundation and Edith Bjornson, Program Officer of The Markle Foundation, who has believed in the idea of seniors and computers and supported this mission over the years.

We also want to thank Kathryn Bates (Chapters 22 and 23), Junior Hansen Jr. (supplementary art), Jeffy Milstead (MacUser/ZD Labs), Alvin Henry (San Francisco Ballet), David S. Mash (Berklee College of Music), Ben Templin (ZiffNet/Mac), Keith Bupp, Anita Mascoli, and Nancy Werthan (Project X), Lynne Leaf and Christine

England (Writers Inc), Robin Merrin, Ken Malucelli, Mickey Stein, Victoria VonBiel, Jesse Greywolf, Michelle Moch, Joanne Reed, Randy Seward, and Ray Walker.

And finally, thanks to the entire SeniorNet gang, including Bradley Haas, Maureen Sullivan, Marcie Schwarz, and Lane Podell; the "Profiles"—Edward Chun, A. Langston Kerr, Greta Lipson, Hazel Phillips, and Nathan Zabarsky; and the thousands of SeniorNet members who have taught us how and why computers have enhanced their lives and provided us with the knowledge to write this book.

FOREWORD

Two major developments are occurring today which should have a connecting point: the aging of America, and the rapid growth of technology. A false assumption has been made that older people either do not have an interest in or cannot learn how to use computers. Nothing could be further from the truth. Given the opportunity and clear instruction, older people can easily learn how to use computers. In fact, according to a recent survey, seniors represent a significant and growing percentage of the computer savvy market.

For over a decade, Mary Furlong and her organization, SeniorNet, have been a driving force behind the movement to educate seniors in computer technology. Founded as a small research project in San Francisco in 1983, SeniorNet has 19,000 members and 78 Learning Centers nationwide. At the Learning Centers, seniors learn computer basics and become connected in the vast online community. Over the years, over 60,000 people have participated in SeniorNet classes.

As the product of these years of experience, **young@heart** may well be the key breakthrough for many older persons who are interested in computers but who do not speak the jargon nor know where to go for help. Clearly written in a "user friendly" manner, this book is a handy reference tool that anyone can use. It will be an asset to those who attend computer classes as well as to those who prefer to learn from a book. For novices, it provides a background in hardware and software basics, an overview of the core applications, and an introduction to the online world. For more experienced users, it offers insights into online resources and more sophisticated technologies.

Welcome to the world of computing.

—Horace Deets
Executive Director
American Association of Retired Persons

INTRODUCTION

It's amazing. With over 34 million Americans age 55 and over—many of whom are very interested in computing—you'd think someone would have recognized the need for a computer book directed at seniors sooner. Maybe computing is too hard for older adults...

Not a chance.

In fact, older adults have proven consistently to be excellent computer students. Older adults are more focused, more patient, and more motivated than many young adults. The addition of life experience, maturity, and perspective give older adults a real edge. The truth is, you don't have to be an Einstein to learn about computers—you don't even need a high school education. You just need to jump in—with this book.

Learning about computers should be an enjoyable experience, not a painful one. This book is intended as a gentle guide for older adults who want to learn about computer technology. The information here is based on SeniorNet's experience in helping over 65,000 older adults learn about computing—without clenched fists and gritted teeth.

This book is written based on the understanding that *you* are the source of inspiration and creativity, not the computer. A computer is just a new electronic tool, no more capable of creating a great work of art, literature, or music than a paper and pencil. Anyone who sits down with paper and pencil can create something unique; a letter—a poem, a story, a joke, a note, a song—but it is the person, not the tool, that guides the process. As such, a computer represents your digital quill. The more you bring to it—a rich life experience, an artistic bent, writing skills, cooking skills, fresh ideas—the more you'll find the computer can do for you.

How the Book Is Organized

Even if you already have a computer, every chapter of this book offers enough information to keep things interesting for you. Here's how the book is organized:

Part I addresses the basics of computing with a focus on your particular needs and clarifying what options are available to you. Basic terminology and concepts are addressed; advice and tips on shopping for computer gear are included, plus a look at setting things up. After Part I, you'll be comfortable gathering additional information and discussing the technology with others.

Part II guides you through many of the software options available. It provides a look at how software can transform your computer and what you can make your computer do for you. Word processing, personal finance, art and music, and many more subjects are covered. Part II also includes a number of User Profiles describing some of the remarkable things individuals—like yourself—can do with a computer.

Finally, Part III looks at "getting connected." You'll learn how to use your computer to communicate with others around the globe. You'll also learn how to access new worlds via your computer and modem. We explore everything from setting up your computer for online communications to exploring the very much talked about World Wide Web.

Staying On Top

This isn't the biggest book in town and that's intentional. We wanted to provide something unintimidating and easy to use. There are thousands of computer books available that address particular subjects, products, and issues and you'll probably want to find some on topics that hold the most interest for you. In the meantime, this book will provide you with a strong introduction to the world of computing—from a senior point of view.

Enjoy!

Learning the Lay of the Land

Getting Oriented:
You Are Here

o, you want to learn about computers.

There are many different kinds of people who want to learn about computers. Which personality type(s) describe you?

I'm pretty "with it." I'm pretty "with it" and I feel the need to stay with it. Computers are affecting everyone (and everything) and I want to know how, too. Every day, the newspapers are filled with articles on new computer breakthroughs, computers for medical rehabilitation, software for reading to the blind, and satellite communications networks. I like keeping current and computers are certainly that.

I'm an active person. I'm not sure how, but I know that if I could put a tool this powerful to use, I'd be able to accomplish even more of the things on my To Do list.

I'm a curious person. Intellectual pursuits and explorations are a great pleasure for me and computing represents a whole new vista. In the world of computers, examination and discovery are the order of the day. This is just the thing to really get my juices flowing.

I'm a working person. I work in an office, and they put a computer on my desk. With little or no training they expect me to jump right in. I want to learn about computers. They aren't about to go away.

I'm stubborn as a mule! There's no way this thing is going to get the better of me! I'm going to learn this thing; no box of electronic parts is going to make me look bad!

3

I'm a family person. I could share a lot more with my family if I learned a little about computers. My kids and grandkids have been working with computers for some time and they are always involved in all sorts of projects. My own kids are using them in their work. The grandkids are playing games and creating reports for school that are out of this world—graphics, sound, animation—the works! Besides, the kids are all over the country and I want to be in touch with them.

I'm loved! My daughter decided to "turn me on" to computing. She graduated to a better computer and insisted on setting up her old computer right in my den. Now I *have* to learn it.

I'm a social person and I like feeling connected. I love meeting new people, making new friends, and sharing with my community. Computing is a wonderful hobby and an excellent way to meet and communicate with people. And everyone I know, from my old college roommate to my teenage grandson, uses e-mail and the Internet. Getting online and getting connected with my peers is a really exciting prospect.

Where Do You Want to Be?

Computers are tools that can help you achieve goals you wouldn't have thought possible. Here are just a few:

- I want to publish a newsletter for our volunteer organization.
- I want to study Japanese.
- I want to write my family history.
- I love photography but I can't afford a darkroom. A computer lets me alter images in much the same way, but without the chemicals.
- I want to make a "collage" for our 50th wedding anniversary.
- My beautiful granddaughter has been diagnosed with diabetes. I want to know more.
- I want to play the stock market and place trades from home.
- I want 24-hour access to the news.
- I loved traveling. I wish I could chat in a cafe on the Left Bank again.
- I want to pay my bills electronically from home.
- I'm going through a difficult period and would like to communicate with others who understand and can sympathize with my situation. I lost my spouse recently and wake up at night with no one to talk to.
- I would like to learn how to play the synthesizer.
- I want to build a congregation database for my synagogue.
- I want to take classes in a variety of subjects—from experts in the field.
- I'm an artist and would like to start a greeting card business.

How to Get There

How can you learn about computers? Start right here. This book assumes that you don't know anything about computers, but that you want to learn. To start you off on the right foot, this chapter introduces you to a basic computer system and only the most basic terminology. It's enough to get you to the next step without overloading you. The material presented is based on conversations with over 50,000 older adults over the last decade.

In some ways, learning computing is like studying a foreign language; there are a lot of things you could do with a language if you knew how to speak it, but you must first learn the basics. Here are some basic concepts and the words associated with them.

What's Hardware?

Hardware is any physical piece of equipment associated with your computer system.

The computer keyboard that you type on is hardware, and so is the monitor that displays what you've typed. The box that you think of as the computer is hardware, and that box contains more hardware, including the CPU or *central processing unit* (the equivalent of the computer's brain). The box also contains a hard drive, a storage area that's sort of like an empty library in which you can electronically fill the shelves. Figure 1–1 shows some of the

hardware that you find with just about any computer system.

The Hardware Basics

Regardless of what kind of computer you have or will get, it will include certain basic components, as shown in Figure 1-1.

Here's a very brief look at and explanation of those components.

Monitor The monitor (sometimes called a display, or *crt* for cathode ray tube) is your window into what the computer is doing. The monitor allows you to view information—pictures, files, musical scores, or what-

Figure 1–1
A basic computer system with a keyboard, monitor, and mouse

ever you type. It also shows messages that the computer may provide regarding its progress in performing some task for you.

Keyboard   A keyboard is the standard way of entering information into your computer. Although the layout of the keyboard is identical to a typewriter, the "action" or "touch" is quite different; on a typewriter, you actually force a mechanical action. A computer requires a less forceful touch since the mechanical action is replaced with an electronic one.

Mouse   The mouse is the computer version of a pointer; when you move the mouse on your desktop, you are moving a corresponding arrow that appears on your computer screen. When the arrow is pointing at something you want to turn on, turn off, or select, you click a button on the mouse to make that change.

Computer   The computer contains all the components that allow the silicon to work its magic. This includes RAM (random access memory)—the area in the computer that "holds" the things you are working on right now, and the CPU (central processing unit)—the brain of your computer.

Floppy disk drive   The floppy disk drive works much like a tape recorder: a diskette is inserted that contains stored information (recording tape also contains stored information). The drive, like a tape recorder, is designed to play the floppy, that is, give

you access to that information. You can also record your own information on a floppy diskette.

Hard disk drive   The hard disk drive or *hard drive* is a super high capacity version of a floppy diskette; it is the storage basement for all of the information, pictures, files, and documents that you create and save. Also, when you install software on your computer, the software is copied onto the hard drive.

CD-ROM drive   CD-ROMS are built into virtually all machines now. A CD-ROM is like a floppy diskette on steroids. One CD-ROM can hold as much information as about 450 floppy diskettes! CD-ROMs are different from hard drives and floppy diskettes in that you can't store your own information on them.

Do They All Look Like This?

Don't be deceived. Two personal computers (PCs) with identical features can look very different: The computer in Figure 1–2 offers the exact same features as the one in Figure 1–1, but some components are built in and others are attached.

What Are Peripherals?

A *peripheral* is any sort of hardware that you can attach to a computer. Your keyboard, your mouse, and your printer are all considered peripherals. There's a multitude of peripherals that let you do lots of things. A scanner for example, is a peripheral that works sort of like a copying machine, but instead of making a paper copy, it "scans" the picture and stores a copy electronically so that you can view it on the computer screen or use the picture in other ways. Modems (pronounced "mode-emz") are used to send and receive information across long distances. You'll be amazed at the special hardware that you'll see attached to a computer: stereo speakers, video cameras, musical instruments, and computerized sewing machines(!), just to name a few. A computer system with several peripherals is shown in Figure 1–3.

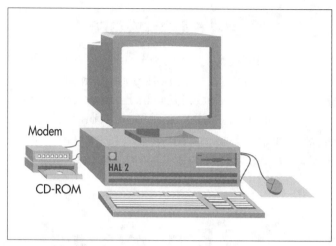

Figure 1–2

Don't be fooled: This computer does the same stuff as the one in Figure 1-1

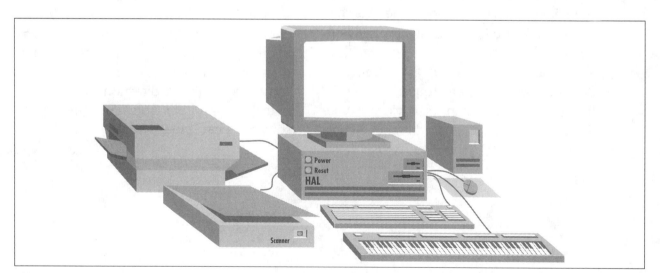

Figure 1–3

A computer system with bells, whistles, and fuzzy dice

What's Software?

Technically, software is a list of (prewritten) instructions that gives your computer some specific capabilities. In English, software is something that transforms your computer into the kind of tool you need. A software *program* or *application* is actually a long list of such instructions.

How Hardware and Software Work Together

You may want to think of a computer as Charlie McCarthy, the ventriloquist dummy of Edgar Bergen. Computers, like that dummy, don't have a brain or a personality of their own. But when someone gets their hands on the dummy, the dummy suddenly inherits the intellect of that person. If an accountant were to pick up the dummy, the dummy could answer questions about finance and give financial advice. If your doctor were to pick up the dummy, it could answer questions about your arthritis or related malady.

Well, the computer is the dummy and it is software that gives the dummy personality. If you want the computer to help with your finances, you load an accounting program, software that imbues the abilities of accounting on the computer—with your guidance. To transform the computer into a formidable chess opponent, you load a chess program (or application). Suddenly the computer is acting like Bobby Fischer—without the eccentricities.

It's true, a computer is a lot more complex than Charlie Bergen's dummy; there's a lot of impressive stuff going on inside the box—it takes a lot of engineers to design a computer—but like a car, you only need to worry about the physical parts of the car when your gas gauge reads empty or when something breaks and needs repair. With a computer, you don't even have to worry about gas. But like the ventriloquist dummy, computer hardware requires someone to give it direction. In the computer's case, that's software. And in the software's case, that's you.

What You Need
for Your Journey

One of the first things to do *before* jumping into the computer game is sit down and figure out your needs. It sounds logical, and on the surface it seems like an easy thing to do. After all, you normally make a shopping list of the things you need and want before you go to the market, right?

Determining What You Need

Actually, it's a lot trickier than it sounds. The grocery list is easy; you always make a shopping list before going to the market, but you have been going to the market for groceries for most of your life. You know what kind of foods you like and what you don't like—what fruit gives you trouble and what vegetables you like in your salad; buying coffee isn't an adventure, it's just restocking the supply of something you've been drinking for years.

Computers, on the other hand, aren't food. They're new and pretty alien. And constantly changing. New computers (and related gizmos) appear virtually every day and the possibilities and potential only seem to expand. That doesn't sound much like food at the supermarket!

If you want to get the computer that's right for you, you have to assess needs that you probably haven't assessed before. Salespeople, friends, and total strangers may offer advice on what computer gear to buy—without bothering to find out what your needs really are. Their recommendations may at times correspond to an expensive array of items that you never knew you needed, and perhaps never will.

Express Yourself

You can be anything you want to be and you can use your computer to help achieve your goals. There's no reason why, as a retired physician, for example, you should not be a poet or a playwright. As a finance-wise housewife and mother, perhaps you'd like to computerize accounting chores and study the ways of Wall Street. Do you enjoy fine art? Painting? Carefully consider the things you would like to do with your computer and then look into the software that you'll need to pursue your goals. (Part II of this book provides an extensive look at all different kinds of software.)

Your individual needs and personal goals will bring your computer needs into focus and largely define what kind of computer you should get. For example, the software program that you saw at a community center and you really want to use, may only run on one type of computer. Or maybe you plan on drawing and painting a lot of pictures with the computer, in which case you'll probably need lots of hard drive space to create and save your work. Everybody's needs are different, but if you spend the time and focus on your needs up front, you'll get the right tools for your foray into the computing world. When you are properly equipped, that foray will be as exciting as it is gratifying.

Are You Currently Using a Computer?

If you are currently using a computer, perhaps at work or for a volunteer organization, there are two very important things to consider before deciding on a machine for your home or home office.

If you get a machine similar to the one at your job, you will be able to take work or projects back and forth between home and office. Or, if you have relatives out of state who have a similar machine, you'll be able to share more easily with them. This is "compatibility"—two machines that are similar enough so that you can perform the same tasks on either machine interchangeably without glitches. What is especially appealing about this is that you can complete some tasks or assignments at home *instead* of at work.

Note: **Talk to your employer first about doing computer-related projects at home. Some employers are not so forward-thinking and may frown on the idea of working "off-site."**

If you are using a machine at work, you have probably gotten comfortable with it. Switching to another kind of machine or different software may mean that you have to relearn a lot of things that you already know on one system. On the other hand, don't let familiarity of one system stop you from moving to another that you think is better suited to your needs.

Software: The Driving Force

Remember, in Chapter 1, we mentioned that a computer is useless without software? Software really is the driving force behind what you need to buy. Even if you already have a computer, you have to think about and evaluate what software you want and need to use. If you don't have a computer yet, your software needs will largely determine which computer you buy.

Once you decide, for example, that you need a program for writing letters and stories, you should research all of the programs that perform that task. That will require a more detailed look at what you need and expect from a particular program (we'll delve deeper into that in Part II of the book to make your research easier). Again, any deci-

sions you reach should be based on your personal needs and preferences. Some people like Tony Bennett and others like Mel Tormé—you need to decide what you prefer.

Requirements: Be Sure to Read the Label

Once you have decided on what software best suits your needs, find out what computers the software will work on and what the software requires. Every program includes a requirements listing on the outside of the package (if you can't find it, ask a friend or find a sales person in the computer store to find it for you). Figure 2–1 shows a typical requirements list from a software product.

There is a trick to reading requirements. First, the list typically includes both hardware and software requirements (you may need certain software to run other software). Second, there are actually two different lists here:

1. minimum requirements, and
2. recommended requirements

You should try to meet the recommended configuration. Normally, your computer also has requirements in order to run, so starting that new program makes even greater demands on your system.

Although the software may work with the minimum requirements, it won't work well. For example, if you have the minimum RAM installed, a program may have to disable some features in order to work,

System Requirements:
Microsoft Windows 3.1 or higher
100% IBM compatible 386 or better (486 recommended)
VGA or higher graphics adaptor and monitor
4Mb RAM (8Mb recommended)
12Mb hard disk space (21Mb for full install)
CD-ROM Drive (3x speed or faster recommended)

Figure 2–1

No ifs, ands, or buts: if you don't have the minimum requirements listed on a program, the program won't work

or it may run painfully slow as it tries to accommodate its memory shortage.

Alert: **To run a program effectively, be sure to have at least the recommended requirements, not the minimum requirements, as specified on the outside of the software package.**

Special Needs

Your computer is a very personal thing. If you have any special needs, begin exploring them early. There are all sorts of simple add-ons like filters to reduce screen glare, keyboards for one-handed typing, and special monitors and additional hardware to accomodate the visually impaired. There are also options for those with limited motor control and programs that can read text files to you.

These special requirements can fill books and are not typically listed or reviewed in magazines. For a more thorough picture of what's available, call the Alliance for Technology Access (1-800-455-7970).

Making You and Your Computer Comfortable

Regardless of the kind of computer you get, make sure that you take space and physical needs into consideration. How much room you have may be a determining factor on what you wind up buying. You should probably know a computer's "footprint"—its dimensions—and how much space it takes up so you'll know what to expect before you bring it home. It's also critical to keep

your computing experience a positive one; you don't want to associate computing with a neck ache or the tired eyes you get from staring at a monitor that's too close.

Comfort Is #1

It's a good idea to leave yourself some extra room when calculating how much space you'll need. Aside from space for your computer and room for your mouse to move on the desktop, you'll invariably need to read or write something while working at your computer. There's nothing worse than trying to read or write something when you don't have room to put it down. If you want to save some desk space, there is a type of computer called a "mini-tower" that is designed to sit under your desk. The monitor and keyboard still sit on your desk, of course, but you get a little extra room up top. If you really want to go the deluxe route, you can get a computer desk. These include such classy extras as a retractable keyboard shelf, which slides in and out of the desk. Figures 2–2 and 2–3 show some layouts; one neat and allowing access, the other too messy and unproductive.

Tip: **Go to a few different computer stores and "test drive" a few machines. Which keyboard feels better? Which mouse? Find the ones that are the best fit and work from there.**

Outlets and Ventilation

You will have at least two power cords looking for wall outlets, so be sure you have outlets nearby.

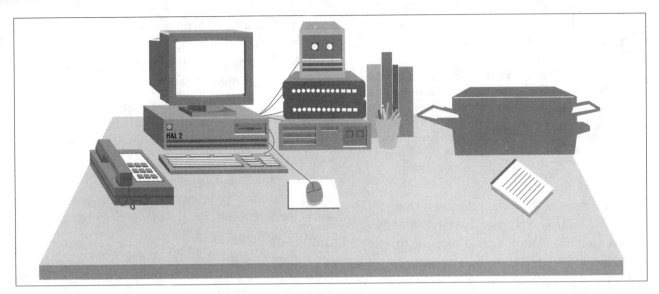

Figure 2–2

Components are stacked to save room

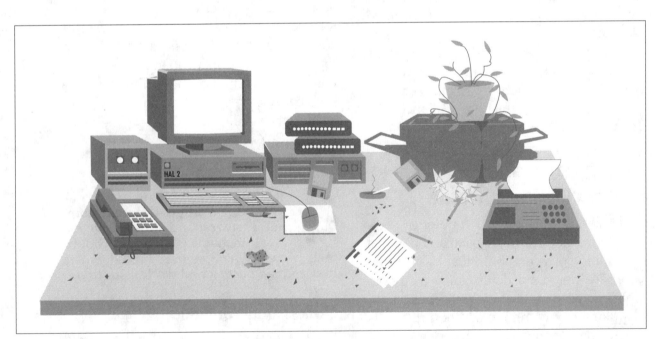

Figure 2–3

Workspace is too cluttered for productive work

Note: **All computers and monitors, and many peripherals, have three-prong plugs which don't fit the common two-prong outlets (see below). If you have two-prong wall outlets, you'll need a few three-prong adapters. You can get them for about a buck each at Radio Shack or any other electronics store.**

You should plan from the start to *telecommute*—use a modem—in which case you are going to need access to a phone jack. If you can't set up near a phone line, you can always run the telephone equivalent of an extension cord from your computer to the phone jack.

If possible, you should put the computer in a well-ventilated area. Both monitors and computers give off a lot of heat. Depending on the size of your room and how well ventilated it is, the heat increase can make things downright uncomfortable.

Not only can the heat get uncomfortable for you, the computer can also have problems. If you have no ventilation and you turn on your machine on a hot summer day, the machine can behave very erratically. Typically, this problem will last until the machine can cool down.

As tempting as it may be, try to avoid setting up near open windows. It's always nice to be near a window, but it may cause a couple of problems. First, you'll most likely have glare problems as the sun reflects off of your monitor at different times of day. Second, computers are very sensitive to dust, and being near an open window could pose a problem over the long haul.

Caution: **Another reason not to put the computer by a window: you may not want that glowing screen to be too obvious to folks looking in your window from the street. People know that a computer can be expensive and you may not want to tempt someone.**

Will Others Use Your Machine?

There are people who you may want to share your machine with; a spouse, friend, or family member may be Lewis to your Clark in this computer adventure. If that is the case, you should think of how their needs could be taken into account. Would you like to make the machine friendly and kid-proof for grandchildren? Should you get a CD-ROM for educational products that they might want to use (you'll use them, too). Talk to your potential PC partner and find out more specifically what they would like the opportunity to do with the computer.

Must It Be Easy to Use?

Ten years ago, ease of use wasn't an issue because nothing was easy. Now, everyone sells computers and software that are "easy to use." The truth is that most everything is a lot easier to use than it used to be. The rest of the story? Some computers are easier to use than others and likewise, some software programs are easier to use than others. The Macintosh, for example, has always had the well-deserved reputation for being easy to use. Microsoft Windows 95 is a lot easier to use than its predecessor, Windows 3.1. Some software is difficult to learn—it has a "steep learning curve" and mastery requires diligence and hard work. Through all of this, you must decide how important "ease of use" is to you and whether you find one computer or software program to be easier for you.

Working Within a Budget

For most people, a budget ceiling dictates how much computer you can get. New computers cost anywhere from about $800 for a basic machine (complete) to about $7,000 for a power user's dream machine. You may want the most powerful machine out there and you may need several sophisticated options, but it may be out of reach financially. Realistically, expect a new system to cost about $2,000.

Striking a Balance

Your best bet is to prioritize all of the things you really want in a system and start cutting from the bottom. Several options—modems, printers, CD-ROMS—can always be added later. If your first priority is to telecommute, then get the modem and sacrifice something else for now. Remember, purchasing a computer is much like purchasing a

home; you can always add on, refurbish, and update as time and money allow.

Think honestly about what you plan to do with your computer. Write down all your requirements and needs. Don't underestimate what you need and don't overestimate, either. And if you expect your computer to help you earn money, be sure to figure that into the equation as well.

The Needs You Didn't Know You Had

When you do all the math, decide what to buy, and get your machine, you will probably discover what many people discover: ways to use the computer you didn't anticipate. Did you get the wrong machine? Should you have gotten the more expensive, faster model?

You did good. If you got a machine and you are working on it enough to see what you want to improve, you have succeeded. And if you got a machine and it does exactly what you wanted and expected it to, you've also succeeded. Congratulations!

> ### Golden Rule:
>
> Don't make yourself crazy over your decisions. Once you have a computer, don't dwell on whether it was the right choice. Use it, enjoy it, and discover with it.

CHAPTER
3

?

Asking for
Directions

It's obvious Mr. Wilde never had to buy a computer. If he did, he wouldn't have been so quick to pass on good advice.

Learning about computers is a lot like dancing: you can't learn if you don't try and you won't get better if you aren't willing to step on a few toes. Great dancers (and computer users) don't hesitate about a few missteps; those missteps are the keys to grace and mastery.

Information and Advice: Where to Get It and Who to Take It from

The easiest way to learn about computers is to listen to what other computer users have to say about their experiences. How do the experts stay experts? By keeping in touch with other computer mavens and giving each other the skinny on what's hot and what's not. There are a lot of good places for you to get information and advice (described in this chapter) and you'll find your time spent researching to be rewarding and invaluable. Some sources will prove more fruitful than others, and a lot of what you get out of any particular source will depend on your style. But all of them, in some combination, will help you get a handle on your computer experience.

When Opinions Differ

If you are shopping for a computer, peripheral, or some type of upgrade, you should get as much information as you can before making your purchase. A good way to ensure the right choice is to get the opinions of others as part of your investigative process. Will some of those opinions be contradictory? Can experts disagree? Sure, but that's to be expected. It doesn't mean that anybody is wrong, it just means that different people come to the table with different experiences and therefore reach different conclusions. You, in turn, may disagree with some of the advice that comes your way, but advice will be helpful at least in getting you to think about things you may not have otherwise considered.

Tip: **Keep a journal or notebook so you can write down and save those important nuggets of information that you gather on your fact-finding missions. Wake up in the middle of the night with an important computer question? Hear a term on the radio that you don't know? Just write it down in your journal/notebook. When you get the answer, write that down too! In a short time, your journal will become an invaluable reference for you.**

Certainly one of the most confounding aspects of computing is the technology's incredible rate of change. Every day, it seems, there is a new breakthrough, a new leap in the technology, that offers us even more computing power and in turn makes last week's technology seem obsolete. With the landscape changing so quickly, it's important to stay abreast of the new technology so that you can better understand and satisfy your needs. Whether you are new to the field, own a computer, are buying a new one, upgrading, or just trying to learn more, staying current is a challenging and important facet of computing. Here are your best potential sources of advice and information.

Friends and Family

If you have a friend or family member who owns a computer, talk to him or her. Friends and family can be a great resource; they know your likes and dislikes, your strengths and weaknesses. Friends and family understandably have a better sense of *your* needs than a salesman in a computer store. Computer savvy friends and family can also be honest and objective when you are having trouble drawing the line ("No, Murray, you don't need computers in the study *and* in the bathroom...yet"). Besides, talking to a friend or relative is a lot easier than talking to a salesperson.

It's best if you can go and visit with your friends so you can get a guided tour of their computer systems. Ask them to show you what they have, what they do with it, and ask them to point out any special stuff they think is of particular interest. Again, don't be embarrassed to ask questions about anything and everything: "What's the black box with the blinking lights?" "Why is the monitor so [big, small]?" "Where is the sound coming from?"

And don't be afraid to interrupt. Computer users are an enthusiastic lot and if an explanation goes right by you, or your friends use mysterious terminology—or you need clarification—don't hesitate to interrupt.

No matter who you are going to talk to, though, be sure to prepare a list of questions beforehand so you can get the most out of your discussion. (A brief list of questions follows this section). You can expect the answers to your questions to generate even more questions. When you think of other questions, jot them down (keep them in your notebook) and get them answered whenever it's convenient. Here's a list of some questions to get you started:

- What do you like best about your computer?
- What do you like least about your computer?
- Is there a computer that you would rather have? Why?
- What do you feel that you needed but didn't get with your computer?
- What software do you use? Did you choose it? Was it included?
- How do you get help when you need it?
- What books or other resources have been the most helpful?
- What store(s) do you frequent? Why? Are the sales people well informed?
- Are the salespeople patient? Is the store really well stocked?
- What is that box on your desk with the flashing lights? What does it do?

The key here is to take advantage of your friend/family members' computer experience: Ask your compatriots what and how they have learned about computing.

Hearing their likes and dislikes, and praises and gripes, will help to illuminate your way. Hearing about their mistakes can prevent you from making (potentially costly) errors. Hearing of their successes will help you stay on the right track in buying and using the system that meets your needs.

Again, working with a person who knows you is a real blessing. They know your quirks and foibles. Friends and relatives can give you tips and point you toward things that a salesperson couldn't know would be useful to you and wouldn't bother to ask. A quick example: most people are right-handed and most computers—including demonstration computers in computer stores—are set up for right-handed people! No right-handed person is going to ask if that's a problem for you—you need to let people know of your left-leaning orientation. In the case of friends and relatives, they already know, but the salesperson does not.

The Computer Store

Many times, a salesperson in a computer store can be very helpful and you may find sales people more likely to help you in a smaller store. Many of these folks are computer hobbyists themselves and will have very definite ideas of what gear is good and bad. You may, however, be disappointed if you try to get help in one of the big computer superstores; these stores can be more interested in selling you whatever they have in stock or the products that give them the largest profit or commission, not in helping you make the right decisions.

Kids

You'll be amazed at how much kids know and how helpful they can be. If there are kids who you come in contact with—delivery boys, the kid down in B5, babysitters, the kids next door or across the street, your grandchildren—don't hesitate to ask them what they know about computers. Computers are so much a part of growing up these days that computing has become second nature for a lot of kids, and many of them have access to computers in their libraries and schools, both public and private. There's no typical computer kid and there's no telling what they may be good at. They may be whiz-bang programmers, or they may be hardware wonders, or they may just be good at playing games. Whatever their particular strengths may be, they are an ideal resource.

 Tip: **If you are near a junior high or high school, call and see if there's a computer club. See if you can get advice from the teacher sponsoring the club or if he/she could recommend a student who could act as a resource for you.**

No doubt many kids won't be able to help you, but for the ones that do know their stuff, they can be a great resource. Having an older person ask them for help can be an opportunity for them to really show off, get your approval, and gain respect (not to mention getting to know you!).

 Tip: **When talking to people about computers, be sure to take regular breaks—at least ten minutes on the hour—so that you can stay fresh, alert, and responsive. It's not easy to listen to someone talk about computers for long periods of time, so don't set unreasonable expectations for yourself.**

Caution: **Beware of that friend who doesn't have a computer (and never had a computer) but volunteers to act as counsel in your every buying decision. If your friend is citing an unknown "expert" ("My boy, Irving, knows everything and he says you should buy a Gribnitz 5000!"), then talk to his source. Advice is cheap enough and you aren't saving anything by getting it secondhand.**

Golden Rule:

Don't be embarrassed to ask questions or to ask for clarification. The simplest questions typically prompt surprisingly complex and enriching answers.

User Groups

User groups are computer clubs that hold regular meetings to commune with computer technology. Characteristically, user groups are nonprofit organizations that are funded by memberships. User group meetings provide a wonderful forum for computer users. User groups typically have weekly or monthly meetings where members and

For the Mac-Minded Only
BMUG: A User Group Success Story

The Berkeley Macintosh Users Group is one of the largest, if not *the* largest, Macintosh-based user group in the world. BMUG (pronounced Bee-mug) was founded in 1984. Over the years, the ranks of BMUG have swelled, with more than 15,000 members in over 60 countries. Weekly meetings are held every Thursday on the University of California campus in Berkeley, California, and without fail they attract a couple hundred people, at least. Each week BMUG hosts a different guest speaker/demonstrator and they have had an impressive roster of speakers including Bill Gates (the richest man in the world and founder of Microsoft Corp.) and Steve Jobs, the cofounder of Apple Computer. You can count on standing room only when a celebrity with the stature of Bill Gates or Steve Jobs is scheduled to speak. BMUG also offers a free help line to its members—personal help on your Macintosh questions—by fax, phone, or in person.

BMUG's twice-yearly, 500-page, professionally bound "newsletter" is really more of an encyclopedia or almanac. Jammed with information—and no advertisements—it is a great sourcebook for tips, tricks, reviews, and advice for Macophiles. It even includes recommendations for coffee shops in Berkeley! BMUG also has a library of public domain software—free programs and software—that is nonpareil. You can get diskettes loaded with fonts, programs, and très cool stuff for $4.00 a diskette. BMUG also has a catalog of all of their available diskettes.

So, what's a typical meeting like? Meetings start with a question-and-answer session that's about as egalitarian as you can get: the questions range from the most basic to the most advanced and all are answered so that the person asking understands the answer. This typically lasts for about 45 minutes to an hour, longer depending on the number of questions on the given day.

After the Q&A session, BMUG will then host a demonstration or product announcement where a company representative demonstrates their company's latest wares. It's all very informal (product demonstrators and company representatives are warned: "don't wear a tie!") and the informality makes it very conducive to learning. If you're more comfortable wearing a tie, by all means feel free. BMUG wants their ranks to feel at ease.

Typically, the meetings end with more discussion about the products being demonstrated, and finally, the moment that everybody anxiously awaits: the product raffle—the presenting company will bring along one or more copies of their product and raffle them off. At BMUG, you don't even have to be a member to win in the raffle! Some of the products that are raffled off would run you a few hundred dollars in a computer store and the price of a raffle ticket—free for attending—can't be beat.

For more information, you can reach BMUG at

1442A Walnut Street #62
Berkeley, California 94709
Voice: 510-549-BMUG
FAX: 510-849-9026

nonmembers alike can learn about the latest and greatest news regarding a particular type of computer and how to use it.

User groups' nonprofit status allows them to maintain a level of objectivity and neutrality, which is your insurance that they aren't trying to sell you something or pull something over on you—they are simply fellow computing fans who take pride in sharing information. User group members are happy to share with you their joys, trials, and tribulations of computing. It's not about greed: user groups are run by volunteers and they are always in need of more volunteers, if you're ever interested.

Extra Special Bonus: User groups do not require membership to attend meetings, so you can walk in off the street and get some really good information. Membership does have its privileges, however. Typically, user groups will have a newsletter and will offer discounts to members on hardware and software. User groups often make deals with a company to sell a product to members at a special discount rate. A user group can organize many people to buy a product as a group and so command a much better price from the supplier.

Tip: **Even if you don't live within striking distance of a large user group, you may want to join one of the big user groups (in addition to your local group), just to take advantage of some of the services the larger group has to offer. For example, newsletters, free software, and discounts are often superior with a bigger user group.**

User group meetings always include a question-and-answer period, which inevitably sheds light somewhere you haven't examined. Following are some typical questions you might hear—or ask—at a meeting:

- I need to get my laser printer fixed. Does anybody know someone who is good and cheap?

- I need to connect a second monitor to my computer. Does anyone know how?

- I've been coin collecting for over 40 years. Is there some software that can help me keep track of what I have?

- My grandson shoved a credit card into my floppy drive and I can't get it out. Can I fix this thing?

- I was mistreated at Acme Computer. Can you tell me a different local store that's good?

If a user group is big enough and/or members show enough interest and the inclination in a particular subject area, they will set up a splinter group called a "SIG" (rhymes with "big"; it's an acronym for "special interest group") that focuses on that specific subtopic. For example, many of the large user groups have graphics, desktop publishing, multimedia, and music or sound SIGS, among others. These groups meet separately and may have just a fraction of the attendance of the regular meetings (and the frequency they meet might be less as well). But if you have a special interest in a topic, check with the user group and find out if they have an associated SIG.

To find a user group that meets near you, contact your local computer store. You might also try the Computing Science Department of your local university or community college, or the computer teacher at the local high school. If that doesn't work,

call the Association of PC User Groups at 914-876-6678 (for IBM compatibles) or The User Group Connection at 1-800-538-9696 (for Mac users). These numbers will refer you to a group in your area code or zip code. (The catch for PC users is that they can only refer you to user groups with memberships over 150.) Although you may not get the most convenient one, you can then call that user group to get the status on a more local user group.

Online Services

Online services are computer networks that you call into with a modem. They provide you with a myriad of services and options. Online services are a great source of information and there are always people online willing to help answer your questions. It may take a little time to learn your way around, but an online service lets you be in constant communication with people all around the world. Not only can you learn all about computers, but you can learn about virtually any and every subject. One of the most popular (and recurring) items that you'll find on the Internet, for instance, are the FAQs (pronounced "fax") or frequently asked questions. Here, you'll find just what the name indicates: the most commonly asked questions that people keep coming back to. Instead of constantly re-answering them, someone sets up a list of questions and answers that you can refer to at any time.

Online services are covered in depth in Part III of this book, but you should know that they can be used to find a great wealth of information.

Classes

Many times, computer stores, community colleges, universities, college extension centers, and others will offer courses in various aspects of computing. These courses vary in quality and you'll find some are more suited to your needs than others. On the up side, a community college or university may offer intensive classes that will provide an enormous amount of information. On the downside, you may be faced with classroom overpopulation and information overload. Don't forget: these classes may be relatively expensive, so be sure the course is offering what you want—at the pace you expect. There's nothing more frustrating than watching an instructor blaze forward without answering important questions that you have.

Caution: **Computer classes may purport to teach you a lot, but the devil is in the details: beware of a class that meets once a week for marathon sessions—4 or so hours. This is way too long to sit in a classroom and it's way too much information for even Robby the Robot to digest!**

SeniorNet Learning Centers

A shameless plug? In this book?! OK, it's a shameless plug, but for a very good *non-profit* resource that may best satisfy many of your computer education needs.

SeniorNet learning centers offer very inexpensive courses in many areas of computer technology, from buying a computer to using desktop publishing programs for creating newsletters to managing your finances. You don't need to know anything to take these courses and you don't even need a computer, making this an ideal way of getting your feet wet. You'll learn a lot in the process.

A class at a SeniorNet Learning Center may meet once a week for two hours (with a break) over a six-week stretch. For a member (fees vary depending on the center), courses are typically $15.00(!). The classrooms are small and each class typically includes at least one coach, a roaming instructor who answers individual questions and otherwise ensures that everybody is following along. For more information on SeniorNet Learning Centers and additional services they provide, see Chapter 23 or call 415-352-1210 for the center nearest you.

Help from the Manufacturer

Computer manufacturers and software publishers can (and do) provide a lot of information about their products, but if you don't own their products, they will typically refer you to your local computer store. There are a number of ways to get information from the manufacturer of a product. If you do own their product, you can expect support and information in the following ways.

Documentation/Promotional Materials

Documentation is the fancy word for all of the literature that a company sends you when you buy their product, including the manual. For many years, documentation and user manuals have gotten a bum rap for being incomplete, vague, and incomprehensible.

Things have definitely changed for the better. Vendors now appreciate that all the bells and whistles in a program or piece of hardware don't count if you can't figure out how to find them or use them. The computers makers have learned from past mistakes and so products and procedures are easier to follow and, generally speaking, better documented.

You can depend on getting a few different kinds of literature with your hardware or software. Typically, you can expect a reference guide that describes all the procedures and options in pretty straightforward language. The reference guide normally consists of dry explanations of a product or program's features along with procedures. A tutorial is often included to provide instruction and step-by-step guidance on the basics. Tutorials are more informal, often chatty, and written with examples that you can install on your computer, as "walk throughs," interactive tutorials that show you exactly how to get results or to successfully complete a task. Finally, the product may include a user guide, a sort of hybrid between a tutorial and a reference. The user guide is not as complete as a reference—it doesn't show you how everything works—but it is more substantial than the tutorial. User guides are also typically easier to read than reference guides.

If you haven't had a chance to browse a software manual, try to borrow one or two from the library or a friend.

Online Help

To make products even easier to use, help information is available online, but not in the "network" sense. Online here means that help screens are built right into the software and can be accessed at any time. That means that when you run into trouble, there is a place on the screen where you can click to get available information. Some programs, you'll discover, have great online help. More often than not, it's the same information that's in the manual with the big exception that you have instantaneous access to it when and where you need it. Once you start using online help, you'll rely on it more and more and the manuals less and less.

Phone Support/Technical Support

If you are having a specific problem with a product, you can call the vendor's "tech support" line. Ideally, you call a toll-free number (1-800) with a question and they provide you with a quick answer. That's in an ideal world. Free telephone support has proven too costly for many companies and not as many provide it anymore.

More than likely, when you buy a product, you'll get free phone support for 30 days or so. Some companies are more accommodating, while some have elaborate plans that cost you money. You may be required to dial a toll call or 900 number (they charge you by the minute). Some companies offer a "support contract," an insurance policy whereby they provide you with additional phone support for a set fee.

 Tip: **Be prepared before you call for technical support. When you call, be sure to be sitting at your computer with the program rarin' to go. The tech support person will ask you lots of questions first, like registration number, type of computer, and how much memory you have. Be prepared to answer these questions—and more—and then be ready to walk through the problem precisely. If your problem results in a message on screen, write down the message exactly and tell them about it.**

Caution: **Some companies may offer tech support but you may have to pay for a toll call. Even if the company has an 800 number, you can get put in a long line of calls, like circling the airport in a holding pattern. A simple "yes or no" question may require 30 minutes of "holding" to get answered.**

Magazines, Newsletters, and More

To judge from the incredible array of magazines, journals, and newsletters that are available, the written word has never been healthier. Even newspapers are getting into the act with lots of articles on computer technologies and Ann Landers-like advice columns for computer users. Each of these different media offer different kinds of information, but you should definitely explore all of them and take advantage of those that best suit your needs.

Books

Nowadays, computer books have become a big business, with publishers offering books on virtually every subject and geared for readers at virtually every level of expertise. For example, there are enormous 1,200-page tomes that tell you everything there is to tell about a product—and then some. These books typically sell for over $30.00 and sometimes include a CD-ROM or floppy diskette. There are computer dictionaries that are useful so you can look up all the weird terms that you hear being bandied about. You'll probably want one of these. They cost anywhere from $10.00 to $35.00. To get familiar with a particular program, you may be best served with books from a "Made Easy" type series. These are introductory books that appeal to the novice user.

Most of the chain stores, B. Dalton and Barnes and Noble, for example, sell the best selling computer book titles. The superstores will have a much better selection than the regular mall-type stores. Depending on the bookstore, you may be overwhelmed by the number of books available. Regardless of how many books are stocked, though, bookstores usually only carry a fraction of the books that are available, so if you don't see something that suits your fancy, don't spend your money.

If you see a book that you like, but it focuses on the wrong product—DOS for Poets instead Windows for Poets, for example—ask a salesperson if such a book exists. If you'd like to see the full range of books offered by a particular publisher, contact the publisher and request their current catalog.

Golden Rule:

Regardless of what book you get, don't judge it by its cover: look at what's inside and make sure it's appropriate for you before you buy. Another way to determine if the book is for you: look in the index for a topic or procedure that you know. Read through that section and if the explanation is unclear or ambiguous, move on to a different book.

Magazines

With the exception of an online service, magazines can provide you with the most up-to-date information available. Unlike books, a magazine appears every month (or however often they are published). Software publishers and computer companies advertise like crazy and they are anxious to see information on their products appear in the magazine. Magazines are usually quite focused, and the title usually tells you what they are all about: *PC Week*, *PC Magazine*, and *PC Computing* are all for IBM com-

patible users; *MacWorld*, *MacUser*, and *Mac Home Journal* are for Macintosh enthusiasts. *UnixWorld* (don't ask!) *NewMedia*, *PCLife*, *NetGuide*, *PC Novice*—the list seems endless. The newsstand cost of these magazines ranges ordinarily from about $4.00 to $9.00 for more esoteric titles. However you cut it, the newsstand price makes it prohibitive to buy more than a few of them. You can always read the more popular ones at your local library.

Magazines are a great resource. They typically contain a blend of product reviews, a few columns by pundits who are sniping at somebody or other, and oftentimes a *Consumer Reports*-like lab report on say, printers or modems. The lab reports are often too dense for a novice to cut through, but they always provide buying recommendations based on their tests.

If you like the style of a magazine and they seem to target a lot of your interests, you should probably subscribe. Subscriptions save you about 50 percent or more off of the newsstand price and it's easy to find deals.

One magazine has been getting a lot of attention lately: *Wired*. *Wired* is a magazine that breaks most of the rules of publishing. The format is difficult to read, many of the graphics are arresting, and the layout is at times disorienting. It can be a challenge to read, but with interviews with politicians and cyberspace movers and shakers, you should definitely take a look at it.

Time? US News and World Report? These are interesting to read, but not as sources for your computer needs. Granted, they do have articles on computing (and an occasional "special supplement"), but you do better with the specialists.

Tip: **Get the best deal on a computer magazine subscription: go to the newsstand, leaf through the pages and a "blow-in" card offering a subscription at a greatly reduced rate will fall out. These promotional cards are designed to fall out when you open the magazine, so don't worry. The publisher will be happy to see the card come back and the bookstore owner will be happy to have one less card on the floor.**

The latest trend for magazines is to provide a free diskette or CD-ROM with the magazine. The good side? Obviously you get to test drive some product or you get some shareware. The bad side is that since the magazine comes in a sealed plastic bag, you can't browse the magazine to see if it has what you are interested in.

Sorting It Out

All in all, there's no shortage of information on computer hardware software, and related products. You'll find sources that you like, other that you don't, but everything helps in the learning process. Once you've gathered all of the information, you'll need to sit down and evaluate what you need. From there, you will better understand how to pick a machine, as discussed in Chapter 4.

Getting the Right Machine

What's the ideal computer? There isn't one that's ideal for everybody. If you are looking for a new machine or you want to upgrade the one you have, you are faced with a dizzying array of options. Even if you already have a computer, this chapter will guide you through the maze.

Types of Computers

Although you'll see and hear lots of brand names, there are two types of personal computers; an IBM-compatible (also called a PC) and an Apple Macintosh-compatible (usually just called a "Mac"). The word "compatible" means that a machine works just like the original and can run all of the same software; a PC-compatible works like the original PCs and a Mac-compatible works like an original Mac.

Isn't the Mac a PC? True, PC stands for "personal computer" and the Mac is a personal computer, but when IBM introduced their computer way back when, they called it the IBM PC—PC was actually the name of the product. The name stuck. Now, people refer to IBM compatibles as "PC compatibles" or "PCs," and the Macintosh, which has a different design, is not compatible with the IBM design. To make things more confusing than they already are (!) the current line of Macintosh computers are called "PowerMacs."

Are PCs and Macs really that different? Well, yes. Because they are designed differently, they typically can't share hardware or software. An easy way to think of it is that a PC speaks French and a

Cutting Corners: How Not to Save Money

One itty bitty clone company that offered clones for a couple of hundred dollars cheaper than the big manufacturers sent a computer to a customer. When it arrived, from the sound of it, something was loose inside the computer. Upon opening the chassis (something you probably don't want to do), everything inside the computer was found to be broken and loose. It seems that the hard drive—a brick-like component—was not screwed in place and so it bounced around within the computer, tearing wires out and breaking parts within the computer. The computer was shipped back immediately—the customer had charged it to a credit card and canceled the charge the same day. Instead of saving the couple hundred dollars, that same computer user ordered a machine from one of the big clone makers. Now he's happy. :-)

Mac speaks Spanish. The French machines can communicate with other French machines and the Spanish machines can all speak with other Spanish machines, but a language barrier prevents a French machine from talking with a Spanish machine.

IBM compatibles and Macintosh compatibles are as American as apple pie—they just see one another as foreign. And there are also a lot more PCs than there are Macs—about ten PCs for every Macintosh computer.

There have also been some very big differences between the two kinds of machines in terms of how easy they are to use—the Mac has always had a reputation for being the easier machine—but those differences have been dwindling over the years as the competing companies borrow and build on one another's ideas. The differences erode further as all of the manufacturers get a better sense of what computer users can really use.

PC Clones and Name Brands

Granted, there are two types of computers, PCs and Macs, but there seems to be an overwhelming number of brand names. What are they? What's going on here?

They are "clones." Clones are computers built to work and behave exactly as the IBM model. Is a clone as good as the real thing? Sometimes a clone is even better. A clone manufacturer may see a flaw in the original IBM PC-based or Mac-based design or think of a clever addition and include that.

Are these "clone" companies trustworthy? The big name clone companies certainly are. You can find many of the big name clone makers advertised in popular computer magazines such as *PC Magazine* and *PC World Magazine*. Many of these manufacturers sell through retail chains and computer stores. Although you can find clone makers who are less than reliable, the name brands have built their success on delivering good products and have reputations at stake. Here is a list of some of the best known PC compatible manufacturers:

AST	Compaq
Dell	Gateway
Hewlett Packard	IBM
Packard Bell	Tandy
Zeos	

Note: **If you are looking for Macintosh compatibles, check out Power Computing, of Austin, Texas, (1-800-370-7693) and Mac Warehouse (1-800-255-6227). Outside of these two, you won't find many—if any—clones in stores. Macintosh clones are a new phenomenon and, excepting those two companies, they are usually custom-tailored machines aimed at the professional user.**

Different Computer Designs

Every personal computer uses the same basic technology; they all include a CPU (central processing unit), a floppy disk drive, a hard drive, RAM, a monitor, a keyboard, and a mouse. Given these ingredients, a computer can still come in many different shapes and sizes. Following is a look at the basic models and what they each have to offer.

PCs and Macs at Home, But Who Are the "Other Guys?"

You won't find them at the computer store, but you read about them in the newspaper, and perhaps you see their associated company stock trading quite high. They are the computers not intended for the home or for the general public. When Macs and PCs don't cut the mustard, these computers are used. Sometimes called "workstations" or less frequently "minicomputers," they are typically more expensive and can execute a particular task especially well. They are used largely for engineering and scientific purposes, although they usually make the news when they are used for creating special effects in movies like *Jurassic Park*.

Sun Microsystems, Silicon Graphics, IBM, and DEC (Digital Equipment Corporation) are a few of the biggest manufacturers. These machines can start at about $5,000 and reach upwards of $100,000. There are also *mainframes*, enormous computers (by today's standards) that service numerous users. Mainframes are used primarily by large corporations and universities.

Stay-at-Home Computers

Stay-at-home computers are computers that are designed for stationary use: you set them up on your desk in one location and you don't move them around. There are two basic designs for these, the mini tower and the desktop.

Mini Tower

The mini tower is physically the biggest model. This is typically designed to sit under your desk on the floor (in the space next to your legs), although you can put it on top of your desk. A big advantage of the minitower design is that it is very expandable—it's built to accommodate all sorts of add-ons. There are lots of expansion slots—special plugs inside for attaching stuff (we'll talk about some of the things you can add to your computer in Chapter 8).

The disadvantages? First, this is the biggest box and takes up the most space. Second, if you set this up on the floor, you'll have to get behind the machine to take care of all of the cabling (if you have

someone else's good, strong, young back to do this, this doesn't matter!). Third, if you put this on the floor, then the on/off switch will sit about a foot off of the floor, so even if you are sitting, you're going to have to reach for it. You will also have to make the same reach to put a floppy diskette into the drive. Your own back and general limberness are the determinants in how important this is.

Desktop Models

Desktop machines are smaller than the mini towers. They are designed to sit on your desk and they double as a platform for your monitor. The super thin models are sometimes called "pizza boxes" because they are so thin—especially compared to how thick computers used to be. They are not always as expandable as a mini tower, but realistically you probably won't be expanding your system *that* much.

Portable Computers

If you don't want to be deskbound, there is a class of computer available just for you. Small, lightweight, and battery-powered, portable computers can be just as powerful as their desktop counterparts, offering you the opportunity to work anywhere you wish.

Laptops and Notebooks

Laptop and notebook computers are portable computers. They are so named because they are lightweight and small enough that you can keep one on your lap and work comfortably with it. When introduced, notebooks were slightly smaller than laptops, but the distinction between them has faded. Nowadays, these little powerhouses can have as much muscle as a desktop machine—weighing in around six pounds or less. The big advantage with these is found in their flexibility: you can work virtually anywhere, anytime.

Note: **Don't forget that if you are carrying around the laptop, you will need to travel with the battery recharger or a power supply. These things can weigh a few pounds themselves, so be prepared.**

Laptops and notebooks are great for the person on the go, or for the person who wants the option of working at the kitchen table one morning instead of being tethered to a big machine that must sit in one room. For most folks, these are very much business machines: a business person can get a lot done even when he or she is on the road. If you do a lot of traveling and you don't want to be away from your computer, these are great. But laptops and notebooks are not typically "first" machines; you usually graduate to one of these if and when the need arises.

Laptops and notebooks also have their own vocabulary associated with them—PCMCIA, dual scan, backlit passive matrix, and active matrix. Because these run on rechargeable batteries, you'll also hear the names of a variety of different battery types.

There are also some disadvantages associated with these machines. For one thing, portables are comparatively more expensive than desktop computers: you pay for that miniaturization. Like any computer, they are upgradeable, but even the upgrades are more expensive than those for a desktop machine. For some upgrades, the parts are not standard and you may have to buy from the original manufacturer at a higher price.

You'll also have to compromise on comfort. Laptop keyboards are much smaller (they call them chiclet keyboards, named after the little Chiclets gum because of the shape and size of the keys) and that can be irksome. They are too small for many hands, so your hands may wind up scrunched up to compensate for having fingers that don't quite fit on the keys. And although the displays on these are greatly improved from the old days, you have to pay a premium for the best displays and there's a lot of variance.

> **Note:** There is a special piece of gear called a *docking station* that lets you use a laptop as both a portable and a desktop computer. A docking station is like a desktop chassis or frame that you slip the laptop into. On top of the chassis, you have an additional monitor—plus all the hookups for your printer, etc. In this way, you only have one machine that you can use at home and away.

Palmtops and PDAs

Chester Gould, the creator of "Dick Tracy," predicted these sorts of devices with Dick Tracy's wrist radio. Palmtops and PDAs, short for personal digital assistants, are used more as personal organizers or super duper communicators. Costing $200 and up, you are paying for the portability factor here since these are small enough and lightweight enough that you can carry one in your shirt pocket. You can carry and update your personal schedule, phone numbers, and all that jazz. As communicators, some of these devices can fax information and even receive typed messages sent by computer users. But they aren't computers as you think of them. Unless you are really on the go and you like to tinker with technology, though, these aren't for you—yet. These are typically purchased as supplementary machines, not in lieu of desktop computers.

Speed!

Regardless of the type of machine you get—PC compatible, Mac, desktop, or laptop—one of the biggest considerations is speed: how fast can the machine process information? Speed is synonymous with power and everybody needs it and wants it. Why do you need so much?

Because we want computers to do a lot for us, the more we expect, the more power we need. In addition, even tasks that seem simple for a human to perform may demand a lot from the computer. For example, it's easy for a person to rotate a picture and look at it from a different angle. For a computer, rotating a picture onscreen requires millions of calculations. To perform these ever expanding lists of tasks, computers need to be fast—and can always be faster.

The speed of a computer is measured with "benchmarks," tests that can provide a numerical measure of how fast a computer or a component of a computer can do something. Everybody likes to point to

Hardware, Software—Wash&ware?

Mini towers, palmtops, laptops; computer companies spend a fortune trying to come up with the Next Big Thing. In one project at NEC Corporation's Advanced PC Design Center, designers were inspired to create a series of wearable computers—a suggestion of what a computer of the future might be. Shown in Figure 4–1, the [not really washable] wearables are unobtrusive and could be worn over your clothing. Would you be interested in wearing one of these?

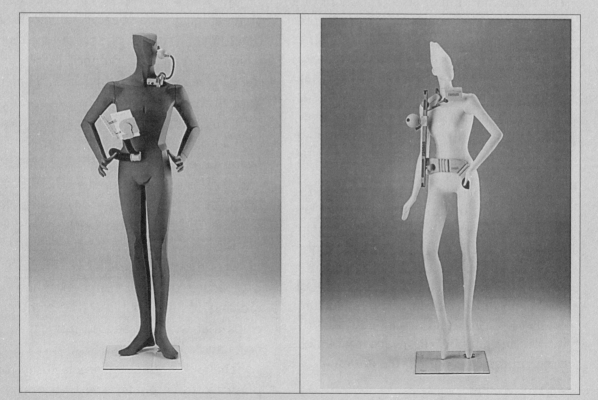

Figure 4–1

Wearable computers—A glimpse into the future from NEC Corporation's Advanced PC Design Center

these statistics and say how benchmarks prove that their machine is the best.

Nearly all of the major components of a computer affect its (and your) speed, so let's take a look at how those parts are rated and why some machines are faster than others. (For more on the speed of individual parts and peripherals, see the following and Chapter 8.)

Getting a Big, Fast Brain

The single most important component of a computer is the computer's central processing unit or CPU. The CPU (sometimes called the microprocessor or just processor) is a chip that does most of the mathematical processing or "number crunching." New generations of CPUs come out every couple of years and each successive generation at least doubles the capabilities of the previous generation.

IBM-compatible computers use the 80386, 80486, and top of the line Pentium processors (the numbered chips are pronounced as, for example, "eighty three eighty six," or just "386;" Pentium is pronounced pen-tee-um, with an accent on the "pen"). Intel is the largest manufacturer of these CPUs, and when you see the words "Intel Inside" it means that Intel's microprocessor is used in the computer.

Motorola is the manufacturer of the central processors used in Macintosh computers. These CPUs are the 68030 (pronounced sixty eight oh thirty or just oh thirty); the 68040; and the current and most powerful, the Power PC series.

Note: **The CPU is the slang for describing a computer type: "she's got a 486 machine" or "he just got a Pentium machine."**

But wait a minute. Not all Pentiums are created equal: The speed of a chip is also determined by its "clock speed," the rate at which information is pumped in or out of the CPU. Clock speed is measured in megahertz (millions of cycles). The clock speed is very important in determining how fast— and how expensive—a CPU can be. The faster the clock speed, the faster the CPU, and the faster the computer. Besides new chips being released, existing chips are often reintroduced with higher clock speeds.

Table 4–1 is a chart to give you an idea of what's currently available. For a little perspective on how fast things are progressing, the first couple of IBM-compatible chips that were introduced more than 10 years ago are also listed.

The CPU is the single most costly component of a computer and prices drop so fast on CPUs now that it's impossible to say how much a computer with one of these chips will cost.

IBM Compatible		Motorola	
CPU	*Clock Speed (MHz)*	*CPU*	*Clock Speed (MHz)*
8086	4.77	6800	7
80386	16, 25, 33	68030	16, 25, 33, 40
80486	25, 33, 50, 66, 80, 100	68040	25, 33, 40, 50, 80, 100
Pentium (80586)	50, 66, 75, 100, 133	PPC 601, 603, 604	75, 90, 100, 120, 132
Pentium Pro	Up to 200-MHz		

Table 4–1

Fast is good. The 8086 and 6800 represent the first generation of current desktop computers—faster clock speeds make for faster computing.

What's the Right Choice?

Again, budget certainly comes first; but, if possible, avoid IBM-compatible 386 machines and 68030-based Macintosh machines since these chips are being phased out (after two or three years as the standard, they become obsolete when the new, improved model appears). If you currently have one of these machines, that doesn't mean you should run out and buy a new one; it just means that there are better buys available today. Intel does not sell them anymore although other companies still produce them. If you do buy a machine with one of these CPUs, it means that you will get the kind of performance that was expected of a computer back in 1990 (way, way, back, ehh?).

Isn't that good enough? Not for the newest programs and CD-ROMs. When a new, more powerful machine is released, developers are anxious to use the added power to perform ever more impressive tasks, so any subsequent versions of a program may rely on that added horsepower. That means that many of the programs that you get now won't run well, if at all, on those older models. As computers become more powerful, software developers write more powerful software and expect consumers to have more powerful machines.

RAM: Random Access Memory

Having a lot of RAM, or random access memory, can make any computer a lot faster. But unlike a CPU, the RAM doesn't have an associated speed. Why then, is RAM so important to the speed of a computer?

Clash of the Titans

Motorola and Intel. No, they aren't Samurai warriors and they aren't warring countries, but they are locked in a battle that by today's business standards is of epic proportions.

What are the spoils of this war? Intel and Motorola design and manufacture the most popular CPUs that appear in today's PC-compatible and Mac-compatible computers. Both companies would like to dominate our desktops and the computers that sit on them. At present, Intel is winning the war, but the war's not over yet. As ferocious as this fight is, in fact, the battle seems to be heating up further. Who benefits from this competition? The consumer. These companies succeed when they produce chips that exceed the capabilities of their opponents. This leads to a sort of leapfrogging of superior technology. What's more, they have to provide this and make the price/performance ratio (i.e., bucks per bang) attractive to consumers. How big are these companies? Big. For the first nine months of 1994, Intel had revenues of $8.29 billion, an increase of 30 percent over the previous year.

How RAM Speeds Things Up: An Analogy

The easiest way to think of RAM is in comparison to your own memory—the more memory you have, the faster you can do things and the better off you are. If you have good short-term memory, you don't have to keep referring to lists, notes, and other memory aids.

Here's an example. RAM represents your short-term memory, that space in your head that lets you remember the directions to the corner store, for example. If you are driving somewhere out of state, however, things get cloudy with so many steps in the directions. You can only remember the basics of your trip—how to navigate from your house or apartment to the freeway, and perhaps to the first exit. Beyond that, what are the names of the streets? Which way do you turn? How many miles do you need to go before the landmark appears? You can no longer rely on what you can store in your own memory. You don't have enough RAM.

So what do you do? Now you refer to the written instructions. You need to take something out of your pocket or glove compartment—a map, for example. That slows you down. You need to slow down even more to study it and get that information into your short-term memory—you're loading new stuff into RAM! Imagine what happens if you only have room in your head for a couple of steps. You would constantly have to refer to a map, and that in

stantly have to refer to a map, and that in turn would constantly slow you down.

Having a lot of RAM is good like having more short-term memory is good: the more information your computer can retain, the less time it spends searching for information and loading it into RAM. More RAM means that you can keep more information loaded into RAM at one time.

One big difference: the computer is nowhere near as flexible as you are. In some instances, for example, the computer can only successfully execute a task if there is enough memory so that *all* of the instructions can be loaded at once. If the computer doesn't have sufficient RAM to run a program, for example, the program will not load and an error message appears to inform you that you do not have enough memory.

> <img> ***Note:*** **An important distinction between your short-term memory and the computer's: yours is better. When you wake up in the morning, you still remember how to get to the corner store. When you turn the computer back on in the morning, it remembers nothing, and everything that you want the computer to use or to know must be loaded into RAM.**

How Much Memory Do I Need?

There's no such thing as too much RAM. Nowadays, most Macs ship with eight megabytes (MB), and many PC clones ship with four, eight, or, with the introduction of Windows 95, 16MB. You can always order a machine with more or upgrade your memory at a cost of about $40 per megabyte. When you get memory, you can't get less than 4MB at a time. (If only it were as easy to improve our own memories as it is to improve the computer's!). Again, as computers get faster and we expect them to perform more and more complex tasks, the need for memory increases—it never decreases. That means that as software becomes more complex, you may discover programs that require more memory than you have. (For more information, see Chapter 8.) Windows 95, for example, says that you only need 4MB of RAM to run it, but you should really have 16MB.

Storage: Your Hard Drive

Your hard drive represents storage space for all of your creations and all of the software that you load on your computer. It's the equivalent of your computer's basement or storage shed. With all of this talk about speed and power, how does "storage space" translate into speed? After all, nobody has a fast basement!

True enough. It's not the basement that's fast; rather, it's how fast you can retrieve things from it. There are two things the hard drive has to do to get that information: 1) it has to find the information, called "access time" or "seek time;" and 2) it has to bring it up the digital stairs and deliver it, commonly called "throughput."

Note: **Floppy diskettes contain much less data than hard drives, so aren't they faster? Not at all. A floppy diskette works differently than a hard drive, so it takes much longer to search for something and to access it; it can take an excruciatingly long time to access.**

Believe it or not, when you collect a lot of stuff on your hard drive—a lot of documents, pictures, sounds, and lots of programs—it slows down your system. Your computer needs more time to search for an item when there's a lot of stuff to search through. The more clutter you have, the longer it takes to find something, just like in your basement or storage shed.

It also takes longer to store a new item when your drive is nearly full. The computer has to sniff around and find unoccupied space. If you have a high-capacity hard drive, then there is lots of space available and it can stow it very quickly. If there is little space, it may have to break up the file and store pieces in different locations (don't worry, it keeps track of all of those details and you don't have to deal with them in *any* way).

Note: **If a lot of documents are stored on your hard drive in chunks, the disk is said to be "fragmented." The computer can track that quite well, but it may still have to go to several different places in your storage space to get it and reassemble it for you. There are special programs for defragmenting a hard drive (one is included with Windows 95).**

How Big Should My Hard Drive Be?

How big is big? When hard drives first came out for personal computers, they were 10 megabytes and that was just grand, which is about what they cost! But now, with thousands of software programs available—some of which demand more than 10 megabytes of storage themselves—many hard drives have over 100 times that original capacity, called "gig drives" for gigabyte drives (1 billion bytes of storage space).

In addition, programs that use graphics and/or sound need lots of room. A single picture, for example, may consume multi-megabytes of space. If you want to put 10 high-quality pictures on your computer, you may need 50MB of space, and that doesn't include anything else on your hard disk.

Aside from sound files and pictures, you can also save or look at video clips—short movies that are saved on your computer. Since a movie is really just a series of still frames (like a flipbook), this takes up a tremendous amount of space, and if it has a soundtrack, it requires even more space—as much as 5MB per minute of sound.

You may be thinking, "I'm not going to make any movies, and I've never owned a tape recorder, and I'm not an artist." You may not be interested in producing a symphony, a work of art, or a movie, but there are a lot of artists, musicians, video makers, and hobbyists out there who love working on these sorts of things. Many would like to share them with you and there's a better than average chance that you will want to oblige them. And when you stumble across a file on the Internet that says "Ella Fitzgerald w. Duke at Town Hall, 1951," or a library of images entitled, "Normandy Reunion Photos," you may want the space to keep those on your computer.

If you don't have enough storage for them, you'll kick yourself. Also, if you don't have much storage, you'll spend an inordinate amount of time negotiating what you can and can't keep.

RAM vs. Storage: Don't Get Confused

The difference between RAM and hard disk storage is a thorny problem for many computer users. Why are RAM and storage so confusing? Largely because they are measured using the same yardstick, the megabyte. When the term "megabyte" gets bandied about, it seems to change scale; a computer person may describe one thing as being enormous at 40MB and then describe another thing as painfully small at 100MB!

Everything is relative. Take fluids, for instance. Is a quart a lot? Well, that depends on what you are measuring. Is a quart enough to wash the car? Not nearly. Is it a lot for a single donation of blood? Too much. Iced tea on a hot summer day? Could be just right. Iodine on a cut? A quart?! Are you crazy?! We're using a quart as our scale, but the things we're measuring are completely different.

In terms of our previous analogies, it's as if we were using the same measuring stick to measure the storage area of your basement and the area of memory in your head. Perhaps now you see that the problem in understanding this stuff doesn't lie with you, but with the terminology computer scientists have grown so accustomed to. Welcome to the megabyte!

Table 4–2 can help you get a sense of the scale of hard disk storage and RAM and just what different animals they are.

Note: **The amount of space a program needs for storage on your hard drive has nothing to do with how much RAM you need to run the program, but both are common facts that you need to know about a program.**

Tip: **A megabyte as a measurement takes time to understand because you probably aren't sure what you are measuring yet. Don't sweat it. You'll get it.**

Storage and RAM	Small	Medium	Large
Hard drive (measured in megabytes)	80MB	340MB	1,000MB (gigabyte) or more
RAM (measured in megabytes)	2MB	4 or 8MB	16 or 32MB or more

Table 4–2
Many PC programs take up several megabytes of storage space. Many programs also require at least 4MB of RAM. With limited storage and RAM, your software options are in turn limited.

When a Speedy Computer Isn't Speedy

All of the things mentioned earlier—a fast CPU, a lot of RAM, and a large hard drive—working in concert will make your machine very fast. But what if one of the pieces is not up to snuff?

Moving information around in your computer—getting what you type from the keyboard to and from the central processing unit to the monitor or the printer or wherever—is very much like plumbing. When you move water through pipes, you expect wide enough pipes to accommodate the water and adequate water pressure to push the water through the pipes. Like your plumbing, if one line is super small or obstructed, you have a "bottleneck" and you won't get the flow of water you would expect. The same is true in your computer. With a fast CPU, your computer can process information quickly, but if you don't have enough RAM, things will still crawl along. All of the components play a part in making yours a speedy machine.

The Art of Compromising

You'll probably discover that you can't have everything that you want. Each feature adds to the price tag and that price tag can really grow. Your dream 133-MHz Pentium machine with 32MB of RAM adds up to a lot more money than you expected to pay for a whole system—keyboard, monitor, and software!

Everybody compromises in this game. Getting a 75-MHz Pentium with 16MB of RAM instead of the monster of your dreams could save well over $1,000.

Regardless of what you get in the beginning, you can always add things and upgrade the computer later—in some computers, you can even change the CPU.

Bundled Software— The "Freebies"

Your computer is useless without software, and many computers come with software "bundles," a collection of free software programs and goodies. Here's what to look for.

Windows/DOS

The first thing you *need* to make your computer work is an "operating system," the software that acts as your computer's manager. You've perhaps heard of Windows or DOS—the Macintosh operating system is referred to as System 7 or System 7.5. These programs give you the basic tools to manage things on your computer—moving information, copying and deleting files—nothing fancy (we'll talk more about this in Chapter 6). The key here is to make sure that the operating system is current for the machine and that it is the right version for the other programs you'll be using. When purchasing other software, the requirements always list what version of the operating system you need to run that particular program.

Nowadays, if the machine has enough memory, new IBM compatibles should come preinstalled with Windows 95. (That means the store takes care of putting it on your computer.) If you already have a machine, it should have Windows 3.1 with DOS 6.2.

If you are using a Macintosh, you should have System 7 or System 7.5. Older Macintosh computers may be running a version of System 6.0. This is not very powerful, but it may be the only thing your old Mac can run. These Macs will not be able to run most current software programs.

What Other Software Is Bundled?

Bundled software can be a really appealing feature when buying a computer. Shop around and see what's being offered. If a computer comes bundled with several programs you would have purchased anyway, consider how much you are saving. Games, online books, financial management programs, and many other offerings can be had.

What "Extras" Are Available to Me?

Like buying a car, there are many extras and options available to you when you buy a computer. When calculating the cost of a computer or getting estimates, the computer dealer must know everything that you want on the computer—whether or not you want a modem and/or a CD-ROM, for example. There are many extras that you need to consider, such as printers, modems, CD-ROM drives, and "sound cards." You can find more information on all of these things in Chapter 8, "Peripherals and Add-Ons: A Hardware Tour."

Where Can I Buy a Computer?

Everybody is selling computers and peripherals these days. Some places offer great deals but you'll have to keep your eyes open to ensure that you get what you really want at the best price. Refer back to Chapter 3 for details.

Assessing the Ads: What Language Is That?

Computer ads are written in a special language, sometimes referred to as "double talk." These ads are devised so that you can't even read between the lines; much of what you need to know from the ad is what is *not* listed in the ad. Figure 4–2 shows a pretty typical ad.

For example, if they say, "extended keyboard also available," well, "available" means "you don't get it, but you can buy it." Or, the ad might say "monitor optional"— if it's an option, then it isn't included in the price. Is the keyboard not mentioned? Surprise: it's extra. Also, of course, you want the computer's memory to be expandable, but if they say "4MB RAM, expandable to 72MB RAM," that means you get 4MB and you would have to pay about $40 per megabyte to increase it— you also have to increase it in increments of at least 4MB at a time, something implied but not stated in the term "expandable."

Tip: **Make your own ad for the computer you want. Write down everything that you need—keyboard, monitor, type of CPU, mouse— and then see if you can find an ad like it in the paper.**

Computer Store/Appliance Store

The easy way to buy a computer is from a computer store. In many ways, buying a computer is the same as buying any other major appliance: you want to buy from a store that is established in the community with a good reputation. You want to know what kind of support they provide, the nature of their warranty, and their return policy should things go awry.

Figure 4–2

A computer ad: You need to know the lingo to know what's what

Nowadays, you can buy most computers and computer peripherals at appliance and department stores. This may be convenient, but more often than not the staff in these stores will not be able to answer many questions for you. You also need to find out what kind of support they provide—warranty options, return policy, etc.—just like in the computer store.

What About a Superstore?

Price Club/Costco certainly do have some good deals. Here's a store that buys so much that they can sell it at rock bottom prices. The dilemma here is that you can only buy one of the few models that they offer and sometimes these are equipped with a confusing hodgepodge of features.

Here's a typical example: Costco recently had a Pentium computer (a very fast machine), but the other components were unacceptably slow—a very old modem that would take three times as long online to access information and a slow CD-ROM. Good price, but a couple of hidden gotchas.

It used to be that the big-name clone makers with a good reputation also came at a premium price. Then the price wars started and they had to provide quality at a low price, which they do.

At the same time, there were guys who would put these together very cheaply in their shops and undercut the clone makers. There are still a number of these entrepreneurial shops in California, but their prices are not much better than the name clone

While Supplies Last!

While supplies last!? Why can't they keep supplies in stock? Probably because this is last year's model that is being discontinued. That may be OK—it could be a great bargain—but the reason the supply won't last is not because of demand, but because these are the closeouts and, more than likely, yesterday's technology.

If a manufacturer can't keep up with demand and stores have to back order, they don't advertise it; misjudging demand is an embarrassment for the manufacturer, indicating unpreparedness.

makers and it's hard to tell what quality the parts are that go into your box.

Mail Order

Scary, eh? You call up and talk to someone you've never met, send them a bunch of money (or give them your credit card number), and they send you a computer.

Well, believe it or not, many of the most successful clone manufacturers can attribute their success to selling this way. Companies like Dell, Compaq, and Zeos offer 800 numbers and very good prices. Is there a chance that your computer will arrive in pieces? Not from these folks: for a high-visibility company, mistreating mail-order customers would guarantee their demise.

In most cases, these companies "pre-configure" the machine for you—they install all of the critical software that the computer needs to run. You just take it out of the box, connect the cables (not nearly as daunting as you may envision), plug it in, hit the "on" switch, and you're ready to rumble! These name-brand clones typically offer very attractive guarantees and many offer on-site service, another important feature. Without this, there is always the risk that if your computer breaks down, you are going to have to drag it to some repair shop and then wait for a couple of weeks until they can fix it or get the necessary replacement parts.

Mail order is quite popular these days for a number of products. Huge ware-houses send out hundred-page catalogs. These companies not only are very competitive, they are incredibly reliable. Here are a few that have great prices and service. You can also call these folks for a catalog of products—both hardware and software. In fact, MacWarehouse and Mac Connection offer overnight service on any product (under 10 lbs.) for $3.

- MicroWarehouse—1-800-367-7080—(IBM compatible—$7 overnight)
- The PC Zone—1-800-258-2088—($3 overnight, up to 10 lbs.)
- Mac & PC Connection—1-800-800-1111—(both Mac and PC products—$5 for orders)

- MacWareHouse—1-800-255-6227—(for Macintosh products—$3 overnight, under 10 lbs.—$1 per pound for orders over 10 lbs.)
- The Mac Zone—1-800-248-0800—($3 overnight, up to 10 lbs.)

Buying Used

Should you buy a used computer or peripheral? If the deal is unbelievable, then consider it. There are folks who need to upgrade or trade in their computers on a regular basis—perhaps every two years—because their work demands they have the best.

Most people who sell these machines, unfortunately, think they should recoup as close to the retail price as possible, but in this industry, that's unreasonable. Even when the owner puts a lot of money into a computer, in a year's time, the price you would pay for a new comparable machine could drop by 20 percent. In two year's time, it could be 40 percent less. The math says that to be a bargain, a machine that someone pays $2,000 for should be sold used for well under $1,000 less.

Someone selling a used machine may try to sweeten the deal with lots of preinstalled software. They certainly need to give you all of the associated disks and documentation. It's easy to put the software on the computer, but legally, ownership may not transfer to you. It's a "magnanimous," although possibly illegal offer on their part.

Buying Through a Newspaper Ad

Be careful of newspaper ads—you need some assurances when handing over a large sum of money. If something is wrong with the machine, it may take a while before you find out what it is. It's also easy to be fooled into thinking you are getting something you aren't. True, a used computer can be a great deal, but you probably need to check out any ads with a computer expert.

Note: **Don't be surprised if the person selling the computer asks you for *your name and number* when you inquire about the machine. Computer crime is on the rise and there is a scam to rob people who are *selling* computers in the newspaper. Here's how it works: Someone calls the person selling the computer and asks a few questions. Then he/she gets directions to the house to come and see the computer. He/she never shows up and a few days later the house is robbed. By getting your name and number, they can call you back to see if you are on the level. It's not foolproof, but it offers some protection.**

Inheriting a Machine

Computers technology moves so fast that many people need to get rid of their old ones in favor of a new, super powerful model. Many such hand-me-down computers are just fine, but many will not be powerful enough to run the software that you are interested in. You may also wind up with a machine that is just not suitable for your needs.

If you are inheriting a machine, be sure to have the donor sit down with you and walk you through all of the different parts. Is something missing? Is there documentation for everything there? Is there something that isn't working? What computers is it compatible with? Is it a dinosaur that is better suited for the tar pit? Can it run the software that you are most interested in? Ask the donor all of these questions. Certainly the price is right, but the computer may not be right for you.

Be wary of older models that are extinct or discontinued. There are some older machines still floating around, but they are not part of the computing mainstream. A few Atari and Commodore computers—Commodore's Amiga, for example—may still be around, but you will find little if any software for these machines and you will not be compatible with other computers.

Note: **Realistically, if the machine is a PC compatible, it must be powerful enough to at least run Windows 3.1—if Windows 3.1 isn't installed and running, the machine will be more frustrating than anything; it will take too long to get anything working on it.**

> ### Golden Rule:
>
> If you are getting a lot of use out of your computer and it satisfies your needs, don't let anyone tell you that it is is no good or too old. Enjoy!

CHAPTER 5

Setting Up

In the good ole days of computing, setting up a computer required the patience of a monk and the intuition of Peter Falk's "Columbo." Fortunately, the good ole days of computing—which weren't really all that good—are behind us. Setting up a computer today is pretty straightforward.

Setting Things Up

You're ready to set up your computer—you've even picked out the perfect spot for it in your home. Unfortunately, most of the stores and dealers that you would get a computer from won't help you out with installation; they'll just sell you the machine. Even the brand names that sell direct typically just have the machine delivered to your house via Federal Express, UPS, or DHL. You will most likely have to wrestle with installation yourself. Here's what to do.

Let a Kid Do It

If you have a young relative, know a neighborhood kid, or you know a local computer saint, definitely try to get one of them to set up the computer for you. The problem with setting up a computer is not that it's rocket science, because it isn't. The problem is lifting and maneuvering a monitor, making sometimes unreasonable bends and twists to attach cables to the back of the machine, lifting the main unit to put it in position, crawling around on the floor, and performing other physically taxing things that many of us think we can—but know we shouldn't—be doing.

What You'll Need

Whether you can get help setting it up or not, you should definitely know the procedure. If someone else is setting things up, stay with them, watch, and ask questions.

The process of setting up a computer has really been simplified, so you really won't need any tools.

Golden Rule:

Save all of your boxes and packing foam. You never know when you may have to pack up the computer.

Cables, Outlets, and Tools

All of the necessary cables are provided with your computer system. You will, however, need an adequate number of power outlets and if you don't have a three-pronged outlet, you'll need those adaptors that we talked about back in Chapter 2. If you don't want to tie up all of your wall plugs, you should also get a "surge protector" or "power strip," a little doodad that safely turns your single outlet into 4, 6, or 8 plugs. Some surge protectors are shown in Figure 5–1.

Surge protectors can protect your computer gear from electrical disturbances such

as unexpected current surges. They are also convenient because the protector has a single on/off switch so you can turn all of your equipment on or off with the flick of one switch.

If you have a modem, your computer also needs to be near the phone jack so that you can connect it. If the phone jack is not easily accessible, you'll need a phone extension cord, available at most hardware stores, appliance stores, or Radio Shack.

How to Set It Up

First, take the main unit out of the box. Most, if not all, of the cable connections you need to make are on the back of the main unit, as shown in Figure 5–2. The plugs on the back of the main unit are referred to as *ports*.

You'll find lots of manuals, diskettes, maybe CD-ROMs, and pamphlets in the box. Take them out of the box, but keep all of the stuff together. You may be opening up lots of other boxes, and they'll also have manuals and instruction guides, so don't mix the contents of the boxes or you'll have to sift through all that stuff just to install a single piece.

Locate the setup guide. Every machine is different and although we can guide you through the basics, you will need to follow the specific instructions for your machine carefully.

There should be cables in the box. If you suffer from cable anxiety, relax. Nowadays most of these cables are designed so that you can only plug them into the right port. For example, some connectors are male and some are female; you can only plug a male into a female (these are standard computer and electrical terms, so please don't be offended!). Both types of plugs are shown in Figure 5–3.

> ## Golden Rule:
>
> Don't turn on the computer until everything is set up and never attach anything to the computer when the computer is turned on. Doing so can damage at least some part of the machine. Have you done it before? Did someone else say that it's really OK? Maybe you were lucky, maybe they were lucky, but this is not a good gamble.

Although some plugs may look similar at first glance, the male plug may have a different number of "pins" inside, or the female may have more or less holes.

Be sure to examine this carefully when connecting cables. You won't be able to connect two mismatched connectors, but the attempt could prove frustrating, nonetheless.

If there is any ambiguity—two cables with the same type of connector, for example, look at the port. Two identical ports will have little pictures drawn above or below them, indicating what you should

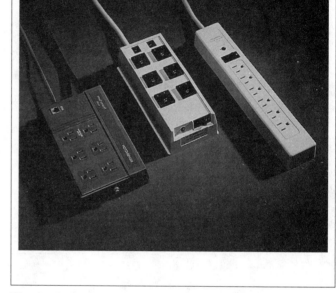

Figure 5–1
Surge protectors guard against electrical damage

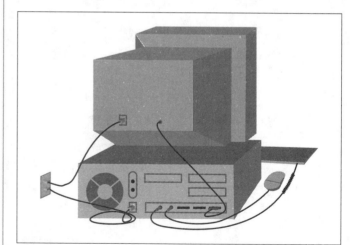

Figure 5–2
The ports on the back of a computer

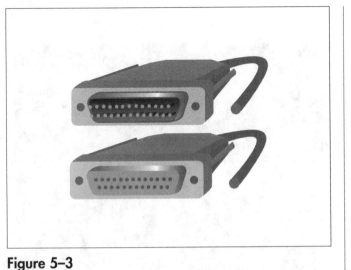

Figure 5–3
Male and female plugs go together

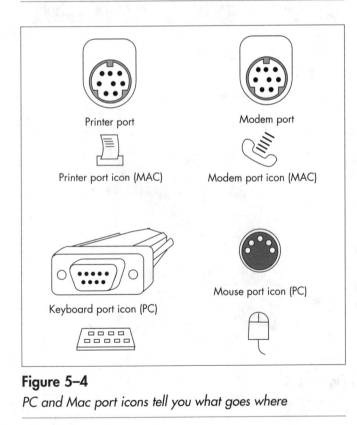

Printer port

Modem port

Printer port icon (MAC)

Modem port icon (MAC)

Keyboard port icon (PC)

Mouse port icon (PC)

Figure 5–4
PC and Mac port icons tell you what goes where

plug into it. Figure 5–4 shows some examples of these graphic guides.

Connecting the Monitor

The monitor normally has two cables, a power cable that runs to your wall outlet and a computer cable that will lead to a port on the back of your computer (remember, outlets on the computer are called ports). Depending on the manufacturer, the cables may be permanently attached at the monitor end of the cable or they may also be completely detachable. Either way, you won't get anything on your monitor screen until both of these cables are properly attached.

For convenience sake, you might be able to plug the monitor's power cable into the computer instead of the wall. This is advantageous because you save yourself a wall plug and the monitor automatically goes on and off when you turn the computer on and off. Check for an "outlet" on the back of your computer that can accommodate your monitor's power cord.

Attaching the Mouse and Keyboard

The mouse and keyboard have their own ports on the back of the computer (sometimes a mouse may have a port in front). The Macintosh lets you plug your mouse into your keyboard. This is where you may have to pay attention to logistics. If your machine is on the floor, the mouse cord should come up behind the desk, otherwise it will be in front and in the way.

Keeping Track of All of Those Cables

Connecting all of those cables can be a real pain, especially when you have to disconnect everything (perhaps to move the computer) and then reconnect them. To make your life a little easier when reconnecting cables, you should label or color code all of the cables and ports. A red star sticker that you placed above a port on the back of your computer should match a red star sticker on each end of the appropriate cable. A green star above a different port should match the green star on the corresponding cable. That way, no matter which cables you disconnect, you'll always know how and where they get reconnected.

Printers, Modems, and Other Stuff

If you have any other hardware to connect, install it now. Follow the instructions carefully and when you are done, hold on to them; once the thing is attached, you may still have to "configure" it—get it ready electronically—before it will work properly.

Knowing All of the Switches

Before you start experimenting, let's take a look at the different buttons that appear on your computer and let's see what they do.

The power switch   The power switch is typically on the front of the machine. When you turn on the machine with this button, you should see an indicator light go on to

let you know the machine is on. On most Macs, the main switch is on the back of the computer, but you can also turn most Macs on by pushing the topmost button on the Mac keyboard, as shown in Figure 5–5.

Note: **Some computers have a key on the front panel. This is not the ignition key but a lock that, when set, prevents the machine from being used.**

The reset button   The reset button is also on the front panel. It allows you to "start over" without turning the machine off. You use this when a program crashes and it won't leave your screen. PC compatibles that are running Windows 95 have a Restart Computer option, available in the Shut Down window. The Mac offers a restart option, available under the Special menu.

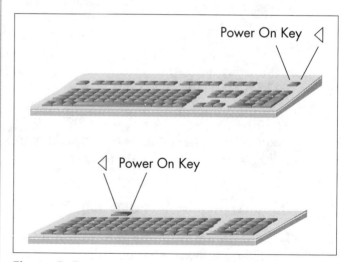

Figure 5–5

Some Macintosh computers can be turned on from the keyboard

The disk eject button The disk eject button is on the front panel of the computer—on the front panel of the floppy disk drive and also the CD-ROM drive. When you want to remove a diskette or a CD from their respective drives, you push the appropriate button. Some computers don't have an eject button. The Mac doesn't have a button on its floppy disk drive. To eject a Mac diskette, you use the mouse to drag the onscreen picture of a diskette into the onscreen trashcan icon and the diskette automatically ejects.

The monitor power switch The monitor power switch is located on the front panel of your monitor, or sometimes on the back. There may be a number of other buttons and adjustments on your monitor. These allow you to "tune" the picture quality. Consult the monitor's documentation for more information.

Installing Software

Whether you are setting up a new computer or you already have a computer, you still have to install software as well.

Exploring Software Options

Once all of the hardware is set up, you can install any software that you may have.

What does it mean to install software? In order for a program to run on your computer, you must actually go through an installation process. Typically, a program comes on one or more diskettes or perhaps a CD-ROM. During installation, the contents of these disks are transferred to your hard drive and the computer is transparently set up to accommodate the program.

For software that you get on floppy diskettes, put the diskette called "Program Diskette 1" or "diskette #1" in the floppy drive. On a Macintosh, a window opens and an Installer icon appears. Click twice on the icon and installation begins. You will be prompted for any additional diskettes. Be sure to insert them in the order requested.

IBM-compatible software installation depends on which version of Windows you are running. For Windows 3.1, you will need to run a setup or install program, but an icon does not automatically appear as it does on the Mac.

Note: **Many Macintosh-based CD-ROM programs don't require any installation. You simply put the CD-ROM into the drive, double-click on the program's icon, and the program begins to run.**

Regardless of the kind of machine you use, refer to the manual that comes with the software for specific installation procedures. Many installation procedures are the same, but even one atypical step can prevent you from getting things right.

Personalizing Your System

Aside from your hardware choices, there are many ways to set up your computer to reflect your personal likes and dislikes. Your computer comes equipped with software that lets you customize in a number of ways. Like a home, however, making your computer feel like home is a gradual process, a collection of ideas expressed and cultivated over time. The software that lets you make many of these changes is located in the Control Panel. (On a Mac, this is a folder with a lot of different options, each dedicated to customizing some aspect of your computer. IBM compatibles also have a control panel.) With that said, here are some of the things you can do to give your machine some warmth and personality.

Background Images

When a computer starts up, you'll notice that an image appears in the background, often the logo of the computer company. You can change this image—you can use any picture you want, actually, and you can change it as often as you want. If your favorite image is small, you can "wallpaper" the background whereby the computer automatically duplicates the image to cover the entire screen.

Startup Sounds

If you have a sound card, your computer can play sounds (or musical snippets) when you start your computer, quit a program, or perform some other action. You can even set up an alarm clock where the alarm is whatever sound you choose.

If you like music and you have a CD-ROM drive, a sound card, and speakers,

you can go out, get Spike Jones on a regular audio CD, and play it on your computer's CD-ROM while you work.

Icons

When you start up your computer, you will see lots of icons representing all the different programs stored on your hard drive. You can customize and change all of these icons any way you please. If you are using Windows 95 or a Macintosh, every document or picture or sound has an icon associated with it. Like international symbols for "don't walk" or "pedestrian crossing," you will quickly learn what the icons represent.

Figure 5–6 shows a set of standard icons associated with programs on the Macintosh. The bottom half of Figure 5–6 contains some fun replacement icons.

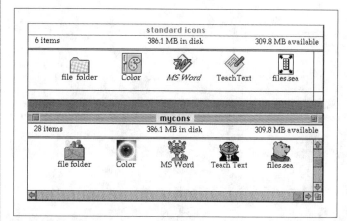

Figure 5–6

Standard icons and some alternate icons

Operating Systems: An Organizing Influence

No matter what you want to do with your computer, you'll need the help of your operating system. The operating system allows you to give commands to your computer and to run any—and every—program you use.

Regardless of which operating system you may have, the purpose is the same: to allow you to manage files and programs on your hard disk (and floppy disks). If you don't take advantage of the primary features of your operating system, your hard drive will have no organization; your computing life will become the digital equivalent of Oscar Madison's world, where chaos reigns supreme.

As you begin to create more and more document, image, sound, and multimedia files, you'll discover the underlying importance and role of your operating system as hard drive housekeeper. Without the functionality of an operating system (commonly called OS and pronounced "Oh-Ess"), you would have no means of organizing and tracking all of your creations. But while an operating system's role is clearly defined, the way it performs the role, the way you issue commands, and the way it shows up on the computer screen are not always so clear.

Why Twin Computers Look Different

It's not uncommon; you have the exact same hardware as your friend, you sit down at his or her machine to do a little work and...everything is completely different. Or maybe the computer

Figure 6-1

Windows 95 has a great look—icons, folders, and documents can appear anywhere on screen

that you test drove in one store appears to be an entirely different animal than the identical model that your sister recently purchased. What's going on here?

In large part, the differences between computers—how they look and how you give them instructions—are due to the operating system. The operating system is software that lets you manage all your files and issue commands to your computer. Different operating systems have very different appearances onscreen.

For example, if you get a new IBM compatible, it will most likely come with Windows 95, the new version of Microsoft Windows. One view of Windows 95 is shown in Figure 6-1.

Figure 6-2 is one view of an IBM-compatible computer running Windows 3.1. The icons—the little pictures that represent programs and documents—are the typical view for a beginning Microsoft Windows 3.1 user. (Keep in mind that you have different programs on your machine, so some of your icons are different.)

A Windows 3.1 user presses a key and the once familiar icons are gone, replaced with a listing of dates, numbers, and peculiar abbreviations, as shown in Figure 6-3.

If you sit down at a Macintosh, the screen will look altogether different, perhaps with a mix of listings and icons as shown in Figure 6-4.

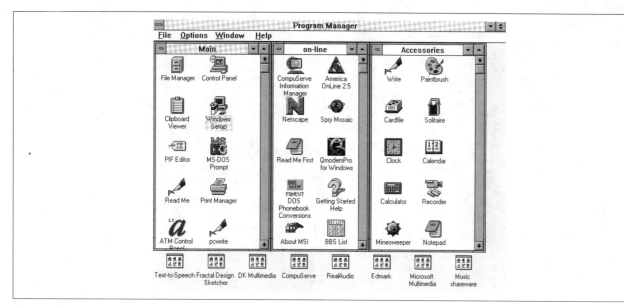

Figure 6–2

Windows 3.1 can have many faces—this is the Program Manager

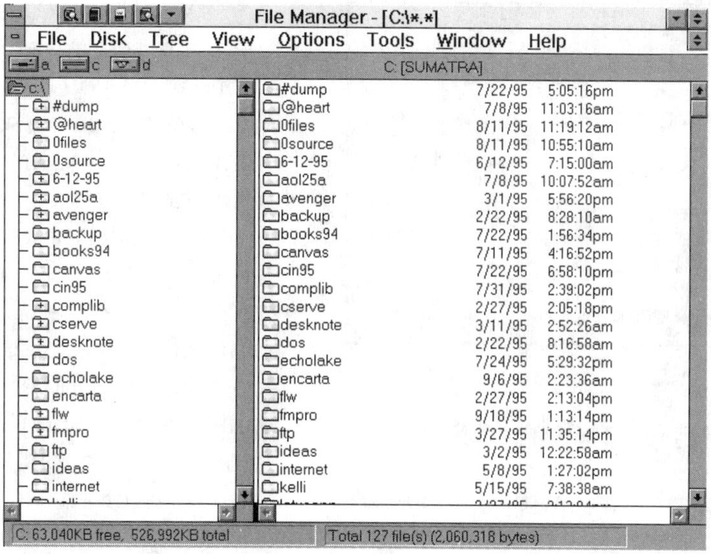

Figure 6–3

Windows 3.1 has a couple of different components—this is the File Manager

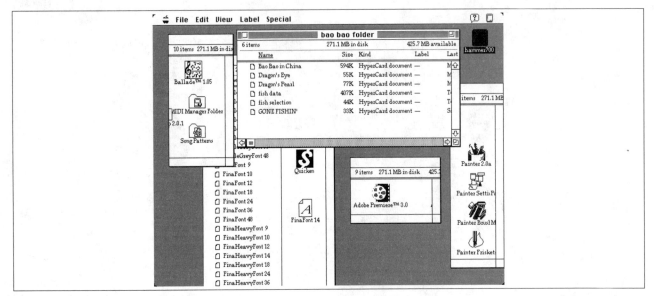

Figure 6–4

The Macintosh looks completely different from Windows 3.1—and a little bit like Windows 95

Golden Rule:

When things get confusing, don't get frustrated. Call a friend, read the paper, or take a walk. Whatever you do, get relaxed first and then take a fresh look.

Operating Systems

Every computer needs an operating system, which is the software that lets you give orders to your computer. It is the operating system that acts on your commands— "delete these files," or "copy this direc-tory." You might consider your computer's operating system as the ultimate govern-ment—with *you* installed as the divine ruler: the operating system gives you maxi-mum flexibility in executing whatever orders or wishes you exalt.

If you declare that all files should be deleted, you want your operating system to efficiently execute your order—but do you want those orders executed without ques-tion? As "computer-dictator-for-life," you want the operating system to warn you before carrying out orders that could be harmful if given in error. Similarly, you probably don't want to issue your orders in some weird technospeak—you want to be able to communicate your wishes clearly and with ease.

The operating system also lets you run all of your different programs. In order to run a program successfully, the operating system communicates with the program to tell it when and how to run. A particular operating system is always provided in a program's list of requirements since a program won't run with the wrong operating system.

Different operating systems offer different advantages, and though there aren't many operating systems to choose from, you should weigh the pluses and minuses of each one and understand what the distinctions are. Regardless of the one you have, you should try to stay abreast of news regarding revisions and updates. Here's a look at what's available and some of the advantages and disadvantages of each one.

Windows 3.1

Windows 3.1 was introduced for IBM compatibles by Microsoft in 1991. Previously, most PCs used DOS (rhymes with "toss"), an operating system that made you remember and type numerous commands to get anything done. Windows 3.1 was a big improvement since it introduced the mouse and on-screen icons to the PC-compatible community (DOS is actually still required on machines running Windows 3.1). Until the end of August 1995, Windows 3.1 was the operating system that was *shipped* with most PC compatibles.

Windows 3.1 really has two components: 1) the Program Manager, a screen filled with groups of icons that you click on to open windows, groups, programs, and files; and 2) the File Manager, a screen used to manage all of your files and programs. Each icon in the Program Manager represents a program (or sometimes a file) that you have installed on your computer. If you want to open a program, you locate the icon in the Program Manager and double-click on it. The program automatically loads into memory and you can do whatever you need to do with the program.

Note: **You have to open the File Manager via the Program Manager. To open the File Manager, locate the File Manager icon in the Main program group (a program group is a uniquely named window that contains a set of icons).** *Double-click* **on it, and the File Manager appears.**

If you have enough memory, Windows 3.1 will let you load more than one program into memory at a time. This can be a real timesaver when you need to go back and forth between two programs. To load another program, return to the Program Manager, double-click on another icon, and the next program is automatically loaded. You can toggle between Program Manager and all of your [loaded] programs via the Task List. When you need it, you can bring up the Task List by pressing the CTRL and ESC keys together.

Toggling between programs is a real help. If, for example, you are writing a report that refers to a picture stored on your computer, you can open the picture in a painting program and the report in your word processor, and switch between them instantly. Without task switching, you wouldn't be able to work with two documents in two different programs at the same, or nearly the same, time.

File Manager, the window that lets you move, delete, rename, and copy files, provides a listing of all of the files and programs that you have access to on your hard drive and floppy drive. The files are stored in subdirectories, the electronic equivalent of dividers in your office filing cabinet and represented graphically as little folders. You can put your files in any subdirectory and move them between subdirectories any time—the subdirectories help you maintain order. You can see all of the files in a given subdirectory by double-clicking on the associated folder icon. In any subdirectory, you can view your files in order based on the date you created the file, time of creation, size of the file, and more. If the information is hard to read, you can change the size of the typeface. Aside from the folder icon and the icon associated with individual files, though, there are no other graphic options here.

Windows 3.1 has some real shortcomings; it's not as easy to use as other operating systems and certain limitations make basic tasks harder than they should be. For example, Windows 3.1 does not allow you to name a file with more than eight characters (and a three-letter suffix) and certain characters in a file name—like spaces—are forbidden. This forces you to assign cryptic names to files and can make the task of organizing your files—and remembering the names of the files—quite difficult.

One of the biggest drawbacks of Windows 3.1 was—and is—trying to get the system to accept the attachment of hardware add-ons. Although a printer, for example, may plug into your computer with ease, the operating system must also make software connections that link the printer to the computer. Windows 3.1 made this, in some instances, a job that required a technician.

Windows 95

Windows 95 is the latest version of Microsoft Windows, the successor to Windows 3.1. Windows 95 boasts a slew of new features and options that make it very attractive for IBM-compatible computers. For one, it's much easier to use than Windows 3.1. (Many people say it is more "Mac-like" since the Mac's operating system is noted for its ease of use.) The Windows 3.1 "division of labor" is gone; there is no separate file management window (File Manager) and no separate window for icons (Program Manager). Windows 95 gives you icons and file management together, so you can click on files, folders, and icons on the desktop and drag things wherever you want them. Your files can also be represented by icons to show what kind of files or documents they are. Windows 95 lets you name your files with up to 256 characters, and spaces are allowed (in general, naming files with 256 characters is not such a good idea!). In a very significant improvement, Windows 95 is *plug and play*—you can add hardware attachments to your system with little or no headache. Windows 95 looks at the attachment and automatically configures it for you.

Like any operating system, there is a downside to Windows 95. For 3.1 users, Windows 95 is a big departure from 3.1, so it means you'll have to learn anew all the commands and locations of features. As a more feature-laden operating system, Windows 95 needs a lot more speed to run effectively, so you should have at least a 486-class machine. Although Microsoft advertises that it can run in 4MB of memory, that's misleading. Windows 95 doesn't perform as it should without at least 8MB of RAM—16 is much better. Without the additional memory and the 486 machine, your computer will run slowly and you won't see the performance you'd expect from this new operating system. In fact, without adequate hardware, Windows 95 can run as slow as its predecessor, Windows 3.1. If you want Windows 95, be sure to have the hardware to support it.

For the Macintosh/PowerPC: System 7.0 & 7.5

When Apple shipped their next generation operating system, dubbed "System 7," back in 1991, they attracted a lot of press for again defining and redefining "ease of use" for an operating system. For dedicated Macintosh users, the shift to System 7 from previous operating systems (System 6.X) was easy: the interface behaved the same and all of the familiar elements were there.

What's in a Name—and Number

For years, software programs and operating systems have been identified by their *version number*, the number that sits at the end of the product name. The number has traditionally been used to indicate the product version. The higher the number, the newer the release. Often, only one digit in a multidigit number changes—Version 3.0 becomes 3.1 becomes 3.11, for example. When the number changes by fractional increments, the developer is acknowledging that the release is incremental—it's not major. When the number is completely revisited—Version 2.13 becomes Version 3.0—that's when the trumpeting really begins.

When describing versions of a product between major releases, people commonly substitute the letter "X" for whatever number(s) changed. For example, Windows 3.X (pronounced "Windows three point ex") describes the family of Windows releases that started with "3."

Microsoft cast convention and tradition to the wind when they renumbered their operating system based on the year. Industry wise guys ask whether the next release will be Windows 95.1!

Network Operating Systems (NOS)

Sometimes a standard operating system isn't enough. When many machines are connected together—in an office environment, for example—another layer of complexity enters the picture, requiring a different kind of operating system called a network operating system or NOS (pronounced to rhyme with "boss"). The two most common NOSs that you'll hear about or see advertised are Novell's Netware and Microsoft's Windows NT.

A NOS still provides you with the same features you need to manage your hard disk. In fact, a NOS can be installed along with another operating system so that the second operating system handles the chores on your machine while the NOS handles any and all communicating with the other machines on the network. Does a NOS prevent you from doing anything? Yes, it does.

Granted, you are the master of your computer and you have the right to manage your hard disk as you see fit, but if you are on a network, everyone characteristically also *shares* access to files on a central machine (called a *server*). You don't want some errant ruler deleting files that you need from the server. Conversely, the errant ruler doesn't want you doing the same thing to his or her files.

A network operating system allows for a *system administrator*, a person or persons to oversee and control the rights of each user on the network. If, for example, you need access to confidential files that others should not see, the administrator can grant you access while preventing other users from even knowing the files exist. If many people on a network share a printer, the administrator can assign you a higher priority so that your documents get printed before other network users. Since the status of users can change (the other errant rulers may complain about another errant ruler or she/he may get a job at another company, for example), a system administrator can change a person's access rights at any time.

But there was a lot more, too. The Macintosh graphical operating system always had many of the best features of Windows 95: plug and play (the ability to attach new hardware and use it without a complicated diagnosis), easy file management (you can drag files, folders, and programs anywhere you want), and more.

System 7 still includes the Apple Menu (in the upper-left corner of the screen) that gives you instant access to a variety of the special features. Installation of additional options is made even easier: you drag the update—say, a new typeface or Control Panel item—to the folder called "System Folder" and it is instantly and automatically installed for you.

In System 7.0, Apple succeeded in making something that was already easy to use even easier to use—and more powerful. System 7.5, released in 1994, was an incremental release, but still helpful to users.

The disadvantages of Apple's newest operating systems are much like the disadvantages of Windows 95. System 7 needs more memory (and speed) than previous versions, so it was the first time that many Macintosh users needed to upgrade their hardware—if they wanted to upgrade to the newest version of the operating system. System 7.5 requires more speed than System 7.0. As such, it is better suited for the newer Mac/PowerPCs.

How to Organize Your Hard Drive

There are some very basic principles that apply to keeping your computer files organized, and your operating system is ready and waiting to help you apply them. Here are the fundamentals.

You can organize yourself in many different ways. The computer won't do it for you, any more than a desk will organize your bills. For example, when you save a document or picture on your hard drive, you will be better able to find it again if you have a system for "filing" your electronic documents. Both the Mac and IBM compatibles let you create folders for sorting documents (IBM compatibles that use Windows 3.1 call these folders subdirectories but they represent them onscreen with little pictures of folders).

Working with Folders and Subdirectories

Every computer system lets you instantly create folders that you name (or label) upon creation. To stay organized, you can create folders for different projects and keep only the relevant files in each respective folder. This is really no different than what you do with all of your important papers at home: a folder for house finances, another for bank statements, doctor visits, and so on.

If you just toss all the bills and receipts in the drawer, your folder system won't work, and it's the same with saving files on your hard drive.

When you get a new program or you start working with a piece of software, be sure to create a folder in which to save your creations. Granted, there are lots of folders that already exist on your hard drive, but you shouldn't use them to store your files. These pre-existing folders may contain lots and lots of files that are used by the computer for it's own maintenance—sort of like the computer version of the boiler room—and it will be difficult to keep track of your work if it is stored with these other files.

The best approach is to start with a folder for each program you are working with. If you are using a word processor for writing and a paint program for painting, for example, you can create two folders, one for your paintings and the other for your written documents.

Folders Within Folders?

Once you get going, you'll discover that having a folder for each kind of program is a good start, but hardly adequate. Between shopping lists, letters, poems, memos, short stories, and other signs that you have become a prolific writer, you may wind up with a couple hundred items in just your word processing folder. That means you're going to have to get more organized.

To add more organization, you need to create more folders, and to make it easier to find things you can create additional folders *within* folders. In your word processing folder, for example, you can keep all of your letters in a folder called "letters," all of your poems in a folder called "poems," and all of your recipes in a folder called "recipes." Now, when you need to find the latest haiku verse you composed, you won't have to search past the Key Lime pie recipe file or the letter to Con Edison about their mistake on last month's bill.

It may sound convoluted now, but you may want to put folders within folders *within* folders (you didn't misread that;

that's three levels). Using the previous example, you may have a "letters" folder in your word processing folder and you may write so many letters that you may need additional organization in your "letters" folder. You may, therefore, have a "friends" folder, a "family" folder, an "e-mail" folder, and a "VFW" folder. The levels of organization that you need will change based on how much you use your computer and how well you can divide things into neat categories. Always keep in mind that an elaborate organizational scheme can also work against you if it is unnecessarily complex.

Naming Folders and Files

Whenever you create something on your computer, whether it is a letter, a picture, a song, a newsletter, or a folder, you'll have to assign a name to whatever it is you have created. Thinking of good names, or, better yet, a good naming *system*, is very important because it will help you tremendously in keeping track of your work.

At first, you might be tempted to enter the obvious file name—"myletter" or poem#1, or "new folder" in the case of your most recent folder. The problems start to develop when you have several similar items with similar names that don't allow you to distinguish between their contents. True, you can open up each and every document to see what's inside, but well thought-out names will tell you the contents without opening each one up. Not using well thought-out names is like canning your garden vegetables and not labeling what you have put in each can!

If you are fairly religious about separating files into well-named folders, then your file names can be more concise. For example, if you are creating a monthly newsletter and you have a folder called "February," all of the related articles can reside in that folder. Each file name can then indicate a particular piece of the newsletter:

horoscope
op-ed-nra
op-ed-fbi
jokes
personals

Alert: **If you are running Windows 3.1, devising good names for folders and files will be more difficult because folder and file names are limited to eight characters. You may have a lot to communicate in a very short name. Windows 95 and System 7.0 don't suffer from this shortcoming.**

In the previous list, you know without opening the document what you are going to find, but don't be lulled by the simplicity of this example. Coming up with file names or file naming conventions can require more creative thinking than you might expect. In fact, you might discover a better name for a file or folder after you have already named it, in which case, you should rename it.

Renaming a File

Renaming a file or folder is a very common task, and every computer system will let you do it. Although the procedure is different on a Windows 3.1 machine than on Windows 95 and the Mac, the end result is the same. To rename a file, you must locate it, select it (highlight it), select the rename function, and then enter the new name. If the new name already exists, the name will not be accepted and you will have to enter a unique name for the file or folder. To rename in Windows 95 and System 7, you click once on the file you want to change and you can then type the new name right in. Press ENTER or click on the mouse and the file is renamed.

Finding Your Creations

No matter how neat and tidy you are, and no matter how well you name your files, there will be times that you can't find that picture or letter you were just working on. You know you saved it, but it isn't in the folder that it should be in. Or maybe you worked on a document and you know you saved it, but now you can only find an old version.

Finding a document or picture on your hard drive is easy as long as you have some idea of its name. Every computer has the ability to search for files, but like renaming a file, every computer does it somewhat differently. Regardless, when you can't find a file, use the find option to track it down. If you discover multiple copies of the same document on your hard drive and you didn't intend to save the extras, delete the unnecessary out-of-date copies.

Making Organizational Decisions: You, Not Your OS

Being neat and organized is economical: it saves time and money. When you create a file or install a program, each takes up storage space on your hard drive. Depending on the size of the program or file, it can take up an awful lot of space. (Some word processors require over 30MB of hard disk space.) When you get pictures or sounds, add new fonts, create that newsletter, or write a letter to your friend, different amounts of disk space are taken up.

But what happens to those files when you stop using them? If you don't need them, you should delete them so they aren't taking up space. The computer doesn't know that you no longer want them and you must therefore delete them yourself. As such, you need to do regular housekeeping to delete those files that are, passé, redundant, or just not wanted anymore. Your operating system can't—and shouldn't—make those decisions for you.

Cleaning House: Don't Throw Out the Baby with the Bath Water!

Being neat and tidy is important, but caution is also in order. In your digital travels, you no doubt will come across many things on your hard drive that you didn't create and that you don't recognize. Don't delete files whose origins you are unaware of. It may be something important. For example, Windows 3.1 creates a folder called "system" that contains all sorts of oddly named files (see Figure 6–5). Without these files, your computer would stop working properly.

> ### Golden Rule:
> Don't delete files on your computer that you didn't create or that you can't readily identify.

Note: **For PC-compatible users only—Programs sometimes build temporary files that are used for handling information. When you finish a project, these files are automatically removed by the program—unless something goes awry, like your computer crashes or you accidentally turn off the machine. In those cases, these temporary files can stay on your hard drive and unnecessarily take up space. You can get rid of them (and you should!) by "searching" the drive for files that end with the extension ".tmp".**

Formatting!

When you insert a diskette in your floppy drive, you may have to format it—or *initialize* it, in Mac Speak. Formatting prepares the diskette so you can write files to it and read files from it. It also erases everything on the diskette. If you want to ensure

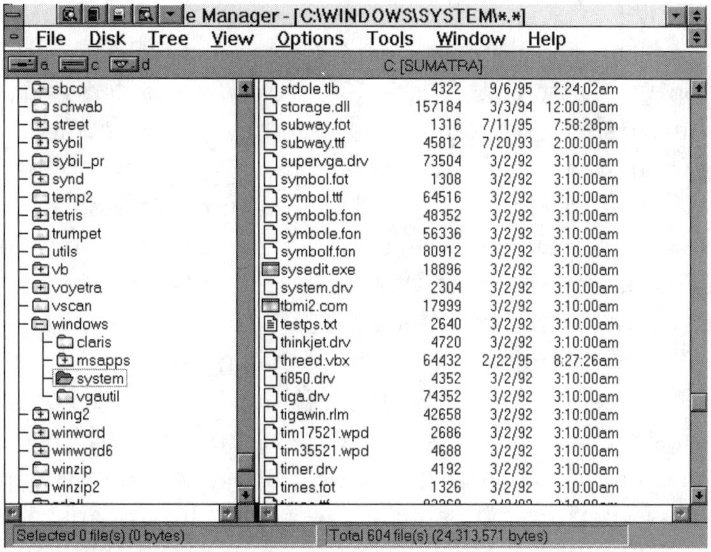

Figure 6–5
Don't delete files that you didn't create

that you have removed everything from your floppy, you should format the diskette.

Format your disks with great care, though. You can also accidentally format your hard drive and lose everything in the process—including your operating system! Be sure to check and double check what disk you are formatting *before* you say "OK".

Caution: **Formatting erases everything from your drive. Don't inadvertently format your hard drive when you just meant to format a floppy disk.**

Turning Off the Computer

When parking a car, you first bring the car to a complete stop, take the car out of gear,

and put it in park. If you had the lights on, you turn them off, and perhaps you do the same with the air conditioner and radio. If you live in a hilly neighborhood, you probably set the emergency brake. Computers, like cars, require that you follow some basic steps as part of turning off your machine. Actually, the real work in shutting down your computer is done by the operating system; you just have to issue the right command.

First, don't just turn the computer off. If you are in the middle of a task (say, writing a letter), finish the task, save anything you have been working on (unless you don't want to save it), and exit the program as the software manual tells you to.

Mac compatibles and PC compatibles with Windows 95 offer shutdown commands that tell the computer to clean things up so that everything will be just right the next time you turn on your machine. Windows 3.1 doesn't offer a shutdown command, but to be safe, you should quit Windows before turning off your machine.

When you ask your operating system to shut down the computer, it cleans your campsite; it puts away programs that are not in use, it tells the programs that *are* in use to close. The operating system then completes any tasks it has running in the background. (Like any good manager, an operating system is performing mundane but necessary tasks without requiring instructions from you. Don't worry. These are "low-level operations" that you don't need to understand. It's enough to know they are performed.)

Not following the proper shutdown procedure can lead to problems. If you don't ask your operating system to shut down your computer properly, temporary files created by a program will be left on your hard drive, taking up space and slowing your system down. Low-level operations that need to be performed will be left undone, another unwanted consequence. Finally, shutting down improperly also leaves you open to losing work that you have not saved.

Be Prepared!—
First Aid and
Precautionary Tips

It's always easy to look fondly on computing when your computer isn't giving you any problems. When things go wrong, though, your sense of delight with this wonderful technology can easily change to contempt for those *infernal* machines.

First Aid

First and foremost, try to be prepared for when problems occur. This chapter will help you pack the right things in your digital first aid kit and show you how to approach a variety of sticky situations. Then, when a problem does arise, if you do some detective work and follow the suggestions in this chapter, you'll be back on track in no time.

Have Plenty of Supplies

You sit down at your computer, write an impassioned letter to your State senator about social security cuts, you hit the print button, and...nothing. A message appears onscreen that indicates that your printer is out of paper. Or perhaps, instead of no paper, the message says your printer is low on ink. Invariably, these problems occur at the worst possible times; on holiday weekends or when you absolutely have to have that letter printed—yesterday.

These kinds of problems are easy to solve. If you have a printer, for example, know what sort of consumables it requires and have extras on hand. For a printer, have plenty of paper and, depending on the kind of printer (see Chapter 8), plenty of ink cartridges, toner, or ribbons.

Along the same lines, if you have a surge protector, it may have a fuse built into it to protect your computer gear from surges in electrical current. If a surge does come across your line, the fuse in the surge suppressor blows. Like a fuse in your house, it breaks the circuit and protects your computer gear from overheating and damage. Check the surge suppressor and locate the fuse. You may want to go to the hardware store or electronics store and get a pack of these to keep in your first aid kit.

Floppy Diskettes

Always label your floppy diskettes and be sure to have several spare diskettes. If you want to take a file over to your community center for printing and they are about to close, you don't want to have to sort through unlabeled diskettes of really important material to find one that is OK to use. When you are done with a diskette and you don't need the contents anymore, delete the contents and label the diskette as "clean" or "blank" so you will always know which ones you can use. When copying files to a floppy with an IBM compatible, you may be prompted to insert another diskette. You need to know—without seeing the contents listed onscreen—whether you have room on the additional diskette. Labeling your diskettes clearly will help keep you safe.

Protecting Your Floppies

When you put something on a diskette that you want to protect, you can lock the diskette so that you can't erase or delete the files on the diskette. If you try, an error message appears on your screen to indicate that your request to delete or erase files cannot be completed.

This is called "write-protecting" the diskette. To write-protect a diskette, find the small tab in the top-left corner of the diskette, as shown in Figure 7–1.

Using a fingernail, the head of a ball-point pen, or the tip of a straightened paper clip, push the black tab down to cover the hole (it might require a bit of force). To remove the protection, slide the tab back to its original "up" position.

Figure 7–1

The write-protect tab protects information stored on a diskette

You will need to be careful with a floppy diskette. Floppies shouldn't be exposed to extreme temperatures—don't leave them lying in the sun or on the fireplace mantel, or you just might lose whatever information you have stored on them. Dust spells trouble, so a storage box (with a lid) for your floppies is a good investment. If your diskettes come in a sturdy box, you can use that as well, but try to keep everything as dust-free as possible.

No Magnets!

Magnets are pretty popular for holding memos, notes, photos, and cards to the refrigerator door, but they are worse than Kryptonite to your computer. The information that is stored in your computer's memory and anything that you save on floppies and hard disks will be erased if a magnet gets too close (a floppy diskette can be erased by passing a magnet over it). This is one thing that can cripple your machine and cause a lot of grief, so keep the magnets away.

Saving Your Work—And Your Time

At times you may find yourself working on a document on your floppy diskette. Working off a floppy is extremely slow and the bigger the file gets, the longer it takes to save. For both speed and precautionary reasons, move files to your hard drive before working on them.

Working with floppies can also be unsafe: if you try to save a document and you are out of room on your floppy, you can lose your work. Vendors may tell you this won't happen with their products, but it's not worth the gamble. Do yourself a favor: copy it to your hard drive, work on it there, and then when you are done, copy it to a floppy as a backup. You'll be glad you did.

Tip: **Don't print from a floppy. This can also take an inordinate amount of time and you can have problems. Instead, copy the file to your hard drive and then print it from there. If you're at a print shop or service bureau, you should still copy your document to the hard drive and remember to delete the file from the hard drive when you're done.**

Mysterious Failures

Everybody's computer experiences mysterious failures from time to time. You can be merrily working away and suddenly your mouse won't respond to repeated clicks, your keyboard stops working, and you seem to lose total control of the computer. Congratulations, you have experienced the ultimate computer frustration, the *crash*. You'll never feel like a true computer user until you experience this rite of passage. Like a crick in your neck, you'll learn to live with system crashes, but you'll never learn to like them.

Ninety-nine out of 100 times, these failures are nothing (or nothing anyone can figure out!). The best way to resolve a crash is to quit whatever you are doing on the computer and restart your computer. On IBM compatibles, press the ALT, CTRL (control), and DEL (delete) keys together to get out of the program that is stuck. When you do, a screen appears asking you if you want to quit the current program or quit everything. If you press just the ENTER key, only the messed up program will close. If you press the ALT/CTRL/DEL key combination again, it will silently restart your machine.

If you are using a Mac and you run into this problem, you can hold down the Command key (with the squiggly clover on it), the Option key, and the ESC key. You are asked if you want to "Force Quit." Click on the OK button.

Alert: **When you restart your computer, anything you have created and not saved will be lost. You should only restart your computer this way when you have to.**

Hopefully that will work—(it's called a "warm reboot" for you Nerds-in-Training), but often it results in a frustrating "beep" sound and nothing more. If you just get a beep (or your screen goes blank or you don't get anything), you should turn the machine off for a few moments. Turn the machine back on and things should be just fine.

My Computer Doesn't Work!

You go through your precomputing ritual—those steps that help get you in the right frame of mind for working on your computer (many of us have one—please write

or e-mail us yours). You turn on your machine and—nothing. Maybe a cryptic message, but no familiar startup screens. What to do? Don't panic. There are a number of things that can give the appearance of computer failure. Here are a few.

Super Common Mistake #7658005-S

There's a floppy diskette in your floppy drive. When you start an IBM-compatible computer, it first checks your floppy disk drive. If a floppy diskette is in the drive, you get this enigmatic error message:

Non-System disk or disk error
Replace and strike any key when ready

and your computer will not start. Just remove the floppy from the drive and press the ENTER key on your keyboard.

Saving a Document

The most important precaution you can take while working is to save your work frequently. Here are some of the most common accidents that can and will befall you when you don't save your work:

Scenario #1   You write a long, heartfelt letter to your sister in Texas—two hours worth of work—and you have been so intent on pouring out your feelings and filling her in on the daily prattle, you don't bother to save the document before you send it to the printer. Zap. Something happens on the way to the printer; your system crashes and you lose *all* of your work.

Scenario #2 You are hard at work and you haven't saved that beautiful picture you created in the longest time. The phone rings, you turn in your chair to answer it and step on the surge bar's power switch *or* you kick the computer's power cord from the wall socket. Sorry. You've lost all your work.

Scenario #3 You are working on an article for the community paper. It's late and you're getting bleary-eyed. You aren't looking at the screen, but you hit a couple of keys and lo and behold, you wind up deleting everything from the page and the "Undo" command—the menu option that lets you "take back" your last action—isn't bringing anything back.

There is a single solution to all of these problems. It can be found in a simple axiom: save your work regularly and frequently.

Golden Rule:

The three most important work habits:

1. Save Frequently,

2. Save Frequently, and

3. Save Frequently.

Backing Up

Imagine lending your collector's item Louis Prima album to a friend who leaves it on the roof of his car and then sheepishly apologizes about how it blew off into the Grand Canyon. The album and your friend's forgetfulness are one thing, but the contents of that album are another. If only you had recorded that album on tape!

That's what backing up is all about. Although it can seem like a real inconvenience, backing up your work—making a copy of something and saving it on a floppy—is an important habit to get into.

Backing things up in an orderly fashion is important. That means labeling diskettes properly, and deleting obsolete documents. Diskette problems? If a floppy diskette starts acting strangely or doesn't seem to be working properly, copy your files onto another floppy (or back onto your hard drive, if they aren't there) and throw out the trouble diskette.

Haunted by the Past—Version, That Is

When you are copying files back and forth between hard drives and diskettes, you might inadvertently find yourself trying to copy two different versions of the same file onto the same diskette or drive. For example: you have been working on a letter for several days. On Day 1 you copy the letter to a floppy disk. On Day 2, you continue to edit your letter and then try to copy it to the same diskette. When you do, a message similar to the one in Figure 7-2 appears.

The message indicates that a file by the same name exists (the date indicates which is the more current copy) on the floppy and you must decide whether or not you want to replace it.

In this instance, the file you are going to replace is an older file, and that's fine. But be careful; it's possible—depending on where and when you copy a file—to inadvertently replace your current file with the old one. When you get a prompt to replace a file, *be sure* the you are replacing the right file. Once you replace a file with another copy of the file, that version is irretrievable.

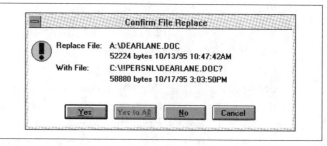

Figure 7–2
Be very careful when copying different versions of a file to the same location

When You Need a Resource You Don't Have

There will be times where you wish you could do something with your computer that you just aren't equipped to do. Perhaps you want a nice color printout of a computer picture, but you don't have a color printer. Maybe you really want a copy of that old photo to store on your computer, but you don't have the tools to capture it.

Help is available. *Service bureaus* are printing and/or copying centers that also offer computer facilities. You pay based on what you use and how long you use it. For example, if you want to create and print a greeting card that has a picture of your spouse, you can go to a service bureau and use their gear.

Alert: **Always ask how much it will cost to print your picture on a service bureau's printer. Depending on the printer used, a single color print can cost over $20.00!**

To find a service bureau, look in the yellow pages under Printing or Computers. If you live near a college or university, you can bet there are several service bureaus nearby. When you find a service bureau near you (Kinko's Copies are everywhere and they usually have computer services), get a rate card to see what they charge. Do they have PCs, Macs, or both? How much do they charge an hour? How much do they charge—per page—on a laser printer? Do they have a scanner? (See Chapter 8.) Finally, what kind of software do they have installed on their computer? You need to make sure that they have software to open your files. If not, you have to bring your program in.

Computer Viruses

As if we didn't have enough problems already! A computer virus is a manmade program that serves no purpose but to inflict some sort of damage to your computer.

The level of ferocity of these programs varies. Some are relatively innocuous, nestling into your computer system and never doing much of anything. Others erase programs, destroy data, and inflict damage to whatever system they infect. In a nutshell, here's how they work. A rogue programmer writes a small program that is "hidden" within some program that people might be interested in, say, a graphics program. The programmer plants the program on an online service and lists it as a graphics program. Unsuspecting computer users download the graphics program, unaware that they have also downloaded a virus along with it. When the program is installed on their machine, the virus comes to life, surreptitiously burrowing itself into other

A Prison Sentence for a Virus Breeder

In 1988, Robert Morris, Jr., a first-year graduate student at Cornell University and the son of a prominent computer security expert with the National Security Agency (NSA) was convicted of violating the Computer Fraud and Abuse Act.

Morris created and released a virus on the Internet. The virus crippled thousands of government and university computers and was estimated to cause millions of dollars in damage. He released the virus on November 2, 1988 through a computer at MIT and then went to dinner. He was surprised at how quickly the virus spread.

During his trial, Morris claimed that the virus was an experiment and that he did not intend to cause damage to any computer systems. The virus was intended to duplicate itself only once and reside innocuously on each "host" machine.

Instead, it duplicated itself hundreds of times, making thousands of computers crash and causing tremendous headaches for universities, private companies, and computer administrators all over the country.

At his trial, Morris' defense cast him as an innocent student who didn't understand the impact and consequences his "project" would have on computer users across the country. He faced charges that could have resulted in up to five years in prison, a $250,000 fine, and restitution costs in the millions. He was found guilty, but only had to perform 400 hours of community service, 3 years probation, and a $10,000 fine. Many computer experts across the country felt the penalty was far too lenient, that a slap on the wrist sentence sent the wrong signal to computer "experimenters," and that he should have served time in prison.

files or duplicating itself repeatedly on the person's hard drive. From there, the user puts a floppy in his or her floppy drive. When the floppy goes in or when the user copies files to it, the virus copies itself to the floppy diskette as well. That diskette winds up in someone else's machine and the virus finds a new home. Most viruses are benign, intellectual exercises for the people who create them. Unfortunately, some are designed to be destructive.

Guarding Against a Virus

In response to viruses, several companies, universities, and individuals have produced virus protection software, programs that you install on your computer and that monitor suspicious background activity, like programs being duplicated without a user request.

If the protection program spots one of these viruses, it either eradicates it from your computer or it announces its find, and then removes it.

These programs, such as SAM (Symantec Anti-Virus for the Mac) and Norton Utilities Anti-Virus (also from Symantec) can be found in any computer store. Others, like McAfee's VirusScan, are also available through online services. You owe it to yourself to have one on your computer.

Tip: **New viruses are constantly cropping up and so virus protection programs are constantly being updated. Keep in touch with the creators of your anti-virus software so you can keep your protection current.**

Rules Around the Machine

Aside from being clean and organized inside your computer, you also need rules to keep your work area neat and tidy.

The Food Rules

A good rule around a computer? No food. Period. A nice cup of hot tea may help you think better, but consider enjoying it in the kitchen! Food accidents with computers—like getting tomato sauce on your good shirt or favorite blouse—are all too common. Knowing what you know about accidents, you'll feel foolish when you spill that beverage right into the keyboard. A food accident usually means one of two unforeseen expenditures: a new keyboard or a new mouse.

Here's the compromise: Two policies, a policy for yourself—when you are alone—and the policy when others are using your computer. Kids? No food, period. *Especially* something they haven't finished chewing! (Tootsie Roll "juice" in a keyboard surely spells disaster. Soda is a killer.) The complement to the No Food Rule is the "Wash Your Hands" rule. It's a simple rule and one that can best be enforced if the kids know that the rule applies to everyone.

Keeping Kids Out

Tiny kids should be monitored at all times (they'll want to show you what they can do with their favorite programs, but anything can happen with a kid and a keyboard. In addition, they are most interested in the moving parts—the CD-ROM tray that can slide in and out—and they size up quickly what to do with the floppy disk drive—like stick pennies in it or credit cards that they just got out of your pants pocket! Stay vigilant (and check out the kid's keyboard in Chapter 8 and the kid's programs in Chapter 17).

Peripherals and Add-Ons: A Hardware Tour

Peripherals and add-ons are "extras"—upgrades that you can attach or add on to your computer system. Peripherals allow you to do more and help you accomplish certain tasks that you otherwise couldn't accomplish. What are the most important peripherals or add-ons? Many people think that a printer is a necessity, while others see a modem as a much higher priority. Certain kinds of musical keyboards can also be considered peripherals or add-ons, but only computer-savvy music hobbyists are interested in them. To accommodate everyone's needs, computer dealers will sell a base machine and then let you accessorize and upgrade—again, much like with the purchase of a car. Not all options and peripherals will be of interest to you, but they are described here so you won't be confused or unclear about them when you see them in the computer store or advertised in a magazine or newspaper.

Compatibility Issues

When you are shopping for peripherals, be sure to communicate exactly what kind of computer you are going to be using the peripheral with. Some peripherals, for example, can be used on both Macintosh and IBM compatibles, but this typically is a feature that costs more—it's for those people or businesses that have both kinds of machines and don't want to buy two of the same peripheral. Overall, you need to announce what you intend to do with whatever peripheral or add-on you are buying. "I want to add memory to my Macintosh Quadra," tells the sales person you want Macintosh memory and the memory that works in the Quadra. Memory is different between IBM compatibles and Mac compatibles, and even between different models. And be sure of product names, because two products can be very different, but their names can be very similar. For example, if you are looking for the Hewlett Packard 5MP, don't accept the Hewlett Packard 5P unless you know how you are compromising. If a sales person says a model is "just the same" or the name is a "spelling error," get more information.

Other peripherals and add-ons, like CD-ROMs, keyboards, and mice are purchased for either a Mac or a PC, but not both, so stay alert!

Printers

One of the most common—if not *the* most common—computer peripheral is the printer.

Everybody wants a printer. Your computer may be fast and your ideas may be great, but you'll have trouble sharing those ideas with others if you can't print them.

There are printers available to fit every need: inexpensive printers, fast printers, color printers, portable printers—one printer company even demonstrated that their printers could print on tortillas! Your needs will probably demand some mix of all of these things (minus the tortilla option).

Printer Technology

There are several different kinds of printers (and about a million different brands), but there are really just three types of printers that you will consider buying: dot matrix printers, ink jet (or bubble jet) printers, and laser printers. Although each class of printer is built using a different kind of technology, they have all proven to be quite reliable. Here's a brief look at what they have to offer.

Dot Matrix Printers

Dot matrix printers have been around for a very long time. A dot matrix printer uses a print head and a ribbon—like a typewriter ribbon—to print a document or picture. Dot matrix printers are the least expensive, the cheapest to operate, and by and large the most reliable. Servicewise, they are like styrofoam at the dump—it takes them about a hundred years to break down! They are also painfully slow and often times very loud. A dot matrix printer also produces the lowest quality printed page. By virtue of its more primitive technology, the look of a document produced on a dot matrix—and compared to ink jet or laser printers—is relatively crude.

Ink Jet Printers

An ink jet printer, as shown in Figure 8–1, is very different from a dot matrix printer. Instead of a ribbon and print head, an ink jet printer uses very tiny nozzles that spray a wet ink onto the page. The nozzles are remarkably precise and can "spray paint"

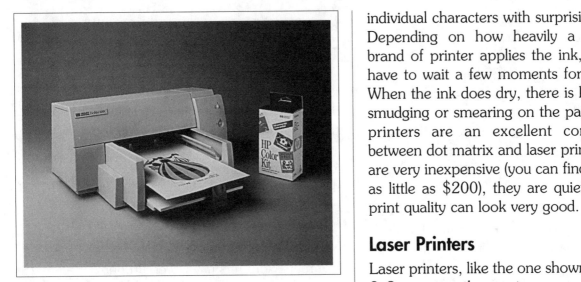

Figure 8–1
A Hewlett Packard Ink Jet: good quality printing at a low cost

Figure 8–2
A laser printer: great quality printing—but at a higher price

individual characters with surprising clarity. Depending on how heavily a particular brand of printer applies the ink, you may have to wait a few moments for it to dry. When the ink does dry, there is little or no smudging or smearing on the page. Ink jet printers are an excellent compromise between dot matrix and laser printers; they are very inexpensive (you can find them for as little as $200), they are quiet, and the print quality can look very good.

Laser Printers

Laser printers, like the one shown in Figure 8–2, are now the most common and most popular printers available. Using a laser beam, a blank sheet of paper is electrically traced with the image or document. Toner—a dry ink—is then applied to the paper and the toner sticks to the traced image. Laser printers are noted for their price, superior printing capabilities, and speed.

The "Other Printers"

There are several other types of printers that you might see advertised, namely thermal wax printers and dye sublimation (or "dye sub") printers. These printers are used specifically for printing color pictures and photographs, and they are quite expensive. Thermal wax printers are often used by design firms or publishers as "proofers" to see how an image will appear when printed. Dye sub printers are used for printing near-photographic-quality images—they often print on special photographic paper and cost thousands of dollars.

Print Quality

Everyone wants their printed pages to look good. The importance of a picture or document's appearance depends on its use: your shopping list's appearance may not matter, but you want a letter to your Congressman to look professional. Letters to friends shouldn't cause undue eye strain for them.

A printer's *resolution* determines the quality of what the printer can print. Resolution is measured in "dpi" (dots per inch), with more dots being better. Nowadays, high-quality laser printers can print at 600 dpi, which means those dots are pretty tiny and the image quality superb, but 300 dpi printers also produce very good quality prints.

If image quality is important to you, you'll do better with a laser printer or an ink jet, since dot matrix printers cannot approach this kind of resolution. Nowadays, 300 dpi laser and ink jet printers are common and available for about $450 and $300, respectively. Ink jet printers are typically cheaper than laser printers.

The Good Looking Type

If a printer includes TrueType or Postscript fonts, you are guaranteed that your type will be the good looking type! TrueType and Postscript are typefaces stored in your laser printer. When you print a letter, the printer uses one of these typefaces, giving your document the appearance of a professionally typeset page. Printers normally advertise whether they include TrueType or Postscript fonts, and if so, they will tell you how many are included.

Note: **You don't have to rely on—nor are you limited to—the typefaces that come with your printer. Every IBM compatible and Macintosh comes with a number of TrueType fonts that you can use in addition to or instead of those that come with your printer.**

If your laser printer does not come with any Postscript fonts, chances are it isn't a postscript printer. Postscript is a product of Adobe Systems, Inc., and as such every printer company must pay Adobe a licensing fee (a royalty fee) on each Postscript printer they build. As you'd expect, when the printer company has to pay for something in a printer, that raises the price of the printer for consumers. If you see two printers that seem identical in features but one is a lot cheaper then the other, check and see if they are both Postscript compatible.

Color vs. Black and White

Color ink jet printers have come way down in price and though they are still more expensive than their black and white counterparts, they are pretty close in price. Color laser printers have also appeared on the scene, but these are expensive and unproven. Options like dye sublimation and thermal wax printers (mentioned earlier) are very expensive. So, if you want to get a color printer and unless you need color for professional use—you are a freelance graphic artist, for instance—you should probably stick with the ink jet options.

A big difference in cost between a color and a noncolor printer is in the *media*—the other supplies you need, like special ink, to print a page. Cartridges for color printers are more expensive and some color printers may require that you use a special paper for your color images. If you are interested in a particular color printer, be sure to check the cost for ink refills and, if required, the cost of any special paper.

Also, watch out for a hidden cost on some ink jet printers. On some early ink jet printers, there was no black ink cartridge. Instead, the printer created black by mixing equal parts of cyan, magenta, and yellow inks. This is really a costly proposition, since the colored inks cost more and you wind up using a lot more ink. It's especially wasteful if you use your printer mostly for printing text, which almost always means no color. If you are getting a color ink jet printer, be sure it has a separate black ink cartridge.

Note: **A color ink jet printer comes with four color inks: cyan, magenta, yellow, and black. Like a professional color printing press, these colors are mixed together on the page (by the printer) so that all the in-between colors can appear in a single image.**

Speed and Memory

Printers are also judged by the speed at which they can print. Speed is typically a much bigger issue for folks who are print-ing a lot of images or long, multipaged doc-uments. Speed is also important when a number of people are all connected to the same printer (in an office) and a slow printer will result in a waiting line for print jobs. That's not to say you don't want a fast printer at home, too. If you have a 10- or 15-page document, a slow printer will have you waiting impatiently.

The standard measure of scale for printer speed is page per minutes, or *ppm*. A superfast laser printer can print 17 pages per minute while a dot matrix printer will print *maybe* 1 page per minute. Ink jet printers and slow laser printers typically print 4 ppm. Depending on what you want to spend, you can find a laser printer that can print 5, 6, 8, or 12 pages per minute.

Note: **The speed of a printer, in pages per minute (ppm) is typi-cally provided in any ad for a printer. If it isn't, be sure to find out how fast the printer is before making any buy-ing decisions.**

You might be asking yourself: what qualifies as a page? (These are questions that sales people don't always like to talk about.) These ratings are based on text documents without pictures. If you print any graphics, expect the printer to slow down dramati-cally. Graphics demand that a printer work a lot harder to print the image (it's not physical work for the printer, but there are more calculations that need to be executed). There is no set time for printing an image because the time to print a page of graph-ics depends on how complex the image is.

Tip: **Look for a printer that has a lot of memory. More memory will allow it to print faster.**

Other Printer Options

There are a lot of features available for printers that you may or may not be interested in. The presence of these features normally means that the printer is more expensive, so if you see a printer that you like and it has features you don't need, ask if there is a similar model without the fins and fancy wheel covers!

For example, some printers can be attached to *both* an IBM compatible or Macintosh. If you only have one machine or the other, you are paying for a feature you don't need. Similarly, some laser printers are "network" printers, printers that include special hardware so they can be hooked up in an office and shared by many people throughout the day. Not buying for your office? Don't pay for the feature.

Storage Options

It's pretty common to buy a computer system and then discover that you need more hard disk storage space. Maybe you get a few new programs that eat a lot of disk space. Perhaps you rediscover your love for painting and begin to explore the possibilities of computer graphics. Maybe you just want to *download*—retrieve from an online service—a lot of pictures and sounds that

hold some special meaning to you. New programs and big files or documents—like graphics and sound files—can whittle away whatever storage you may have left on your computer system. In fact, Windows 95 can easily take more than 30MB of hard disk space alone!

When your needs and interests demand more storage, you'll find yourself first cleaning up and getting rid of unwanted files. After that, you may feel pressed to delete things you don't want to delete, or maybe you'll weigh cutting back on downloads, explorations, and other disk hungry activities. Does a storage shortage mean it's time for a new computer?

There's no need to buy a new computer when you need more storage, you just need to get more storage. The most common type of storage is a hard drive, and you may choose to just buy yourself a bigger hard drive than what you currently have. But a hard drive isn't your only option; there are several different kinds of storage, each offering different advantages and disadvantages. Regardless of the option you choose, you want more room, quick access to your programs and documents, and a reasonable price.

Note: **"Size" is not a reference to the physical dimensions of a hard drive but to its storage capacity.**

One of the biggest considerations with storage is speed—how fast you can get your information "out of storage." The comparisons can be striking, like comparing the time it takes to get stuff out of the basement versus how long it takes to get something from your safety deposit box at the bank. You should look for a drive with an *access time* (sometimes called the *seek time*)—the average time it takes to locate the information you request—of 12ms (milliseconds) or less. The lower the number the better, so expect to see a higher price tag for 8 or 9ms drives. Do a few milliseconds really make much of a difference? They sure do. Your computer may access your hard drive many times in a single work session and the delays add up fast. Here's a look at what each storage option has to offer.

Hard Drives

Back in the early 1980's, it was the lucky hobbyist, indeed, who could afford a 10MB hard drive. Now, a 1Gb (gigabyte) drive (1,000MB or 100 times the size of early drives) is common at a fraction of the cost. Currently, you can get a 1.2Gb (that's 1,200MB) hard drive for under $300 and prices continue to drop. Hard drives are even available in the 10Gb range. Access times of 10 or 12ms are pretty standard on these drives.

Hard drives are available both as internal models installed within your computer's chassis and external models that sit next to your computer. If you like to tinker and you want to install the drive yourself, it's pretty straightforward, though you should probably have an experienced hand nearby to help guide you the first time around.

If you're like the rest of us and you don't want to be bothered with the innards of the machine, be sure to ask how much more the drive will cost to have it installed when you buy the drive and how long they will keep your machine (the job only takes about ten minutes but you never know how long it will take for them to get to your machine).

In most machines, you can just add another drive right into the computer, so that you will have the combined storage area of the two different drives—your original and your new one. Many Mac models, unfortunately, can't accommodate more than one internal drive. So if you get a new internal drive for your Macintosh, you'll need a way to transfer all of your files from your old drive to your new drive. Your best bet? Have the new drive installed when and where you purchase it and request that they transfer all of the information from your original drive. Also, if you are replacing an old drive with a new drive, be sure your new drive is big enough to accommodate everything from your old hard drive and all of the new goodies you expect to get.

The other option is to have a hard drive next to your computer, called an *external drive*. For an IBM compatible, you'll need to first install a SCSI (pronounced Scuzzy) interface card inside your computer. For a Mac, a SCSI port is provided on the back of the computer and your external drive attaches to it. External drives cost more because they come with a separate power supply and because of extra parts (like a case), but they offer some real advantages.

You can remove an external hard drive (they weigh a few pounds) and attach it instantly to another computer. That's especially convenient if you have two compatible computers (two Macintoshes or two IBM compatibles) in two different locations and you don't want to copy lots of stuff to floppies when you are traveling from one machine to the other.

Tip: **Be sure the drive you get has a good warranty—name brands like Conner, Seagate, and Quantum Corporation offer at least a couple of years—and be sure it's from a company that has been in business for at least a couple of years. Lifetime warranties aren't worth much from companies that aren't planning on staying in business past next Tuesday.**

Zip Drive

The Zip Drive from Iomega (1-800 my-stuff) "plays" a diskette that looks very much like a 3.5-inch diskette, but with a couple of very big differences: the Zip diskette holds up to 100MB of data and the diskette only costs about $15! A lot of people have stood up and taken notice of this, including Iomega's competitors. Shown in Figure 8–3, The Zip Drive itself costs about $200 and it comes with one blank diskette. You store these diskettes in little "jewel cases," like the plastic cases that you use to store audio CDs. If you have lots of graphics or big files that you want to keep but you don't want them cluttering up your hard drive, you can save them on a Zip

Compression: Getting More from Less

If you need more storage space but don't want to invest in new hardware, you might want to try compression software. A compression program "dehydrates" your files and stores them in much less space (sort of like a trash compactor for software and files). Some files can be reduced by more than 50 percent in size. When you want to use or open a compressed file, the software automatically "reconstitutes" or uncompresses the file. Any compression program you choose will slow things down a bit since it takes a few moments to both compress and uncompress the file. One important caveat: you can't share a compressed file with someone on another machine unless they have the same compression program loaded. If your friend doesn't have the program, you must first uncompress your file before giving it to that person. Windows 95 users get compression free: Windows 95 includes DriveSpace, Microsoft's own compression program.

Two popular compression programs are Stacker from Stac Electronics (1-800-522-7822) for IBM compatibles and DiskDoubler for Macintosh compatibles from Symantec Corp. at 1-800-441-7234 (they both retail for about $100).

Figure 8–3

The Zip Drive is a great solution to many storage problems

diskette. As you obtain more sounds, images, and other files, you can buy the necessary Zip disks and store them there. It's a great system because it's cheap and it allows you to expand your storage when and as needed.

Compared to the speed of a hard drive, floppy drives are very slow and copying files to and from a floppy diskette is as aggravating as it is time consuming. Although not as fast as a hard drive—the Zip Drive has a seek time of 29ms (about three times as long as a fast hard drive)—it is much faster than a floppy, making the Zip Drive an even more appealing choice. The Zip Drive appeared for the first time in late 1994 and, based on everyone's response, it will probably become the next "floppy" standard. Iomega has even announced a new variation on the Zip Drive, the Jaz Drive

that uses diskettes that hold 1Gb of information. The Jaz drive costs $600 and the 1Gb cartridges cost $100 each. The Jaz Drive also has a 12ms seek time, making it as fast as most hard drives!

Removable Storage— Syquest and Bernoulli Drives

Named after the companies that first introduced the technology, Syquest (shown here) and Bernoulli drives are like oversized floppy diskette drives that play oversized plastic cartridges.

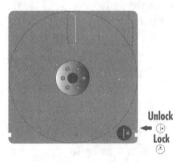

To use one of these drives, you plug the drive into an available parallel port or SCSI port. Each cartridge can hold 44, 88, 105, or 270MB of information. These have been around for a long time and they have been a standard form of storage. Nowadays, you can get a Syquest drive for a few hundred dollars and a cartridge for about $50 (and up), depending on its storage capacity. They have been a favorite of publishers, graphic designers, and artists who create big files. Syquest cartridges have been the accepted standard for a long time, but with the constant price drop for hard drives and the introduction of the Zip Drive, it's difficult to recommend them. They are much slower than the Zip Drive and the cartridges are quite delicate. If you happen to inherit one of these or if a Syquest drive comes with a system you are getting for super cheap, be careful of the cartridges; if you damage the cartridge in any way, you can lose all of the data that you have stored on it.

Tape Backup

Tape backup is a kind of mass storage that saves information to a type of recording tape. A single tape can store huge amounts of information. Tape backup is best suited for archiving; that is, storing enormous amounts of data that aren't currently needed but must be saved and must be accessible—like your safety deposit box.

The Mac uses a DAT machine (digital audio tape) as a tape backup device. DAT machines are a lot more expensive, easily three times as much as tape backup machines for IBM compatibles.

Tape backup can look appealing because the tape player may cost as little as $100-$200 and a single $10 tape can store hundreds of megabytes of stuff. But tape backup isn't good for home use. Although tape drives are relatively inexpensive, they offer the slowest access to your data of any product. Why so slow? Because it is tape, just like a cassette tape or video tape. If you need to get something that is stored at the end of the tape, you have to "shuttle"—rewind the tape or fast forward

Why Do Obsolete Technologies Hold On for So Long?

Floppy drives are slow, but every machine has at least one of them built in. Syquest drives are still everywhere, even with newer, superior technologies available. Why do these products persist even when newer superior technologies are available to replace them?

Any new technology that is overwhelmingly accepted by the computing community typically becomes a standard. It points the way, everyone follows the lead, and a new standard is born. But when a technology defines a standard, it takes a long time to move past it, even when a newer technology proves to be a better standard. When unleaded gasoline for cars began appearing at the pumps, car owners understandably wouldn't junk their older model cars for cleaner burning gas, and so leaded gas remained available at many gas stations. Zip Drives, for example, would be a great replacement for current floppy disk drives, but virtually every machine currently has a floppy and all of those users won't, don't need to, and can't upgrade. In time, newer standards take hold and replace the older ones, but it usually takes a while.

the tape—to get to your information. Unlike a CD or a phonograph record, where you can lift the tone arm and skip to the song you want, tape doesn't give you "random access." That means it could take well over 30 seconds just to find a piece of the information you are looking for.

Who uses tape backup? Big companies that may have to store hundreds of thousands of pages of records. Or perhaps a company that automatically archives (backs up) the contents of all of their computers, which are all connected to a network.

Monitors

Your monitor is your window onto your work and your creations. For most users, the monitor that ships with the computer (most likely the least expensive one that the company sells!) is good enough. For others, however, the display capabilities need to be superior. If you are an artist (or you aspire to be one), a 14-inch monitor won't satisfy your needs. If you expect to have a few things going on at one time on your computer and you want to be able to see them all onscreen at the same time, then you definitely need more screen "real estate."

Size

People are often satisfied with how their monitor looks, they just want more of it. Nowadays, 14-inch monitors are standard, but if the dealer offers a 15-inch and you can afford it, by all means get it. Even one extra inch makes a surprisingly big difference.

Big monitors can be a pleasure to work with. If you are interested in a really big monitor, you'll be able to find 16-, 17-, 19-, or 21-inch monitors. A 17-inch monitor should really satisfy your needs, unless you are laying out magazine spreads or a big city newspaper! With an oversized monitor, you'll get a whole lot more room to work on your projects, and it's a lot easier to work when you can see everything you need to on the screen at one time. There are, however, some other things about large monitors—some drawbacks—that you need to know about.

For one thing, big monitors weigh a ton. The bigger picture tube and supporting electronics weigh an awful lot and that weight will definitely make you think twice before moving your computer (ever). Not only is the monitor heavier (and taller), but it is also deeper, requiring that you have enough room *behind* your monitor so that it doesn't bump up against the wall. With that added monitor size, you'll also need a little more distance in front, between you and the monitor screen. Without that, an hour on the computer will have your eyes spinning like Percy Dovetonsils—remember the character on Ernie Kovacs' TV show?

To get an idea of how big these monitors can be (and how much room you'll need), get some measurements (especially monitor depth) for a couple of monitors you are interested in and see if and how it affects your setup. Regardless, you'll find that bigger monitors demand a whole lot more space. Be prepared.

> *Note:* **You'll find that bigger monitors (17 inches and above) require a lot of power to run and they can heat up a room in a pretty short time, so be prepared for a boost in room temperature and your electric bill.**

Getting a Clear Picture

Having a large enough monitor to meet your needs is certainly important. Regardless of the size, though, you'll need a monitor that's easy to look at. The quality of the image is critical because, unlike a TV, there is a tremendous amount of text that you will read from your monitor. You'll probably hear the term *noninterlaced* (versus *interlaced*) to describe computer monitors. This is a technical term that distinguishes the nature of a computer display from a regular television. Computers use a noninterlaced display.

Resolution

One important feature of your monitor is *resolution*, the clarity of the display. Resolution can actually be measured. Every monitor's display is made up of a grid of dots called pixels. The artist, Seurat, created images using nothing but thousands of fine dots. The more dots you can use—the more pixels, in the computer's case—the clearer and more precise the image appears. The common resolution these days

is 640×480 pixels, which defines the number of pixels across the screen versus the number of pixels from the top to the bottom of the screen. A resolution of 1,024×768 is clearly a better display—more dots—and 1,280×1,024 is fantastic.

Dot pitch is also important in identifying the quality of a monitor's display. Dot pitch defines the distance between each pixel, measured in millimeters (mm). To ensure a good display, look for a monitor that has a dot pitch of .28mm or lower. The lower the dot pitch, the better the resolution. Monitors with a high dot pitch look muddy and unclear.

Color

True, virtually every computer sold today comes with a color monitor, but the color may be less than great; perhaps a beautiful sunset appears to have bands of orange instead of a smooth gradual shift in color. That's because the computer systems are set up to display only a few colors onscreen at one time, and each shade of the same color counts as a unique color. Here's an example. Figure 8–4 shows a black and white landscape.

Figure 8–5 shows the same image as it might appear on a computer system with banding.

> *Note:* **Sometimes two colors are put together in a checkerboard fashion to fool your eye into seeing the pattern as a completely different shade. This effect is called *dithering*.**

Figure 8–4
An image as you would hope to see it on your computer

Figure 8–5
The same landscape as it may appear on your computer screen

Expanding Your Color Range

To get "full color" so that you don't get that banding or dithering effect, you need to change the display settings to the highest number of colors possible. Most systems shipped today are set to display 256 colors, and on some systems that can be changed to over 16 million colors.

This option is not available on all systems and unless you are working with high-quality images or a good graphics program, you won't notice any difference. If you want to expand your color range, here's what to do.

On a PC

On an IBM compatible, open the Main Program Group in Program Manager and double-click on the Windows Setup icon. The Windows Setup dialog box appears. Click on the Options menu. The first field that appears is the display field. Click on the associated down-pointing arrow and find an entry that ends with 640×480×16.8M. Click on that line and then exit. Windows will prompt you to restart your system. If you can't find the line, check with the computer manufacturer to find out if and how you can get full color.

On a Macintosh

To expand your color range on a Macintosh, locate the Monitor control panel. Double-click on it and the characteristics of your monitor appear. The top of the window lists your color options. If the word "millions" appears, you're in luck. Click on it and your system shifts automatically to the greater color range.

Note: **Simple changes to your computer system always seem to bring on the unforeseen. For example, expanding the color range of a computer can affect the speed of your computer when working with color images. The following section describes this problem in greater detail.**

Graphics Boards for Speed

You already know that speed is an important consideration when evaluating just about every component of your computer, and your monitor is no different. When you get a larger monitor, when you increase your resolution, when you expand your color capabilities, or any combination of these things, your computer has to work harder to fill the larger screen area with a sharper image. Every time you make changes onscreen or change your onscreen view, the computer has to calculate and fill in all of the extra space. For the computer, that means sending out more information, and that means it slows down. The way to avoid the slowdown is to purchase a new *graphics card*, or *graphics adaptor*, a board that plugs into a slot inside your computer to speed up the computer's flow of display information. Some of these boards are called "graphics accelerators" and the prices typically start at a few hundred dollars and can run over $1,000. Graphics cards also have special memory built on to the board called VRAM (for video random access memory). The more VRAM you

have, the faster and more capable your graphics card will be.

Every computer has a graphics adaptor in it: when you plug your monitor into the back of your computer, you are actually plugging your monitor into a graphics adaptor. You may be able to upgrade your current card, so before investing in a new card be sure to investigate exactly what the limits of your current card are. It may be able to provide the power you need with a couple of minor and relatively inexpensive changes by the manufacturer.

Alert: **Every monitor gives you some control over brightness and contrast, for example, but many of the controls are accessible only by trained technicians. If there is a serious calibration problem with your monitor, carefully document the nature of the problem and call technical support at once to get things straightened out. A bad display can be a source of eye strain and bad headaches and will quickly discourage you from using your computer.**

Every monitor is different, even when they come from the same manufacturer. When you see a monitor in the store, assume that it has been set up for its maximum display quality. Before a monitor leaves the warehouse, it is calibrated—the electronics are fine-tuned to provide a high-quality image. It's a process that requires precision, and if the monitor gets badly jarred (or dropped from a delivery truck, for example) the calibration will be lost.

Modems

A modem (short for modulator/demodulator) is a telecommunications device that lets you send information across telephone lines to other modem-equipped computers. Modems are de rigor these days. They often come as standard equipment on new computers, and you can't experience the Internet—or any online service, for that matter—without one.

Internal vs. External

There are two basic types of modems: internal modems that are built into the computer, and external modems—like the one shown in Figure 8–6—that sit next to your computer and attach to your computer's serial port. Internal and external modems each have advantages and disadvantages.

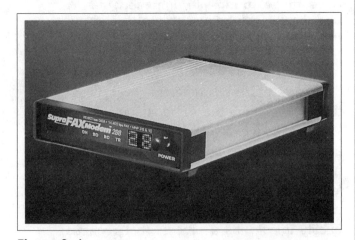

Figure 8–6

An external modem provides indicator lights to let you know if things are OK during an online session

For an internal modem, the biggest advantage is that it's built in! You don't have to worry about an "extra" part bouncing around on your desk. An internal modem is also cheaper; it works off of your computer's power supply and doesn't require a metal chassis or cables like the external modem does. Unfortunately, when your internal modem goes on the fritz, someone has to open the computer to repair or replace it. If you purchase an internal modem separately, after you purchased your computer, someone has to open your computer to install it as well.

External modems have a lot going for them. They are attached with just a cable, so you can easily disconnect them. You can always use them with a different computer, if and when you wish. Most models have front panel indicator lights that let you know when various things are happening. For example, one light blinks when you connect to another modem, another light blinks to indicate that you are (successfully) sending information, and still another indicates that you are (successfully) receiving information. Those signals are important because they let you know whether or not your modem is doing what you expect it to be doing.

Unfortunately, external modems use an external power supply, a black box at the end of a power cord that requires a wall outlet (or power strip). By virtue of bad design, the black box on these power supplies can block off a second outlet when you plug them in. All in all, it's an inconvenience, but a minor one.

For Laptops: One More Option

If you have a laptop computer manufactured in the last couple of years you may have another modem option. Late model laptops usually have a small slot on the side, called a PCMCIA slot (pronounced letter by letter and short for Personal Computer Memory Card International Association). You can get a PCMCIA modem that is about the size of a credit card and fits right into that slot. These are somewhat more expensive (about $350 for a 28.8-Kbps PCMCIA modem) but they keep the laptop experience as light and compact as possible.

Speed

Speed, you are probably not surprised to hear, is how modems distinguish themselves from one another. A modem is very much like a water pipe leading to and from your computer, but it is pumping data, not water. The faster the modem, the faster you can send and receive information. And you do want fast: a slow modem can turn a 10-minute task into an aggravating multi-hour mess. To add insult to injury, slow modems can cost you more in the long run; you are charged a by-the-minute usage fee when using various online services (more in Chapter 20), and so you want to do things fast to minimize these.

Nowadays, the fastest modem you can get for home use—and the speed you want—is 28.8 Kbps. That's 28,800 bits per second. The next fastest is half that speed, 14.4 Kbps, and then 9,600 bps. There are older modems that are slower, but you really don't want to use them and you certainly should not be buying them now. The fast 28.8-Kbps modems cost about $200 and the 14.4-Kbps modems cost less than half that. What you spend for the faster modem, you'll save in time and frustration. Here's the math: a file that takes 20 minutes to send with a 28.8-Kbps modem (or to receive) will take at least 40 minutes with the 14.4-Kbps modem and 60 minutes with a 9,600-bps modem. Most of the time, you will have to pay for your "connect time"—the time you are online—so you save money by minimizing that time. If you currently have a slow modem and you spend much time online, a new fast modem represents a very sensible upgrade.

Fax Modems

Many of the modems that are available also offer fax capabilities from your computer, so that you can send "facsimiles" from your machine. This is a great little feature, but don't overestimate it. For one thing, you can't fax a document unless the document is already stored on the computer. For another thing, your computer must be turned on in order to receive a fax. These two things can greatly reduce the value of fax/modem capabilities. If you want a fax machine for sending comic strips from the newspaper, recipes that you've cut out of the paper, or handwritten documents, this won't work without a scanner (see later in this chapter). In addition, leaving the computer on eats a lot more electricity than a fax machine.

Translating Modem Standards: Hieroglyphics Made Simple

If you've looked at any modem ads lately, you have probably discovered that the ads read like the alien cast from a Star Wars sequel. Instead of R2D2 and C3P0, though, you get MNP5, MNP10, V.32, and V.32bis. This sort of techno jabber may seem impenetrable, but it really isn't.

Here's the key. Each name—like V.34 (pronounced vee dot thirty four)—means that the modem is capable of doing a particular thing. The designation V.32, for example, means the modem can send and receive information at 9,600 bps. Each name represents a standard defined by the CCITT (Consultive Committee of International Telephony and Telegraphy), an international group of telecommunications professionals. The standards ensure that modems from different vendors will work with each other. Each time the committee decides on how new modems should work, they issue a new standard, with the requisite unfathomable name. If a standard is revisited or revised, then the name is appended with the suffix "bis" (rhymes with "miss"; French for "again" or "encore"), hence V.32 and V.32bis (pronounced "vee dot thirty two biss").

If these standards weren't established, modems from two different companies probably wouldn't be able to communicate. As such, any modem ad should tell you that the modem supports or adheres to particular standards. The problems arise when a modem ad indicates that it offers particular features associated with a standard, but in a *nonstandard* way. That's no good. It's not enough that a manufacturer tells you that the modem can achieve speeds of 28.8 Kbps if it can't connect to another modem. The CCITT V.34 standard indicates that, yes, the modem can send and receive information at 28.8 Kbps *and* it does it the way other V.34 modems do it.

Caution: **Modem standards—as confusing as they are—are there for your protection. If a modem says that it is 28.8 but not V.34, don't buy it.**

Following are translations of a few of the more important, and in some instances older, standards.

Standard	What it Means
V.32	Indicates that the modem can send and receive information at 9,600 bps
V.32bis	Indicates that the modem can send and receive information at 14,400 bps

V.34　　　Indicates that the modem can send and receive information at 28,800 bps

There are many different specs associated with a modem, but the most important one now is V.34. If it conforms to this most recent standard, it will satisfy your needs.

CD-ROM Technology

CD-ROMs (compact disc-read only memory) have become the hot computer technology of the 1990s. It is this technology that has helped usher in multimedia—computers and software that use graphics, sound, and animation to educate, entertain, and inform. CD-ROM technology is really divided into two parts: 1) CD-ROM drives, and 2) CD-ROMs, the discs.

CD-ROM Drives

A CD-ROM drive, as shown in Figure 8–7, "plays" a CD-ROM or CD. By comparison, a CD-ROM drive is like a turntable and the CD-ROM is like a phonograph record.

CD-ROM drives can be installed internally in your computer, like your floppy disk drive. You can also get external models that sit on your desktop and attach to your computer with a cable. The CD-ROM drive, however, typically has some sort of tray that the CD-ROM sits in. Push a button on the CD-ROM drive, and the tray appears. Put the CD-ROM on the platter, lightly push the loaded tray back in, and the CD-ROM drive is ready to go.

What to Look for in a CD-ROM Drive

Although you are probably tired of hearing about speed, speed is what you need with a CD-ROM drive. CD-ROM drives are rated to indicate how fast you can get information off of the disk in order to look at it (or listen to it). The speed of the drive is usually referred to as "spin" (like the old 78s, which referred to the number of revolutions per minute on the turntable). Currently, the spin speeds are 2X (referred to as double spin drives, and slow), 3X (triple spin, and faster), 4X (quad spin, and very fast), and now the 6X drive. If you like numbers, these drives are rated as shown in the following table:

Rating	Transfer Rate (kilobytes per second)
1X	150 Kbps (the slowest)
2X	300 Kbps
3X	450 Kbps
4X	600 Kbps
6X	900 Kbps (the current reigning speedster)

The 6X drives are currently the most expensive at about $400, but like everything else, the prices will drop in a very short time. If you can, avoid buying 2X (double spin CD-ROM drives). The 4X spin (quad spin) has become the standard, and they aren't that much more expensive than 3X drives.

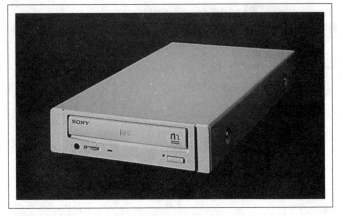

Figure 8–7

An external CD-ROM drive. Many computers come with these built in

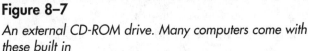 *Note:* **If you already have a 2X spin drive, there is no upgrade path (a way of converting your current CD-ROM drive to the faster kind). So, if you want a faster drive, you'll have to replace what you have.**

CD-ROMs

A CD-ROM is like a turbocharged phonograph record. Instead of just sound on the diskette, you can also have pictures, text, animation, even snippets of video. The CD-ROM drive plays the disc and the computer allows us to see and hear the information that's stored on the disc.

Note: **When describing a CD, the term "disc" is used as opposed to "disk." They are pronounced the same.**

A single CD can give you all of this because it has an enormous amount of storage on it; a CD-ROM can store upwards of 700MB of information. But don't be misled; many people, books, and magazines describe a CD-ROM as a storage device, which isn't altogether true. A storage device lets you store things, but a CD-ROM doesn't let *you* store anything. A CD-ROM may come with hundreds of megabytes worth of programs, files, pictures, and more, but you can't erase anything from the CD-ROM and *you can't save* any of your own work on the CD-ROM—hence, the name ROM, for read only memory.

What's Available on CD-ROM

There are CD-ROMs for everything now; you can get encyclopedias, thesauruses, dictionaries (including the *Oxford English Dictionary*), national phone directories, and more. In fact, some Kodak film development centers, for about $10 more, will give you a CD-ROM with *your* pictures stored on it. There is a small program (free from online services and user groups) that you'll also need, and with that installed, bring home your PhotoCD, pop it into your computer's CD-ROM drive, and you can view the family shots onscreen!

But all that glitters is not gold. Just because the technology holds great promise, doesn't make every CD-ROM worth owning. For example, many manufacturers boast that their CDs contain "hundreds of megabytes" of valuable infor-

CD Content—What About Quality Control?

"Content" is how people refer to the material included on a CD-ROM. Many people have been very critical of what is available thus far on CD-ROM, with some justification; for every great CD-ROM, there are 30 that are mediocre. There are certainly some great titles available, but perhaps a little patience is in order.

Without trying to be too melodramatic, think about the impact that Gutenberg's printing press had on content. People then couldn't think in terms of books or magazines because the only things worth publishing when moveable type was introduced were classic or epic works—like the *Bible*. With the advent of the printing press, people were free to write about and share ideas they were never able to share before. But it took some time for people to figure out what they could share (we are still figuring it out!). Content has evolved since that time, but it has taken more than 500 years to get today's published options.

Multimedia and CD-ROMs hold a lot of promise for publishing, and many see them as a whole new medium whose horizon and potential have yet to be defined. Most of us conceive of communicating as either writing or speaking to others. CD-ROMs change the format so that we can easily include animation, audio, text, and video, and these have not been part of the currency of communication for most people. Most important, however, CD-ROMs can be (and are) designed to be interactive; the user can participate in the work itself and guide what he or she wants to happen. Unlike a book, where you go from the beginning to the end, an interactive CD-ROM "branches"—it lets you decide which of many directions to go in. Some interactive CD-ROMs let you put together a musical composition using the instruments, tempos, and rhythms that you specify. These are new concepts and capabilities, and if the history of publishing is any indicator, it will take some time for "content pioneers" to surface.

mation, as if quantity could somehow ensure quality. It doesn't. In fact, there is a term for this kind of CD-ROM—"shovelware"—so named because the manufacturer just "shovels" stuff onto the CD to try to impress the consumer. Before buying any CD-ROMs, at least try to find a couple of reviews of them. (Several educational CD-ROMs are mentioned in Chapter 16, "Education and Do-It-Yourself Software.")

Alert: **Don't buy a CD-ROM drive to store files or documents on; for all practical purposes, you cannot save any files on a CD-ROM. You can't copy any files to them and you can't use them to back up your system as you would a floppy diskette.**

Capturing Pictures: Scanners

It's certainly fun to look at and even to play with other people's images, but at some point you probably wondered, "How can I get my own images into the computer?" You can get your images into the computer using a *scanner*, a device that "reads" your image and duplicates it as an image inside your computer, sort of like a copying machine without the paper.

You use the scanner's accompanying scanning software to start the scanning process (by clicking on an OK button, most likely). Inch by inch, the document will appear on your monitor. Once scanned, you can save this document for later manipulation and editing.

Scanners really vary in cost and quality. You can get a cheap handheld scanner (it looks sort of like a broad electric hair trimmer) for $50 or you can pay over $1,000 for professional-level scanners. Chances are you'll wind up somewhere in between.

Aside from the hardware, you need to pay close attention to the software that comes with your scanner (and it *should*

come with some software). Depending on the quality of the software, it should let you adjust the contrast and brightness of the image (unlike a copying machine, you control these things via your computer software) and it should also let you edit the image in various ways. For example, if you put the image on the scanner upside down, it will show up on your computer monitor upside down. Instead of turning the actual picture around and rescanning, the software should have a rotate function; click on rotate 90 degrees and the image turns 90 degrees (from 3 o'clock to 12 o'clock) on the computer screen. Click on 180 degrees and the image turns 180 degrees on your computer screen (from 12:00 to 6:00). No matter what kind of scanner you want to get, be sure to sit down with a couple different ones first and see what they offer, both in terms of the hardware and the software.

Note: **Scanners are great for capturing images, but remember that images are typically "owned" by the individual who creates them. It is certainly possible to scan your favorite cover of *Time* magazine, but Time-Warner gets very upset when they become aware that you are using their property without their permission—and without paying the appropriate royalties.**

Color vs. Black and White

You can get both gray scale (no color) or color scanners. A color scanner is more expensive and color scans (what you produce and save on your hard drive when you scan something) are much bigger and require more hard drive space for storage. A full-color scan, for example, requires four times as much storage space as a monochrome (black and white) scan.

Resolution

Scanners are also rated based on the quality of the image that can be captured. Here, resolution is measured in dots per inch, or dpi. Good scanners let you scan at any number of resolutions. Less expensive scanners can't scan an image at the higher resolutions. Again, like a Seurat painting, the scanned image is actually composed of lots and lots of dots. But the precision of a scan is greater than what your monitor can display and it can even be greater than what your printer can print. A good scanner can easily capture an image at 600 dpi or higher. In a black and white image, that means that a picture that is one square inch will take up $600 \times 600 = 360,000$ bytes of storage space. A 3×5 inch picture will require 5.4MB of storage space! Gadzooks! If you are planning on high-resolution images, you'd better have plenty of storage space.

 Tip: **If you are scanning documents for the purpose of printing them on your printer, don't scan them at a higher resolution than your printer can print. No matter how good your scanner is, your printed scans will only look as good as the resolution of your printer.**

Regardless of what kind of scanner you get, you will be able to "grab" images—photos of loved ones, pets, stamps, coins, whatever, and use them in your computer projects. Scanned images can be included in letters that you print (say goodbye to scotch tape and glue) or newsletters, not to mention a little creative mischief, as shown in Figures 8–8 and 8–9. Here's a look at the two types of scanners and what they have to offer.

Flatbed Scanners

A *flatbed scanner*, as shown in Figure 8–10, is designed like a copying machine. The scanner has a glass panel, called a platen, where you put the document for scanning, and a lid that closes on top of the document. Flatbed scanners can also be quite large; a flatbed scanner may need as much desktop space as your computer does and it will add to your electric bill.

Flatbed scanners, starting at about $250, are really convenient: you put a page or picture on the platen, click OK, and you'll have a digital copy of the image stored on your computer in no time.

Handheld Scanners

A *handheld scanner*, as shown in Figure 8–11, is the cheapest way to get into the scanning game, and its size and portability let you use it wherever you want, with whatever (compatible) computer you want. Handheld scanners do not occupy much space at all and they start at about $50.

Figure 8–8

Once you scan the image of a loved one...

Figure 8–9

...you can give him a free facelift!

Handheld scanners work the way you use a squeegee: you move the scanner over the document to capture a strip of it, move over to the next unscanned strip, and repeat the process until the entire image is scanned. The number of strips you have to take depends on how wide the document is and how accurate you are with a squeegee! Because you can't get much width in any single pass of the scanner, handheld scanners are best suited for grabbing notes, comic strips, and columns of text that are no wider than the scanner.

Stitching Software

If you are trying to scan a wide page with a handheld scanner, you will need to use a "stitching program." This is software (that should come with your scanner) that lets you "sew" the scanned strips together so that your document or image looks like it should. Trying to get a single page stitched together can require a lot of patience, and after trying to put together a few pictures you may come away with a greater respect and appreciation for what Dr. Frankenstein

Figure 8–10

A flatbed scanner lets you save and view your own pictures on the computer

Figure 8–11

A handheld scanner for quick and small scans

tried to do with his monster! This inconvenience—having to digitally stitch a family photo together, for example—may be a convincing enough argument that you go buy a flatbed scanner. The real test? Try one in your nearby computer store and see how hard it is to reassemble a photo or letter.

OCR-Scanning Text

One feature provided with many scanners is OCR, *optical character recognition,*

software. This software is designed specifically for scanning text. Instead of taking a snapshot of your document, however, OCR "reads" a typed page and then puts the text in a file for you so that you can edit or reuse the text with a word processor.

This is great if you want to save articles or documents that are already typed. OCR does have limitations, however. It won't read your handwriting (it can't read your doctor's handwriting either, but then, who can?). When the OCR program can't read

A Rose Is a Nose Is a Pose

You have always taken pride in your penmanship, but the scanner's OCR software can't read it. Are these substandard products?

Not at all. OCR can recognize all of the different characters in a printed typeface because they always look the same. In a handwritten page, however, characters never look the same. Some people always write in a cursive style, others print, and some use a combination of the two. Some people close their o's and a's, while others leave them open, and T's are crossed in a million different ways. Computer scientists are trying to tackle this vexing problem, but for now, all of these variations make it impossible for the computer to accurately and consistently translate what a handwritten note actually says.

Note: When you are using OCR software to read a document, it will not retain the formatting for you. If the text uses a fancy typeface or all different type sizes, don't count on capturing these aspects of the document.

The Mouse and Other Input Devices

The mouse is a pointing device and selector. It takes a few minutes to get used to it and, in fact, some people (you may very easily be one of them) never feel comfortable with it. Fortunately, there are a lot of alternatives to the mouse. How comfortable are these alternatives to use? This is probably one of the single more subjective calls in computing. Here are the basic alternatives.

Trackball

The trackball, as shown in Figure 8–12, is like an upside-down mouse; if you look at your mouse, you'll see a little ball on its underside that you are rolling across your tabletop. Instead of rolling a ball across the tabletop, a trackball holds a ball in a stationary position and you roll the ball with your finger. Buttons next to the ball let you make selections. Trackballs, like mice, also take some getting used to and, like mice, people either like them or they don't. One advantage with a track ball? You don't need a mousepad and you don't need so much room, since your mouse isn't moving all over the tabletop.

a character, it leaves an empty box, and perhaps a question mark, to let you know that it has missed something. It can also mistranslate—you need to correct these things manually.

Tablet and Stylus

A tablet and stylus, as shown in Figure 8–13, are the digital equivalents of a pen and pad. The combination plugs into your computer and you hold the stylus as you would a pen. When you want to make a selection, you either press down with the stylus or click a button on the side of it. This little gizmo can feel pretty good—assuming that using a pen feels pretty good to you. This option is probably the most costly, though, ranging from $150–$400.

Why would anybody pay so much money for this when a mouse ships with every computer? Because a stylus has a special feature: it is "pressure sensitive"—it can send a different message to the computer depending on how hard you press down on the tip. For artists who use a tablet and stylus to create, it's the technology that dreams are made of. When an artist draws using a computer and stylus, more pressure results in a heavier stroke; less pressure results in a much lighter stroke, just like painting. The tablets come in different sizes, the larger tablets costing considerably more and taking up more desk space.

Joystick

A joystick, as shown in Figure 8–14, is probably the strangest pointing device of the lot, but in many ways the easiest and most logical of all. Joysticks were made popular first on video games and are commonly seen on motorized wheelchairs where they act as the pilot's steering wheel.

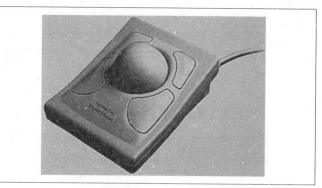

Figure 8–12
A trackball may be easier to handle than a mouse

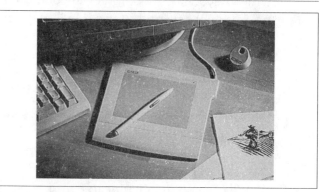

Figure 8–13
The stylus and digital tablet: an artist's dream come true

Figure 8–14
A joystick offers ease of use

The joystick can move in any direction and requires little muscle control. A button near or on top of the stick allows for selection.

Keyboards

Keyboards are your means of entering information into the computer. You can select things with the mouse, but the keyboard is pivotal to the free flow of your ideas.

If you are used to a traditional typewriter keyboard, a computer keyboard can be downright painful to use. Unlike a typewriter, the act of pressing a key on a computer keyboard does not result in any sort of mechanical action; rather, it completes a circuit. That may sound like less strain on your hands, but it actually increases the stress on your hands. Carpal Tunnel Syndrome, a distension of muscles and tendons due to overuse, befalls many typists who migrate from a typewriter to a computer. If you feel any pain or discomfort in your hand, wrist, arm, or elbow, and you can associate it with working on the computer, talk to your physician.

 Alert: **Carpal Tunnel Syndrome can be brought on or exacerbated by use of the mouse as well as the keyboard.**

The Ergonomic Keyboard

Although it looks bizarre (and feels bizarre at first), the ergonomic keyboard, as shown in Figure 8–15, is built to inhibit Carpal Tunnel Syndrome and related muscle problems.

The ergonomic keyboard is more expensive (about $250), but if you fear the consequences of using the standard keyboard, this could be worth the investment. Both Apple and Microsoft make versions of the keyboard.

One-Handed Keyboard

The BATkeyboard ($200, Infogrip, Inc., 1-800-397-0921), as shown in Figure 8–16, allows the user to type on a seven-key keyboard with one hand. All letters of the alphabet are achieved by "chording," pressing multiple buttons simultaneously.

The Kiddie Keyboard

If you have grandchildren in the house, My First Keyboard ($100, Kidtech, 1-800-681-4056), as shown in Figure 8–17, may be just the thing. Indestructible (it's "spill proof"), color coded, and fun to use, the kiddie keyboard allows kids to compute without damaging your no-fun, adult, and easily damaged keyboard.

In addition, you don't have to unplug your own keyboard if you don't want to. They can both be plugged in together.

RAM

You've probably gotten the message "Out Of Memory" by now. If you tried using Windows 95 without 16MB of RAM, you probably got it pretty fast; or, if you tried to start two or three programs on your Macintosh, you got the same message.

Figure 8–15
The ergonomic keyboard is designed to lessen the muscle stress associated with typing

Figure 8–17
The kiddie keyboard won't suffer at your grandchildren's hands

Adding RAM is probably the single most popular upgrade for a computer. Adding RAM makes your computer work faster and in turn allows you to work more efficiently by keeping more programs and/or more information loaded. If you want to add RAM to your system, you must install small memory clips called SIMMs (single inline memory modules) inside your computer. A technician (or yourself, if you want to learn how) clips the SIMMs into *SIMM slots* inside the computer. This job should take a technician less than ten minutes to actually perform. It's not hard, but be sure to ask how much your computer store charges for memory installation *before* taking in your machine. RAM doesn't seem expensive at about $40 per megabyte, but since you buy it in 4, 8, or 16MB measures, the price can definitely climb.

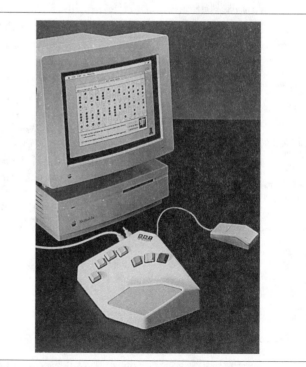

Figure 8–16
A keyboard for those who can only type with one hand

How Much RAM Is Enough?

You can never have enough RAM, but budgetary considerations may say otherwise. Most machines indicate the maximum amount of RAM they can accommodate by saying something like "expandable to 128 megabytes." At about $40 per megabyte, that's over $5,000 worth of memory! Although that's a bit much for a home machine, you should certainly consider having 16MB, especially if you are running Windows 95.

You should also purchase the largest SIMM (measured in megabytes) you can get because your computer has only a limited number of slots to accommodate these, so if you fill all of the slots with 1MB SIMMs, you'll have to discard one (or more) to put in your new, higher capacity chips.

Alert: **If you're working with a laptop, you have a unique set of problems. Your laptop's memory may best be upgraded with a PCMCIA card (personal computer memory card international association). This is a credit card-sized item that slides into a slot on the side of the computer and is significantly higher in price than standard SIMMs.**

Multimedia, Music, and Sound

The multimedia craze has descended full force, and it's impressive. To take advantage of it, you'll need a CD-ROM drive (described earlier) and a few other components.

Sound Cards and Audio Add-Ons

A sound card is a special add-on that goes inside your IBM-compatible computer. A sound card makes it possible to hear your CD-ROM play back with high-fidelity audio and to record sound onto your hard drive as well. It is also an important addition for game aficionados; games often have elaborate sound tracks with all sorts of sound effects and music. If you don't have a sound card, you are out of luck. If you own a Macintosh or you are thinking of getting one, you don't need sound cards because sound capabilities are built in.

Many IBM compatibles ship with a sound card already installed. If your IBM-compatible machine doesn't have one and you want to get one, you can get a decent sound card starting at about $80. These cards have a special SCSI connector so that they can be connected to the CD-ROM drive.

Granted, you can get a very inexpensive card, but be sure to get a card that provides "CD quality sound" (both for recording and playback). This term implies certain technical characteristics that are required for good fidelity. (Again, for you tech nerds, that means 16-bit sampling at frequencies of 44.1 kHz or 48 kHz.) In addition, make sure that the card is "certifiably" Sound Blaster-compatible. Sound Blaster, the original [and best-selling] sound card from Creative Labs, has been accepted as an industry standard. If your card is not 100 percent compatible, you could easily run into problems.

Alert: **If you are using Windows 3.1, even if the card is 100 percent Sound Blaster-compatible, it's probably a good idea to let someone else put it in because these cards can be difficult to install. (If you have Windows 95, it's not a problem.)**

MIDI

MIDI (rhymes with G. Gordon "Liddy") stands for musical instrument digital interface. MIDI is another format that many games and some CD-ROMs take advantage of. If your card does not have MIDI capabilities, then you won't hear these sections.

Most sound cards do have MIDI capabilities built onto them. Earlier sound cards provided something called FM synthesis, which has been eclipsed by wavetable synthesis. In a nutshell, the music that you hear generated by FM synthesis pales in comparison to that generated via wavetable synthesis. If you can, get a wavetable card.

Listening to Your System

Your sound card will let you experiment with sound and listen to your CDs, but you are going to need some speakers to plug in to your sound card if you want to hear anything. Nowadays, everybody is offering low-cost, self-powered speakers, including some of the sound card companies. These are not especially hi-fidelity systems—many

of the low-cost brands are accompanied by a bad buzzing and/or hissing. If you want to ensure good sound and you have a decent stereo system, you can connect your sound card to your home stereo system. The downside is that you have to turn on your stereo system when you want to do anything with your sound card.

Tip: **If you want good sound but you don't have a good stereo and you don't want to invest in a good self-powered speaker system, try a set of good headphones. You can plug these into the sound card or into your CD-ROM drive's headphone jack. You can get a pretty decent set of headphones for about $25—you'll get good sound and you won't disturb others late at night. The downside? Two people can't listen at once.**

Multimedia Upgrade Kits— The Easy Way

If you don't have a CD-ROM drive for your computer, a multimedia upgrade kit is the best way to go. You want a kit that provides a CD-ROM drive, a sound card, speakers, cables, and a microphone. Some of the kits available include a boatload of CD-ROM titles that would cost you as much as the upgrade kit if you bought them separately (not that you can use or want all of them). You can get these kits for about $400.

What Are All Those Weird Peripherals in the Magazines?

All of the peripherals and add-ons discussed here address the "traditional" needs of almost all computer users. There are a lot of other, nonstandard things, though, that people want their computers to do and they need different peripherals to get those things done, or to help them get those things done. Some things are more serious in nature, like in the scientific community where scientists or physicians use a computer to run or monitor experiments or procedures. Other things are slightly more, well, unconventional, like a special Lego controller that lets you create and program Lego Robots. Or a sewing machine that plugs into a computer and lets you program embroidery patterns (with multicolored threads). There is even a cake icer that takes any photograph, scans it, and then recreates the photograph—in icing—on the cake!

If there is a peripheral that you could use, but that's not listed in this chapter, investigate—through magazines, online groups, user groups, and other sources.

Aside from the specialty stuff, though, you'll see a lot of other peripherals advertised, the bulk of which are for computer people who work with networks. You'll see or may already have seen advertisements for bridges, routers, ethernet hubs, token ring cards, network interface cards, Netware, 10 base-T products, AppleTalk hardware, and a slew of other products that have odd names and seem to have a lot of flashing lights. Not to worry. These products are only of interest to those computer people who are connecting lots of machines together. They don't serve any purpose for a home machine.

PART II

Applications

CHAPTER 9

The World of Software

> **"Measure a thousand times and cut once."**
>
> —A Turkish proverb

Software is what gives your computer identity and functionality. With the right software, your computer can help you with virtually any subject or discipline.

So Many Choices, So Little Time

There are thousands of programs available to help you perform various tasks and there are usually numerous competing programs for any given task. There are programs for word processing, finance, publishing, graphics, entertainment, and more. There are numerous programs available for IBM compatibles, many others for Macintosh computers, and many others available for both kinds of machine. This section of the book looks at the world of software and provides valuable information that will help you in evaluating, buying, and using different software programs.

Don't Rush

As you start to see all of the programs available to you, you'll be tempted to go out and buy a lot of software, but you'll do better to temper the impulse with a bit of caution. Software, by and large, is not cheap, and making hasty decisions can cost you a lot of money. In addition, price is not an adequate indicator of whether the software is good for what *you* need. As often as not, an inexpensive program is as well-suited to your needs as the big sticker program.

Like anything else, you don't want to spend your money on something that you don't really need.

Popularity Contest?

As price does not always correspond to the best choice, neither does the popularity of a program. Although everybody down at the art school may be buzzing about a particular program (Photoshop, for example), that doesn't mean it's the one for you. Popularity does ensure that the program does something that a group of people are really impressed by. Without sounding facetious: it may not be what you need, but for a lot of people to like it, it must be really good—for something. Programs don't get popular, though, unless they perform well for a lot of people. If it's a popular program and it does what you want it to do, then go for it.

A Few Freebies

Windows users get a few programs installed for free—Microsoft calls them "applets" (short for "little applications"). Applets, a few of which are shown in Figure 9–1, are not especially powerful, but you can experiment with them and learn from them. Applets give you a taste of what's available—at the right price.

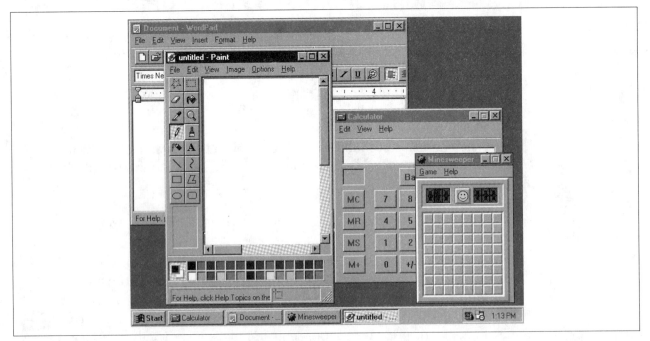

Figure 9–1

A few of the popular applets in Windows

Windows comes with a few programs that let you experiment without buying any software. WordPad is a low-end word processor; Paintbrush, a painting program; and just for fun, a game—Minesweeper.

Alert: **Windows also comes with a couple free games. For the uninitiated, games can be very addictive; you can start playing a game at 2:00 P.M., look up at the clock in what feels like twenty minutes and it's 4:00 P.M.—you've lost two hours!**

Software that Comes with Your Computer

Many computer companies are including free software with their computers as an added incentive to get you to buy a particular machine. These are full-fledged programs that are often quite powerful—and popular. These deals can often be very good, but you should pay attention to the list of programs the manufacturer is providing to see which of them suit your particular needs. These software incentives may also be offered with various peripherals, like multimedia upgrade kits, printers, and/or scanners.

Paying the Price

Finding the right price for the software you want can be really confusing. Software companies, like car companies, sometimes attach a suggested retail price to their products. A dealer can then discount the pro-

gram as he or she sees fit. The suggested retail price is always quite inflated, so if that's the first price you see advertised, you should shop around before buying. A reputable mail order outfit will typically have all the best selling programs at very low prices and your neighborhood computer store might have a good price. The big warehouse stores like Price Club/Costco offer great prices, but they usually have a very limited selection—they only sell the few top selling products. If you join a user group, check for specials that the group may offer from time to time. Lastly, you can buy from the software publisher, but they usually only sell at the suggested retail price.

Tip: **Software companies will often offer university and college students (unbelievably) good discounts on their products. If you are taking classes at a school, find out what software specials are available to you and take advantage of them.**

When the Discount Is Too Deep

If you see an offer that's too good to be true, be careful; it just may be. If a [popular] program is deeply discounted, be sure to check and make sure the version number of the program is the most current. Popular computer programs are updated and improved on a fairly regular basis (perhaps yearly) and, like cars, last year's model is old news—and not worth its original retail price.

You should also check to make sure the program is not a "limited edition" or "lite" version—a scaled-down version of a program priced much lower than the full-blown program. Unless it's what you are looking for, don't buy a lesser product.

Upgrades: A Great— but Exclusive—Deal

A software upgrade is an inexpensive revision of a popular program. Upgrades are available to users who have already paid full price for a different—earlier—version of the software. Don't be misled, though: an upgrade requires that you own a previous version of the program. Think you're going to outsmart Bill Gates and buy it anyway? After all, how does he know if you have it or not?

Guess what? Software developers can know and they do. When you install the software, the program *looks* for a copy of the previous version on the machine. If you don't have it on your drive, the computer won't install the new version. If you call the developer for assistance, be prepared to have a serial number for your original purchase—typically on the master diskettes. When they ask for this and you don't have it, surprise—you're caught!

"Bootlegged Software"—It Isn't Really Free

If you have any software that you like, or if any friends or family members have any software that you like, the thought may have occurred to you that "we can each copy our software and pass it around. This way, we each pay for one program and we each get several programs."

Can you do this? Well, physically, you can (unless the program is on a CD-ROM), but it is unethical and illegal. A single program can easily take a developer a year to create, requiring the skills of artists, programmers, designers, and others; in short, software development costs a lot of money up front and there is never any guarantee of a return for the developers. The only return they see is if the program is a success and people buy it. The companies that develop these programs cannot continue to develop cool programs if people don't pay for them.

You may ask "But isn't Microsoft wildly successful? Do developers really need my money?" Yes, to both questions. Yes, Microsoft has been wildly successful, but their success is hardly sound justification to bootleg software. The vast majority of software companies are small, independent businesses, and pirating software can put them out of business.

There are other problems with copying software. You can't get technical support when things go wrong. When you call a company for support, they ask for your product's serial number or registration number. If you don't have the original number, or if you acknowledge that you "pinched" your copy, you won't get help and you might get into trouble. This can prove especially embarrassing if and when you have a bad system crash and someone has to help dig you out. It may be all the more difficult if you are trying to explain what all that unregistered stuff is doing on your machine.

What's worse is relying on a product that could fail and not having any way to recover from the failure. If you are working on a deadline to finish that newsletter with unregistered software, and the program stops working, you are totally out of luck unless you want to go out and buy the program that minute.

Aside from all of the negatives that can befall you—and the pressing guilt that you may experience—you'll really benefit from buying the software. In doing so, you get the manuals and the tutorials that accompany the product. That can save you hours of trying to figure out how to do something that has a simple explanation.

> ## Golden Rule:
>
> Pay for software that you use. It will reduce your [product-related] headaches and allow the software developer to create even better products.

Getting the Latest Version

Is it really important to get the latest and greatest version of a program? Yes. A new version can be a completely different program. The interface can change, the commands to perform tasks can change, irksome bugs may be fixed, and more. Nowadays, version changes are almost always for the better and a newer version is more than likely easier to use and understand. If you get an old version of a program, you'll meet with other problems as well. Getting support and getting questions answered is also a more difficult task.

Tip: **It's not always so easy to know when a new version of a program is about to appear. When you do buy a program, be sure to send in your registration card. The company will then send you all sorts of product literature, including news on future releases.**

Stay on Your Platform

In nerd talk, a type of machine (IBM compatibles, for one; Macs for another) is described as a *platform*. A lot of excellent programs are cross-platform—there are versions available for both Macintosh and PC computers. When you are shopping for software, though, be sure to specify which platform you are buying for. Even though a program may be cross-platform, the Macintosh version only runs on a Mac and the PC version only runs on a PC. And even though a program may be available on both platforms, the version numbers may be different for each platform. The newest Mac version may be 3.5, for example, and the newest PC version of the program may be 2.0. To complicate matters further, a new version of a cross-platform program may appear on one platform months before it appears on the other. If you see a cross-platform program that you like, evaluate it on the machine you intend to use it on. Some cross-platform programs are slightly different on each platform, so be sure the version you are getting has the features you expect. Finally, some products that are sold on CD-ROM include both the Mac and the PC versions on the same disc! (Some CD-ROMS can be formatted so that the same disc can work in both machines. If the software box indicates the CD-ROM is Mac/PC-compatible, you have such a disc.)

> ## Golden Rule:
>
> When you hear about a new version of your favorite program, make sure the program released is intended for your particular platform and not some other kind of machine.

Get the Right Kind of Disk

Be sure to get your software on a disk format that you can use. More and more programs come on CD-ROM discs, so if you don't have a CD-ROM drive, you'll need the floppy diskette version of the program. For big programs that come on lots of floppy diskettes, a CD-ROM version is preferable. Not all big programs are available on floppy diskette, however. CD-ROMs hold hundreds of megabytes, and if the program uses all of that space, then the floppy disk alternative is out of the question. Programs that are small and can fit on

one or two diskettes are not necessarily available on CD-ROM, either.

Note: **When buying companion books about a particular software program, pay close attention to what version the book addresses. A book about an older version of a program may be useless if you're trying to learn about the newest version. Ditto for taking classes. Be sure the class you want to take addresses the same version of the program you are interested in. Otherwise, you may find yourself lost in a discussion of a product you are unfamiliar with.**

Software Protection

Some programs, usually from smaller companies who can afford piracy the least, will build some form of *copy protection* into their program. Copy protection is intended to prevent users from making illegal copies of a program. There are a few different types of copy protection, and although not so common anymore, you might run into one kind or another.

The most aggressive form of copy protection is the *dongle*, a custom-made attachment that a user must plug into a designated port. Before the program can start, the program sends a message to the port and awaits a message back from the dongle. If you don't have the dongle, the program won't get the go-ahead message and will never start. A dongle appeals to software developers because the user can copy the program to a million different machines but can only use it on one machine at a time. Dongles are bad news for consumers, though. They raise the price of the software enormously, and you know who pays for that!

Another more common form of copy protection allows you to install the program only a set number of times. If you try to install the program on three machines when you only get two installs, it won't let you. If you want to delete the program from your computer, you must go through an "uninstall procedure" to reclaim the copy. Many people have complained bitterly about this form of protection and as such, developers are using it less and less. If this form of protection is used on a program, the developers will tell you about it in the installation chapter of their manual. If you don't like it—and no one does—you should let the company know how you feel.

Another, less intrusive form of copy protection prompts you with a question before running the program. For example, "What is the 5th word on page 157 of the manual?" You, in turn, open the manual and type in the 5th word from page 157. If you don't have the manual (a common problem for bootleggers) you can't enter the word and the program will not start. Of course, a more enterprising—make that determined—pirate will copy the manual, and herein lies the real problem: pirates are always figuring out how to get around copy protection, so a developer must keep changing and perfecting the copy protection scheme. But to change and perfect the protection means time and money devoted to something other than the program. That

International Piracy, Software Style

Software developers depend on copyright law—and the enforcement of it—to protect themselves against the illegal duplication of their products. Outside of the United States, this can be extremely difficult, as in the case of China.

China flagrantly violates international copyright agreements and the computer industry is losing big time. Between 1993 and 1994, China acquired over 3/4 of a million PCs, yet less than 1 million dollars in business software has been sold there, representing an average of about $1.00 per computer—an outrageously low number. Estimates put the rate of software piracy in China at greater than 94 percent, indicating a flagrant disregard for the rights of all developers.

With the explosive growth in the CD-ROM market—and the ease with which professionals can counterfeit these programs—U.S. software developers fear the threat of increasing Chinese piracy; several Chinese underground CD-ROM counterfeiters have already surfaced, churning out counterfeit products at an ever-increasing rate. Unfortunately, the counterfeit software is not just used in China. A formidable export business thrives in China and threatens U.S. software developers even more.

Software Freemasons—Beta Testing

They sometimes wear their status as a badge of honor. Sometimes, like secret agents, they will hardly (if at all) even acknowledge that they are a part of the team. They are beta testers, those select few individuals who have chosen and have been chosen to use and test a software program before it is released to the general public. Who gets enlisted into these beta test programs and just what exactly are they doing?

Before a company can release a software program, they must test it to make sure that all of the features are working and that the software does not unexpectedly do something it was not intended to do (like crash your computer or format your hard drive!). In their quest for perfection, the developers assemble a number of dedicated users—power users and nonpower users alike—who they believe can put the product through its paces. The testers' mission is to find and report any bugs or problems the software has. Beta testing doesn't pay anything, but it does carry with it the honorable distinction of making you an industry insider ("*I beta tested the Icelandic release of PowerWidget!*"). It also gives you the best "sneak peek" possible of the next release. The downside of beta testing? Sometimes you do find those bugs that crash your system, delete files, and/or format your hard drive. It's all part of the job, and it can be especially unpleasant.

Who gets to beta test? If you have to ask, you're out of luck. If you're interested, though, here's one way to stack the deck in your favor: If you use a product and you would like to get on the beta test team, try to find a bug or two in the current release. Call the technical support people and discuss the problems, and, after things are reported, mention that you sure would like to beta test the next release. When the beta release approaches, a software company often searches their user base for those who are good at sniffing out bugs.

means we all wind up paying more for the program.

The Software Police!

The Software Publishing Association investigates cases of piracy (they even have an 800 number to report scoundrels) but they aren't coming after small home users—yet. The SPA focuses on larger companies that buy a single copy of a program and then install it on lots of machines throughout the company. They also investigate counterfeiting by looking for companies that illegally duplicate and sell copies of software programs.

Freeware and Shareware

After seeing how expensive some software can be, it may not seem possible that free software could exist. Well, it does, and while some freeware programs may not be worth much, others can prove indispensable. Freeware is written by people who are willing to share their work with others, gratis. Software companies rarely give things away, but some individuals do.

Shareware, freeware's conceptual cousin, introduces another approach to getting a program out in the public eye.

Shareware programs are often more sophisticated and elaborate than freeware programs. With a shareware program, you get the program—fully functional—and you can test drive it to your heart's content. If you like it, you are asked to send a [relatively] small payment to the author. When you do, you become a registered user and you often receive a manual and update information. In some instances, the shareware version works fine, but some of the features are missing until you purchase the product and become a registered user. There are some great shareware programs out there, most easily accessed via the various online services or from your local user group.

Golden Rule:

When you find shareware that you really like, send in your money and become a registered user. Shareware developers are not "big players" and their alternative approach to selling software needs to be supported.

Word Processing
and Desktop
Publishing

Judging by the success of word processing and desktop publishing programs, the written word won't be replaced any time soon. These programs offer a bevy of formatting options for the written word previously available only through commercial print shops and publishing houses.

Word Processors

A word processor is like a supercharged typewriter that lets you get your ideas and thoughts out quickly. A word processor gives you incredible flexibility in formatting and presenting whatever you choose to write.

Word processors have become necessary for effective writing, helping to automate and remove the drudgery many of us associate with the writing process. Coming up with ideas, stories, screenplays, and poems is the fun part; accurately typing any of it without making tons of mistakes, however, is the "not fun" part. Getting your thoughts down on paper can be extremely tedious and time consuming—without a word processor, that is. Word processors are invaluable because they so effectively reduce that tedium. The writer, Peter DeVries, said it best: "I love being a writer. What I can't stand is the paperwork."

To make the job of writing easier, word processors these days offer everything from grammar checking and spelling correction to built-in reference works like synonym finders and almanacs.

With a word processor, your words and ideas can flow onto the "page" as effortlessly as you can think of them. If you make a mistake in typing, you see the mistake onscreen and you can correct it any time. The image of the frustrated writer yanking, crumpling up page after page from the typewriter, and filling a waste basket to overflowing is a thing of the past; your words don't show up on paper until you are happy with them—only then do you send your document to the printer. For many of us, a word processor is the single most important program on a computer because it allows us to capture our thoughts and feelings and communicate them to others.

Alert: **If you're a person who never learned how to type, a word processor may prove frustrating at first. Don't be discouraged; the more you write, the more familiar you'll become with the keyboard, and the faster you'll begin to type. If you are interested in working on your typing skills, there are software programs available (like Mavis Beacon from Mindscape, 1-800-234-3088, or Expert Typing—$14.95!—from Expert Software, 1-800-759-2562) that make typing drills more like video games.**

What Can a Word Processor Do for Me?

When first introduced, word processors were clunky programs that used hard to learn commands for even the simplest writing chores. Today, they are enormously powerful programs that can perform tasks

more commonly associated with the neighborhood print shop. Figure 10–1 shows what you can expect to see when you open a powerful word processing program. A program that offers so much may strike you as unwieldy, however, with the powerful and complex features obscuring how to execute the easy tasks.

Typically, the more powerful the program, the more intimidating it is to learn, right? Not really. Not anymore, anyway. Granted, a word processor for the writing professional includes a larger number of complicated features, but there are also a lot more easy-to-use features as well.

> ### Golden Rule:
> Word processing should mean more communication with friends and loved ones. You can become a word processing master by writing letters to friends and family. The practice will teach you how to word process and the end result is lots of contact.

Word processors offer features aimed at all kinds of writers, so don't be put off by the abundance of what may seem to be useless features for your particular needs. For example, if you just need to write letters, poems, or short stories, options such as footnoting, indexing, and cross-referencing are not important to you. If you are writing

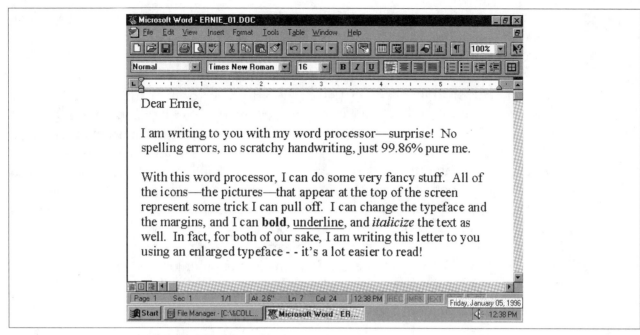

Figure 10–1

Word processors provide all sorts of features so you can focus more on being creative

your autobiography, college dissertation, or some other long and complicated document, though, you'll be grateful for such features.

Regardless of what kind of documents you write, there are many features in word processors that you would no doubt use if you knew they existed (and if they were easy to use). Here's a look at a few of the basic features of a word processor that are both powerful and easy to use. These features alone make a strong case for becoming computer and word processor literate.

Typing Without a Care

Word processors let you type nonstop. You don't have to worry about a carriage return (starting on the next line when you approach the right margin) because the word processor does it automatically. If you *don't* want a line to go all the way to the margin or you want to start a new paragraph, then you hit ENTER—which is the equivalent of a carriage return. If you want, you can just type away and then worry about the formatting when you're done writing.

Word processors offer a lot of margin options. As with a typewriter, margins can be set to provide more or less white space on the left and right edges and at the top and bottom of the page. Instead of sliding a metal tab like you use on a typewriter, a word processor lets you set the margin by sliding an onscreen tab (at the top edge of the page) with your mouse. Here's where a typewriter gets left in the dust. After you have written a document, a word processor lets you change the margins on all or part of your document and it will automatically (and instantly) reflow the text to fit the new margins.

You can even change the fundamental layout of the page. Good word processors, for example, let you put text in a multicolumn format. You get to define how wide the columns should be (each column can be different) and how much margin should appear between the columns. Figure 10–2 shows a multicolumn format for the Gettysburg Address.

Editing Your Work

Word processors are superior to typewriters in many other ways. Whenever you put words to paper, you often want to rearrange or reorder what you have written. Aside from the myriad formatting options in a word processor, you can also reorganize and shuffle the contents of your document however you wish. Word processors let you cut, copy, and paste any segment of a document to another location in the document—even to a completely different document.

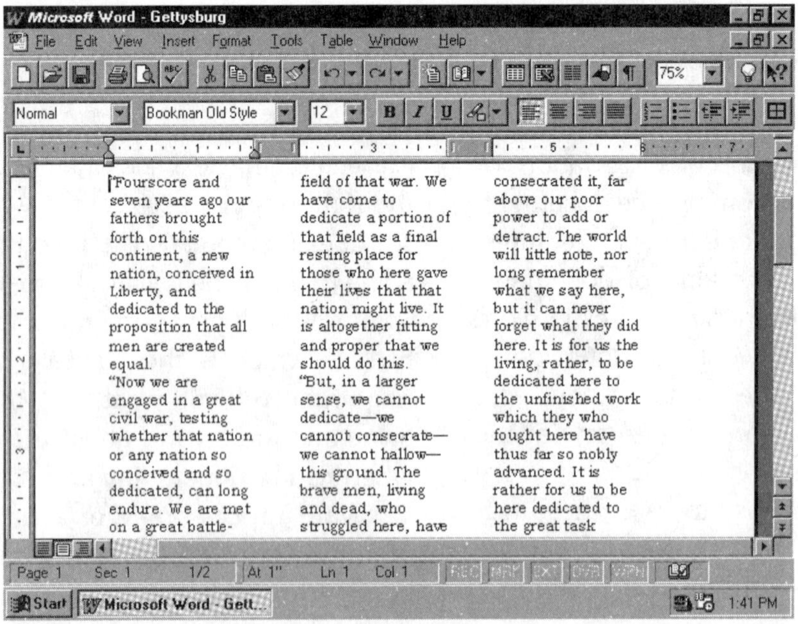

Figure 10–2

You can easily change the format of your document to include multicolumns—a Herculean task when attempted with a typewriter

The Cut command, represented by little scissors, lets you highlight a section of your document and cut it from the document, as if you snipped it out with a scissors. The Copy command, represented in MS Word by a picture of two identical pages, lets you highlight a section of your document and copy it—it doesn't disappear from the page—as if you made a quick Xerox of the section. In both cases (cut and copy), the section of the document you selected is held in the computer's memory so you can paste it somewhere else. To paste your section, move the cursor to the spot in the document where you want it to appear and select the Paste option, represented by a glue brush or jar of glue.

Here's an example. Let's say you want to make paragraph 5 of a letter you've just written into paragraph 1. To do so, you highlight the paragraph, click on the cut icon, move the mouse to the top of your letter, click the mouse, and paste the paragraph to its new location. Word processors let you organize on the fly—you can change the order of anything at anytime—and you don't have to use a scissors and tape to put it all together!

Caution: **You can only cut, copy, and paste one text segment at a time. If you cut a segment and then cut another segment before pasting the first one, you lose the first one.**

Spell Checking and Reviewing

For many users, spell checkers make a word processor worth the price of admission alone. Anytime you want to proof your writing for typos, select the Spell Checker option and the software will go through the document, showing you misspelled words and prompting you for corrections. Spell checkers also catch errors like "don;t," "I am am writing," and "english" (the language requires an upper case "E"). When possible, spell checkers offer suggestions for what you may have been aiming for. Spell checkers will not catch misspellings that turn out to be words, so if you mistyped "I spotted my dog" as "I potted my dog," you'll have to correct that manually. If your spell checker comes across a proper name or words it doesn't know, you can always add them to the spell checker's vocabulary—its word list—so it won't flag it again unless you misspell it.

> ## Golden Rule:
> Always spell check your documents. Spell checkers don't miss many errors (they won't get misused homonyms, true) and they pick up some nonspelling errors that everyone typically misses. For example, a spell checker will identify the duplication error in *this this* sentence and alert you to the problem.

Repeating Your Efforts—Effortlessly

The ability to make multiple copies of a document and vary each slightly can be a phenomenal timesaver. If, for example, you need to send the same letter to 25 people, you can create 25 copies with the same content but using a different name and address. In fact, a feature called *mail merge* even lets you automate this process. You write a single letter or document and specify a mailing list—perhaps a group of names in your electronic phone book. The word processor then goes through the specified list and inserts the appropriate personal information in each letter and prints the required number of "personalized" letters.

Note: **Mail merge is a great feature, but it's really only worth the trouble if you have 20 or more people to send your letter to.**

Keeping Your Pages Straight

If you write a story or essay that is several pages long, a word processor can automatically number your pages, meticulously placing the page numbers in the same place on each page and not interfering with the text you have written. No matter how much you edit your document, the word processor will automatically *renumber* your pages correctly.

If you want to include more information than just a page number at the top or bottom of the page, you can use a *header or footer*. A header is a line of information that appears at the top of the page independent of the text. Header information can include a title, chapter number, page number, time, and/or the date—whatever you want, really. You typically enter the information you want via a menu com-

mand and it is automatically placed on each page accordingly—you only type it once and the computer deals with proper placement on each page. If you want to include the date and time, don't type it in manually. Instead, click on the date and time icons. In this way, your date and time displays are automatically updated; if you print the document again next week, the document displays the new print date. If you want to include this sort of information, but you want it at the bottom of the page, you can use a *footer* instead. Headers and footers work the same except one appears at the top of the page, the other at the bottom.

Creating Elaborate Documents— With a Little Help

Some word processors provide step-by-step guidance in creating very complex documents. In Microsoft Word, for example, when you create a new document, you are first prompted with a list of "templates"—predefined document forms. With a template, you write your document and then assign predefined formats to the different sections. Some of the templates—called "Wizards" in Microsoft products—are actually walk-thrus. When you opt for a Wizard, the program prompts you to enter individual sections of the document—it does the formatting for you—and then generates the document. Once generated, you can add and change the text as needed.

With the Newsletter Wizard, for example, Word prompts you for a banner, the number of columns to use, the number of pages in the newsletter, and a few other facts. Word then generates the newsletter and all you need to do is fill in the news. Figure 10–3 shows what less than two minutes with the Newsletter Wizard can generate.

Printing a Document

Creating and formatting your document onscreen is great, but when you want to give or send what you have written to someone, you'll need to print it out.

You have a number of options available. For example, you can change the page orientation from portrait to landscape (8.5 × 11 versus 11 × 8.5). You can reset margins

and, with many printers, you can specify the quality of the print (the better the quality, the longer it takes to print). One of the most powerful and important features, however, is the Print Preview option. With Print Preview, you can view the layout of your document to ensure that everything is formatted as you intended. Figure 10–4 shows a typical Print Preview screen.

If you see a problem in Print Preview, you can return to the document and adjust it accordingly—before you print it.

Note: **When using multicolumn layout, the actual multicolumn format only appears in Page Preview mode or Page Layout mode.**

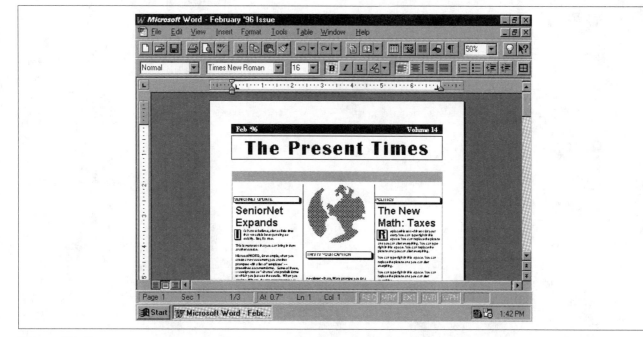

Figure 10–3

Sophisticated word processors like MS Word 6.0 let you build complex documents in minutes

CURIOUSER AND CURIOUSER

When you work with a word processor, you will be looking for answers to some frequently asked questions. Here are a few of those questions—with the answers.

Q: I only want a few lines of text on page two of my document, but my word processor insists that I fill the page. How can I get to the next page without filling up the previous page?

A: When you want a new page—before the word processor thinks it's time—find the menu option that designates "insert page break." This forces the word processor to start on a clean page, regardless of whether the previous page has been completed. A *soft page break* is when the computer automatically inserts the break. A *hard page break* is when you insert the break.

Q: My document looks very different when I print it than it appears onscreen. Is there a way to see how a document will print before I print it? I'm wasting a lot of good paper on this!

A: Yes. Before you send your document to the printer, look for a Print Preview option (typically under the File menu). This will show you how each page of your document will look when printed. The term for seeing things as they really are is WYSIWYG (pronounced Whissy-Wig) for "what you see is what you get."

Q: I was working in my word processor and I used the Search/Find command to find a poem I wrote last night. I can't find the poem. Could it have been erased?

A: If you saved your poem before turning off your machine, it's on your hard drive, but try using your computer's Search/Find command—not your word processor's Search/Find command—to find it. The Search/Find command in a word processor is searching through the text of the document you have open, not the different files on your hard drive.

Q: There are so many buttons, pictures, icons, and options at the top of my screen that I'm getting dizzy! What do they all do?

A: Those toolbars and icons are shortcuts to many of your word processor's options. Every software program has its own set and you can even change the ones that appear onscreen at any given time. The best way to learn them? Experiment!—but don't get footloose and fancy free with a document that you really care about or that you haven't backed up. Use a copy or a test document that you can lose. Once you have a test document, open it, highlight a piece of text, and then click away on the toolbar and see what happens.

Q: My friend and I both have the WonderWrite word processor from ACME software. When I send him files on disk, he can't open them. What's wrong?

A: Sounds like you have the same program but you have a more current version. Find out what version your friend has. Newer versions of a program can always read documents created in the older version, but the older version can't read the newer documents. Newer versions of a program can also save documents using the older version's format. If your friend doesn't want to upgrade, then you need to save any shared documents with the older version format.

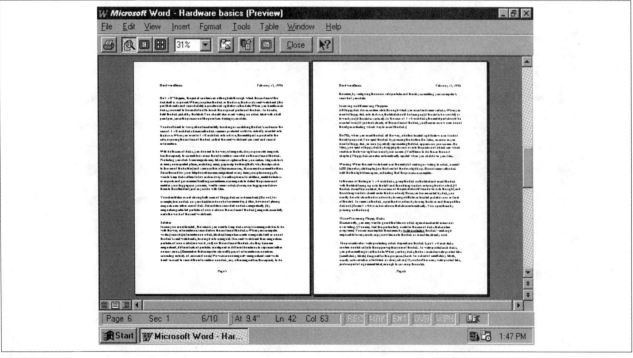

Figure 10–4

Print Preview lets you check your document before you print it out. Although you can't read the text, you can see the big picture

Anatomy of a Word Processed Page

Word processing has come a long way in the last ten years. Word processing software used to provide the functionality of an advanced typewriter, and although it still does, it also offers a whole lot more. Basic features now include the ability to format a document with columns and to include graphics within a document. Here's a look at the sort of document a good word processor can help you create.

1 The size of the type is variable, so that you can turn anything into a headline.

2 Any amount of text and any size text can be italicized.

3 Any amount of text and any size text can be underlined.

4 Any amount of text and any size text can appear in bold face.

5 You can apply several different effects to the same text—this text is **bold**, *italic*, and <u>underlined</u>.

6 Word processors also let you "pour" any of your document into columns, like in a magazine or newspaper.

7 The text can be aligned to the left, centered, or to the right. This headline is centered.

8 You can easily add fancy touches such as drop caps—oversized leading letters that give your document a nice touch of elegance.

9 There are numerous fonts—typefaces—that you can use to spice up your document.

10 You can insert graphics or clip art into a document.

11 We left this mistake in, but your word processor would tell you about it: if the same word appears twice in a row, the spell checker asks if you want to delete one of them.

12 This mistake would also get caught by the spell checker: the spell checker would flag this—just add a space between d and t.

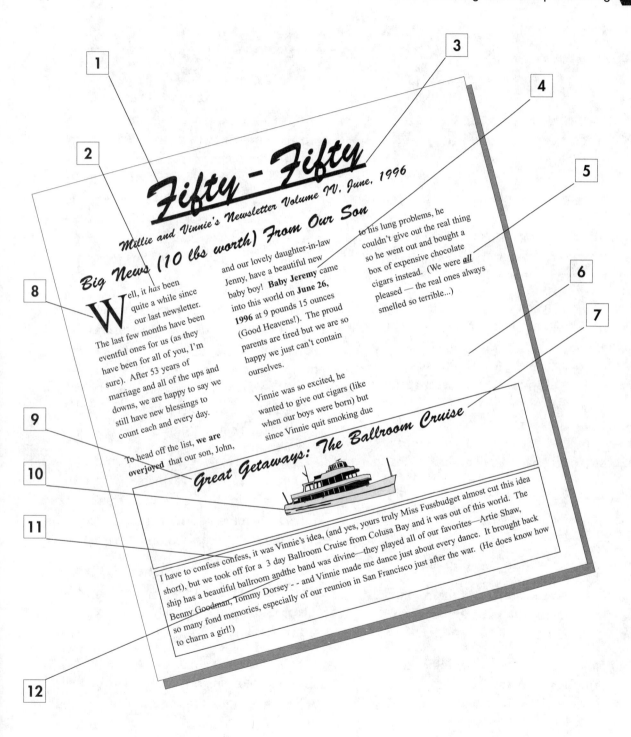

1
2
3
4
5
6
7
8
9
10
11
12

Word Processing:
Just a Few Words

A whole vocabulary has sprung up around word processing. In fact, it is very much the language of professional editors and publishers. Here are some of the terms you may hear when people discuss word processors. You may not want or need to know them all, but it's nice to have them when you read related articles or hear others using the terms in conversations.

ASCII text (pronounced "ask-ee") is any text that is free of any formatting—no italics, no fancy typeface, no underlining, and no borders or graphics. ASCII is a universal text format, and every word processor can open, edit, and save ASCII files. ASCII stands for American Standard Code for Information Interchange. ASCII files are sometimes referred to as "plain text" or "text" files.

Alignment is the generic term for left, right, and center justified text.

Flush left/flush right describes text alignment along a margin (see also *justification*).

Footer refers to the line of informational text that appears at the bottom of each page, independent of the main text.

Header refers to the line of informational text that appears at the top of each page, independent of the main text.

Hypertext is a specially formatted word, phrase, or sentence that lets the reader jump to a different piece of text by clicking on it. In an "electronic" advertisement for the *Mercury Cougar*, for example, clicking with your mouse on the word "Cougar"—if designated as hypertext—could take you to a definition and description of this member of the cat family.

Justification is the term to describe text alignment along a margin. *Left justified* means that the text is aligned with the left margin. *Right justified* means that the text is aligned with the right margin. *Justified* or *centered justified* means that the text is aligned with both margins.

Landscape refers to orienting an 8.5x11-inch page so that it is 11 inches wide and 8.5 inches high. This is the preferred way of printing when the information or picture is longer than it is high (see also *portrait*).

Macro is a set of steps that can be performed with a single action or keystroke. Macros allow you to quickly perform often-used procedures.

Margins are the white space around a document. Margins are designated by their position: left, right, top, and bottom.

Orphans occur when the first line of a paragraph is printed alone at the bottom of a page. Orphans are considered inelegant formatting (see also *widow*).

Portrait is the standard orientation of an 8.5x11-inch page(see also *landscape*).

Ragged right/ragged left refers to the effect of text that lines up on one margin but is not flush against the other margin—it appears *ragged*.

Text editors are programs used for opening and/or editing ASCII text only (not for editing formatted documents). When you open a word processed document in a text editor, a jumble of added characters may appear. These are formatting commands that are nonsensically translated into text.

Widows occur when the last line of a paragraph is printed alone at the top of the next page (see *orphan*). A widow represents inelegant formatting.

What Can't a Word Processor Do for Me?

A word processor can be a magical tool. But as significant a technology as it may be, there are things a word processor can't do. They do offer a wide range of formatting options to help make your document look good, but there are formatting options that word processors are not capable of performing. If you are interested in focusing on the layout and design aspects of your document,

then consider getting a desktop publishing program—in addition to your word processor. (We describe desktop publishing programs at greater length later in this chapter.)

Note: **Many of the limitations of a word processor are not really in the word processor itself, but in perhaps overly high expectations. These programs aren't supposed to do everything, they are just supposed to make writing and communicating with words easier and at that they succeed admirably.**

What's Available

Word processors represent the meat and potatoes of computing; software companies have sold millions of them. That means that the competition is fierce with some excellent products available. The big word processors are Microsoft Word, Novell's WordPerfect, and Lotus Word Pro (this was called AmiPro but no one knew how to say it).

One of the nice things about choosing one of these word processors is that all the files you create in one can be read by the others; You don't have to worry about reading other folks' files, so don't worry about being locked in; all of the formats are readable or convertible by the other programs.

First Class Options

They may be too much for some users, but the feature-packed, professional-level word processors really let you compose your prose with style. Here's a look at what's available.

- **Microsoft Word**—PC/Mac—Now the most popular word processor. About $275 (street price).

- **Lotus Word Pro**—Formerly AmiPro. Not as popular, but just as powerful. They have been selling this program for under $100—a phenomenal deal.

- **Novell WordPerfect**—PC/Mac— WordPerfect was the most popular word

processing program until Microsoft Word overcame it. About $150 (street price).

- **MacWrite**—Strictly for the Mac—also powerful, MacWrite is significantly cheaper than the competitors.

Great Deals

The following products are inexpensive and include scaled down versions of the top-end word processors just listed. They all cost about a hundred bucks and you get a lot more than just a word processor (for more information see Chapter 13 on integrated software programs).

- **ClarisWorks**—Mac/PC—includes a scaled down version of MacWrite. $70 (street price).

- **WordPerfect Works**—PC only—includes a scaled down Version of WordPerfect. $70 (street price).

- **Microsoft Works**—Mac/PC—includes a version of Microsoft Word with less horsepower. $70 (street price).

Test Drives

Windows 95 includes a small word processor called WordPad that will be OK for your short-term needs, but will probably not satisfy you in the long term. Windows 3.1 includes Write, WordPad's predecessor.

Desktop Publishing

Desktop publishing or *dtp* (pronounced dee-tee-pee, as the individual letters sound), gets an awful lot of attention these days, and well it should: computers have turned the publishing industry on its ear, revolutionizing the world of type and design.

How does desktop publishing differ from word processing? Desktop publishing focuses almost exclusively on the format of the document; it's about how the page looks, not about the content. Magazine and book publishers, for example, leave the writing to professional writers and authors. The authors and writers compose and create the content in a word processor, and, once finished writing (and they are *always* late!), the material is edited and *then* brought into a desktop publishing program—"imported" or "poured"—for layout. Dtp programs let the designer juggle tables, graphs, charts, images, text, and many other elements with considerable ease. These are the sorts of elements you commonly find in magazines, newspapers, and books.

Page design is especially demanding because it typically includes so many different elements. In addition, articles often start on one page and continue onto other pages. Page design requires a real attention to detail and the eye of a graphic artist who can visually integrate graphics and text.

Professional desktop publishing also requires precision. Figures must be positioned precisely and text must not overflow its borders. To help maintain that precision, desktop publishing programs provide rules around pages so that every element can be placed precisely. Figure 10–5 shows these rules in a document in Quark Xpress, a popular desktop publishing program.

Dtp for the Common Person

Aside from the high-end programs, there are a number of products that provide remarkable desktop publishing capabilities—without the exacting precision. There are programs for creating flyers, business cards, greeting cards, awards, and a barnload of other things. Figure 10–6 shows a card put together in Microsoft Publisher in under five minutes. Color graphics, borders, and text are all provided along the way, with suggestions for what works best.

Programs like Microsoft Publisher and Broderbund's Print Shop Deluxe help you create items, providing lots of handholding. If you prefer, Microsoft Publisher can walk you step by step through production to ensure that your end result is attractive and professional looking.

As such, these programs can be great fun; they allow you to generate greeting cards, certificates, and other "publishables" that you would otherwise never be able to produce. The following is a partial list of what you can create—effortlessly—with these programs:

Banners	Business cards
Calendars	Flyers
Greeting cards	Invitations
Labels	Newsletters

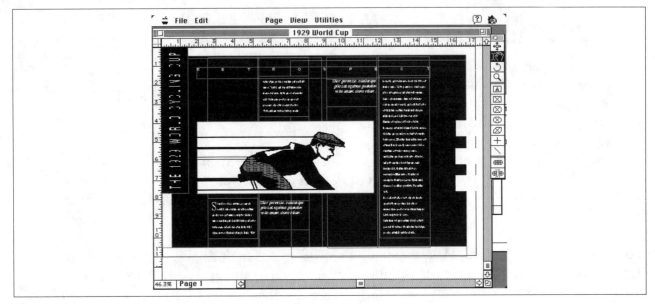

Figure 10–5

Professional dtp programs must meet the exacting standards of publishing professionals

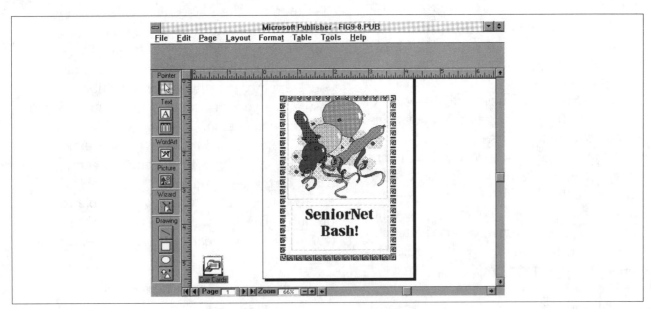

Figure 10–6

Desktop publishing can help design and print an incredible range of printed materials

Just a Few Words About dtp

Although desktop publishing has spawned some of its own language, many of the terms you'll hear define the publishing vernacular. Here's a smattering of what you may hear.

CMYK is an acronym for cyan, magenta, yellow, and black—these are the four primary colors of a color ink press. Using these primary colors, all other colors can be derived by blending them correctly. In order to attain accurate color representation, dtp software must be able to simulate or reproduce the CMYK color range.

Dtp is short for desktop publishing.

Kerning is the adjustment of space between letters.

A pica is a typographic unit of measure equal to .166 inches. One pica is equal to 12 points.

Point is another typographic measure used as a common measure for the size of a typeface. A larger number indicates larger type; 10 pt. Helvetica is smaller than 24 pt. Helvetica. There are approximately 72 points to an inch.

A pull quote is a phrase or sentence taken from the main text, enlarged, and embedded in the main text. Pull quotes entice the reader into reading the article.

Registration marks are placed by professional dtp programs on the outer edge of a page so that a color press can be properly aligned as each color is applied.

Reversed text is white text surrounded by black background.

The separation process distills a full color image into four separate negatives and plates, one for each of the component colors; cyan, magenta, yellow, and black (CMYK).

A service bureau is a computer/printing center that takes your computer-based document or graphic and prints it according to your specification.

Thumbnails are very small copies of graphics. The thumbnails demand far less computer time to manipulate and display. They are not intended to look good, only to let the designer know what the image is without loading it into memory.

What's Available

The range of dtp programs—and the size of their price tags—is quite varied. If you plan on creating high-end, publishable quality documents, be prepared to spend a lot of dough. If you want to experiment, create some nice cards for friends or your organization—or just have some fun—go for a low cost (but still powerful) alternative.

For Blue Bloods...

...and desktop publishing professionals, there are several choices. All of these programs offer enough features to lay out and design a book or magazine (this book was done with Quark Xpress) and all but one of them carry a price tag fit for a king (or queen)—over $500!

- **PageMaker** (from Adobe Systems, Inc.) was the first and reigning dtp program for many years. Both Mac and PC versions are available (Adobe Systems, 1-800-833-6687). Street price: $600.

- **QuarkXpress** (Quark, Inc.) was once the upstart in desktop publishing, and has since challenged PageMaker's industry lead with special features that address high-end color printing (Quark, Inc., 1-800-788-7835). Both Mac and PC versions are available. Street price: $650.

- **Frame Maker** (Frame Technology Corp.) was long seen as the most advanced dtp package but was originally not available on the Mac or PC. Excellent for technical documents and long documents (Frame Technology Corp., 1-800-843-7263). Street price: $650.

...For The Masses

- **Microsoft Publisher** (Microsoft) provides the power and features to make greeting cards, flyers, signs, and whatever else you can dream up at a very reasonable price (under $99). (Microsoft: 1-800-426-9400.)

- **Print Shop Deluxes** (Broderbund Software, Inc.), like Publisher, offers lots of features to design and print anything with ease! Priced at under $100, Broderbund also offers a variety of add-on products (special backgrounds for holidays, seasons, etc.) starting at about $30. (Broderbund: 1-800-521-6263.)

- **Laser Award Maker** (Baudville Computer Products) is a more specialized product, intended primarily for making awards and certificates. The quality of the output (assuming you have a decent printer) is superior, it comes with a package of high quality paper, and the program is easy to use. $100 (Baudville: 1-800-728-0888).

The Currency of Desktop Publishing

Law enforcement officials recognize desktop publishing for a different reason: it ushers in a whole new approach to counterfeiting.

Consider the ease with which an image, with today's computer technology, can be duplicated and then printed. The problem is bad enough that manufacturers of color laser printers have safeguards built into the printers to prevent using the machine for counterfeiting.

Although money is more difficult to counterfeit—it is printed on special paper that has silk threads woven into it—counterfeiting is still proving to be quite a problem for police. The problem has become bad enough (more so overseas, where American 100 dollar bills have become the currency of choice) that a new 100 dollar bill has been designed in an attempt to thwart the new "desktop counterfeiting."

Specialty Printing

Aside from the more "traditional" desktop publishing programs, there are also desktop publishing programs aimed at small niches. These programs do one kind of document exceptionally well. One such program is Laser Award Maker, a program that lets you design and print beautiful awards and certificates. With Laser Award Maker, you'll be able to create diplomas to prove to your friends—once and for all—that you hold graduate degrees from Harvard, Yale, and Princeton, and any medical and law schools of your choice!

Figure 10–7 shows an example of what you can do with Laser Award Maker.

There are hundreds of awards you can generate with this program, from certificates of appreciation to diplomas, and even small signs. There are business awards, community awards, and sports awards, to name a few. The program also comes with a selection of high-quality papers, with and without borders, for creating extra special awards. The program lets you design your own awards if you wish, but when you choose a preexisting template, the program takes you through, step by step, all the way to completion. The results are quite impressive.

Anatomy of a Desktop Published Page

Desktop publishing has come a long way since its inception a decade ago. Ideally suited for creating awards, flyers, and newsletters, desktop publishing programs are now used by most newspapers, magazines, and book publishers. Here's a look at what a professional dtp program can do.

1 Text can flow around an image frame automatically, based on your specifications.

2 If you move an image, the text reflows automatically.

3 This empty frame is waiting for imported text.

4 Inset boxes can be created.

5 Text from the front page continues on different pages. If more text is added to the first page, it automatically pushes the text to the continuation page.

6 This is a big document that incorporates many separate typefaces and graphics. Special document inventory options tell the editors what is used and helps to keep track of all the pieces.

7 You can specify different shaped frames for your images.

8 A border can be defined instantly. You just specify which type of border (or customize your own) and how wide you want it to be.

9 Color is very complicated in the world of publishing. A number of tools have been developed so that negatives are generated for four-color separations. To ensure accuracy, the colors are calibrated by special software.

10 Rulers and grids can be used to provide precise layout and design.

11 On output, a professional package can provide registration marks for press alignment.

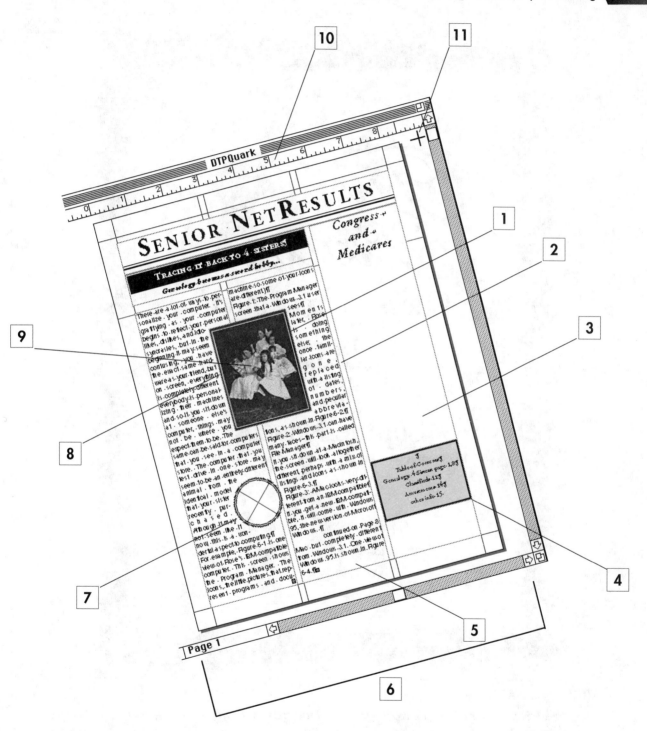

Chess Tournament

This award
acknowledges superior performance in
The Annual Chess Tournament
on the part of

Sophie Mascoli

someone who doesn't settle for second best.

Nathan Marnoff

Alfred Newman

February 18, 1996

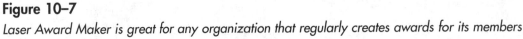

Figure 10–7
Laser Award Maker is great for any organization that regularly creates awards for its members

Fonts

In the world of electronic publishing, "font" is the fancy term for a typeface. Typefaces are used to set the tone of a document and help you communicate or reinforce the message or information you are trying to convey. When you see a cartoon about cavemen, for example, the font used in the cartoon caricatures stone carvings: you understand, without thinking about it, that what you are reading is fun—it's not serious.

Fonts used to be produced by craftsmen who created the letters in steel and iron molds. Because of the difficulty in producing a font and the complexity of the technology required to set a printing press, type and typesetting options were not available to the common man.

With the computer revolution, fonts are created digitally; there are no molds, just talented artists sitting in front of computer screens, designing. Fonts are now for everybody, with thousands of them available for use. Figure 10–8 shows a small sample of the range of fonts that are available.

What can you do with them? A lot of people like to browse the enormous online font libraries, pick the ones that catch their fancy, and save them for the right project.

Tip: **Fonts say a lot about us, and when overused, they say we don't know a lot about how to use fonts! For overall readability, stick with more traditional typefaces, like Helvetica and Times Roman.**

> ## Golden Rule:
> Don't use too many fonts in any single document. Too many fonts in a document make a document hard to read, and multiple fonts often get in the way of whatever message you are trying to convey. More often than not, the more fonts you use, the less you communicate with the reader. Likewise, the more you use bold, underline, and italics, the less impact they have.

Word Processing with a Personal Touch

As grand as all of this font technology is, it falls flat in comparison to the personality and warmth you get from a handwritten letter. Until now, that is.

There are now fonts that give the appearance of being handwritten. When you type using this kind of font, it doesn't look like type at all, but like someone's handwriting! Figure 10–9 is a brief note that uses "Lefty Casual," one such True Type font. With Lefty Casual, your writing is perfectly ruled, your i's are dotted, your t's are consistently crossed. Nothing is ever scratched out and your margins are straight enough to make any nun proud.

If fonts like Lefty Casual aren't personal enough for you, Signature Software (1-800-925-8840/503-386-3221) has

THIS IS A HEAVY COMIC FONT. LIKE SOMETHING OUT OF A CARTOON.

Vivaldi is very ornate - - and hard to read!

Aristocrat: for the well-turned nose!

Book Antiqua is rather elegant.

Some fonts, like Fitzgerald, are designed in the spirit of a certain era.

THIS FONT, CALLED BAZOOKA, HAS A PLAYFUL, YOUTHFUL FEEL TO IT - - REMINISCENT OF A CERTAIN BRAND OF CHEWING GUM, NO?

Figure 10–8

Fonts are fun! There are fonts to help convey virtually every message and mood

devised a way of converting your handwriting into a custom font. That means you can have a font that looks like your own writing when you type.

 Note: **There is some irony here; we strive for machine-like perfection and once we achieve it, we use our new tools to regain what** we have lost.

Alert: **Not all fonts are free. Adobe Systems, Inc., the original digital type "foundry" has hundreds of fonts for sale. Other fonts from type foundries can be more or less expensive, depending on the complexity, elegance, and demand for the font.**

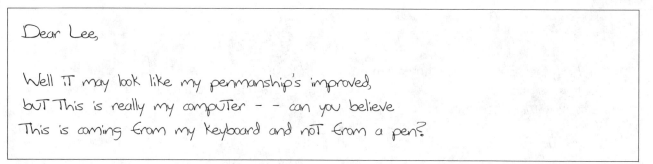

Figure 10–9

Lefty Casual gives your word processed document real warmth—even though your pen never touched paper

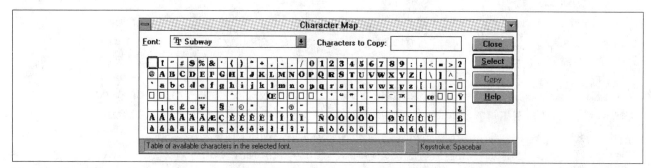

Figure 10–10

Many fonts have additional characters that you can access via Character Map on a PC compatible (shown) or Key Caps on a Macintosh

What a Bunch of Characters: Things You Didn't Know You Could Type

When you get a new font, it will include more characters than there are keys on the keyboard. Little graphics, bullets, Greek or Latin characters; there are a lot more characters within the font that you can't readily see. But there is a way to see them. On the Mac, you can pull down the Apple Menu in the upper left corner of the screen and select Key Caps. On a PC compatible running Windows 95, you click on the Start button, select Programs, then select Accessories, and then Character Map. In Windows 3.1, you should go to the Accessories window and select the Character Map icon. When you double-click on this, a guide to all of those characters appears. The Character Map in Windows 3.1 is shown in Figure 10–10.

CURIOUSER AND CURIOUSER

Selecting the right typeface may seem an easy task, but the range of choices can make it a lot tougher, not to mention technology issues that arise. Here are the answers to some questions you might soon have.

Q: I just got some fonts, but I can't open them. How can I use them?

A: Fonts need to be installed. In Windows 95 and Windows 3.1, you do this with the Fonts option in the Control Panel. On a Macintosh, you drag your new fonts into the System Folder.

Q: What programs will let me use my new fonts?

A: Any program that lets you manipulate text: word processing programs, graphics programs, desktop publishing programs, even spreadsheets. If your fonts are installed properly, they appear in the font list of your program.

Q: I want to send a letter to a friend in a foreign country. How can I place an accent or a tilde over the character?

A: You use a special character that includes the tilde. You can use the Character Map to locate the character you need and paste it into your document. Some word processors give you the ability to paste a special character or symbol without accessing the Character Map. See your word processor's documentation for more specific instructions.

Q: Can I type in a foreign language?

A: You can get a foreign language font, but remember, it may not be easy typing in Thai or Hebrew on an English-based keyboard.

Special Effects

Not only are there lots of fonts, but there are also special effects that can be applied to these fonts. For example, there are programs that will make your fonts into three-dimensional characters with all sorts of surface textures. Pixar's Typestry, for example, lets you generate 3-D type, as shown in Figure 10–11. To generate these effects, you should have a computer with lots of horsepower, though. Creating special effects with Typestry can easily take a couple of hours of computer processing time.

Typography:
Just a Few Words

Typography has been around for over 400 years. Here's some of the terminology—with a few 20th century computer terms thrown in—and what they all mean.

Dingbats is a font consisting of small graphic elements. Each graphic in the font is assigned to a key on the keyboard. Like any typeface, Dingbats are measured in points. Dingbats include bullets, arrows, and other small graphics often embedded within text.

Ligatures are two characters or letters that may be connected, such as fi or fl.

Monospaced type is a typeface in which all characters occupy an equal amount of space. Typewriter fonts are monospaced.

PostScript font is a scaleable (resizable) typeface that retains a high-quality appearance regardless of the size at which it is printed. Developed by Adobe Systems, Inc.

Proportional type is a typeface where each letter occupies only the amount of space it needs, as opposed to monospaced type where each character occupies the same amount of space. Proportional typefaces, such as Times Roman and Helvetica, look superior and are easier to read.

Sans serif is a typeface that uses no flourishes or added strokes. Sans serif is a more functional looking typeface. Helvetica is a common sans serif typeface.

Serif typeface is a typeface that uses small flourishes or curves at the end of the character's main strokes. Times Roman is a common serif typeface.

TrueType font is a scaleable type technology—like PostScript—introduced by Apple, Inc.

Type 1 is a type of PostScript font that typically takes less memory and prints faster.

Type 3 is a type of PostScript font that can include special effects, such as gray shades.

Weight describes a font's variation from light to bold.

Figure 10–11

Pixar's Typestry lets you bring fonts to life—in three dimensions

Profile:
Edward Chun

Project/Activity
"Words of Wisdom"
A collection of wise sayings and poems

Project Start Date
1941 (collection)
1989, 1995

Hardware/Software Used
Acer Pentium 75, Macintosh Performa
Macintosh Plus
Hewlett Packard Laser Jet III
Microsoft Works
Broderbund Print Shop Deluxe
Novell's WordPerfect

Contact
Edward L.S. Chun
c/o SeniorNet Profiles
1 Kearney
San Francisco, CA 94108

Profile
When we finally caught up with Edward Chun, he was just coming in the door from one of his many whirlwind trips, this one to Japan for a no-holds-barred celebration. "My friend really knows how to throw a party!" Edward says enthusiastically.

Who
Edward Chun knows how to live. When he retired from the U.S. postal service at age 60, he was enjoying his new found freedom in Honolulu. Then he got a call from a travel agent. "They heard I could speak several languages," he says, matter-of-factly. "They wanted me to escort a group of travelers to Tibet. I led the group, and the trip was a big success, so they keep asking me to lead trips. I love it!"

Edward's certainly racking up the frequent flyer miles: he's taken over twenty such trips in the last ten years with destinations including China, Japan, Mongolia, Fiji and the Cook Islands, and Malaysia. His wife, Louise, restores jewelry and so Edward always knows what to bring home.

What
Edward graduated from high school in 1941, right before the war started. "I started saving poems, wise sayings, and proverbs in a big file," he says. "My ambition was to make a book of sayings that would be cherished."

Edward's publishing vision became a reality about fifty years later when he began taking classes at the SeniorNet

Learning Center in Honolulu. A fellow student, Edward Lee, liked the book concept and helped to create a spiral bound booklet entitled *A Collection of Favorite Words of Wisdom*. Figure 10–12 shows one of the entries from Edward's collection.

The verses, poems, and sayings, reflect the many sides of Edward, reflecting on such themes as friendship, aging, and lifelong learning. Although Edward has a Mac Plus at home, he used a PC compatible at the SeniorNet Center to design and print the booklet. All of the text was originally entered using WordPerfect. The booklet cover was designed using PrintShop, and the book was laser printed and spiral bound at a local print shop.

"I actually have two collections of sayings," adds Edward. "The second collection of limericks, jokes, and cartoons, was collected during the war years and let's just say, it's a bit risqué. I've been saying that I'd get the second collection done for a while—I'm taking a class now in Claris-Works so I'll be able to do a lot of the work at home on my computer."

On Computing

Edward certainly enjoys a challenge, and before joining SeniorNet, he didn't know how to use a computer. "Getting started really wasn't that hard," he says. "I still have a lot to learn about computing—I'm no power user—but it sure is a lot of fun and I really enjoy the time I spend doing it. It's been really enjoyable."

Edward Chun is a live wire. He plays tennis, takes aerobics classes once a week, plays ukulele and guitar, and is involved in numerous organizations, including the Shriners. Aside from being a past president, he and other Shriners play music for patients at the local hospital. And somehow he still finds time to take computer courses.

At 72, Edward L.S. Chun is Honolulu's guarantee that there will be no island energy crisis.

IF THE RIGHT MAN USES THE WRONG MEANS,
THE WRONG MEANS WORK IN THE RIGHT WAY.

IF THE WRONG MAN USES THE RIGHT MEANS,
THE RIGHT MEANS WORK IN THE WRONG WAY.

KUNG FU TZU

Figure 10–12

An excerpt from Edward Chun's A Collection of Favorite Words of Wisdom

Accounting
with Taste

Spreadsheet programs are responsible, in large part, for the widespread use and success of the personal computer in corporate America. Spreadsheets allow you to execute bookkeeping procedures automatically, as you enter numbers into the ledger.

Spreadsheets: Making Numbers Easy

Spreadsheet programs let you create electronic ledgers in which calculations can be done instantly and automatically. You enter information in boxes, called *cells*, that are arranged in rows and columns. You can also assign formulas to cells so that calculations can be made instantly. With a spreadsheet, you can calculate in a moment's notice, for example, the effect of refinancing your mortgage.

Figure 11–1 shows what you see when you open a typical spreadsheet program (in this case, Microsoft Excel). The rows and columns are where you enter your information, the columns are marked alphabetically across the top and the rows numbered down the side. The row/column layout helps keep things well organized, but the seemingly simple appearance conceals the real power of a spreadsheet. The buttons and Menu bar across the top offer a bevy of editing and formatting controls.

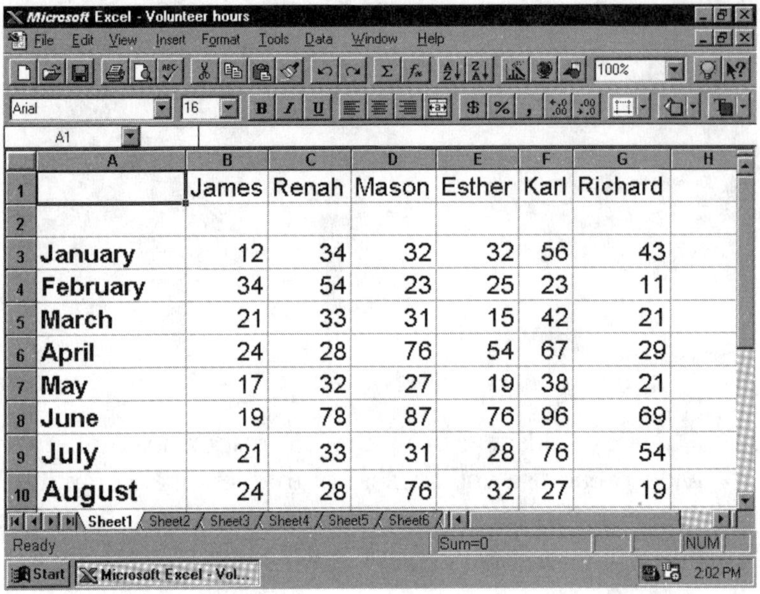

	A	B	C	D	E	F	G	H
1		James	Renah	Mason	Esther	Karl	Richard	
2								
3	January	12	34	32	32	56	43	
4	February	34	54	23	25	23	11	
5	March	21	33	31	15	42	21	
6	April	24	28	76	54	67	29	
7	May	17	32	27	19	38	21	
8	June	19	78	87	76	96	69	
9	July	21	33	31	28	76	54	
10	August	24	28	76	32	27	19	

Figure 11–1

In Microsoft Excel, numbers are entered into the small boxes or cells

What a Spreadsheet Can Do for You

Spreadsheets are very powerful programs used by accountants and other financial professionals everywhere. You won't find a Fortune 500 company that doesn't use a spreadsheet program in creating budgets, building forecasts, and figuring out payroll. Spreadsheets aren't just for accounting professionals, though. Any adult who has to do any personal accounting can benefit from a spreadsheet program. In fact, spreadsheets serve a dual purpose. Since they can also accommodate text, they are also ideal for creating tables that mix text and numerical information. Figure 11–2 shows an example of a [mostly text] chart created with a spreadsheet program. You could do this in a word processor, but it's a lot easier with a spreadsheet.

Editing Your Work

A spreadsheet program has all of the advantages over a pen and ink ledger that a word processor has over paper and pencil or a typewriter. Like a word processor, spreadsheet programs have a number of standard features to help you make improvements, additions, and corrections to your spreadsheets quickly and effortlessly. To begin with, you can click on any cell at

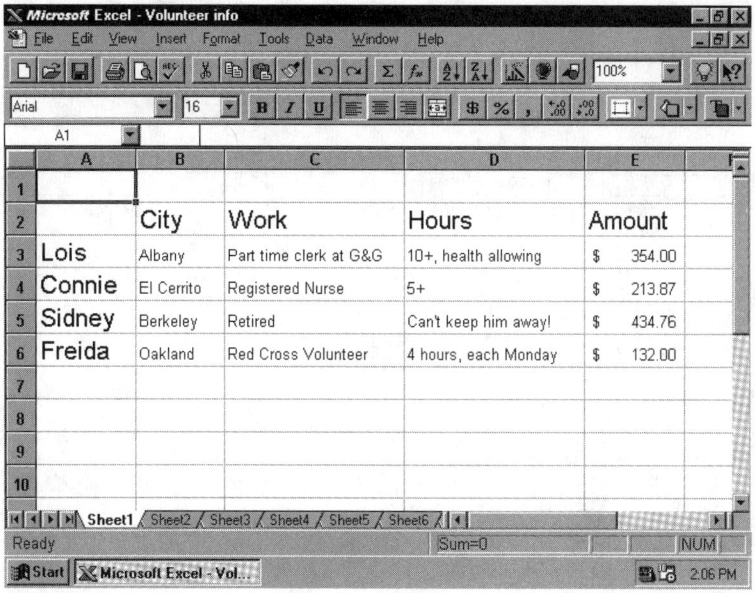

Figure 11-2
Spreadsheets let you create and elegantly format data in tables

any time and place any number in the cell. You can edit the contents of a cell, just like editing with a word processor. You can delete the contents of a cell or group of cells, and you can move or copy cells to different locations.

Since spreadsheets accommodate text, you can insert titles for rows and columns at any time. If you lay out rows to represent the months of the year and discover that you have skipped April (tax month!), you can insert a row for April by highlighting the row (below where April should appear) and clicking on "Insert." You can do the same with columns by selecting a column and clicking on the Insert command.

As you create a spreadsheet, you need to specify what kind of numbers you are working with, or, more accurately, a format for the numbers. Figure 11-3 illustrates some of the different formats that are available. You may want one column in your spreadsheet to represent percentages, another column to represent dollar amounts, and another column to represent a numeric quantity (say, the number of hours worked in the week). When you assign the format to a row, column, or cell, any number you place in the preformatted cell automatically takes on the corresponding format. For example, once a cell has been formatted to contain a dollar amount,

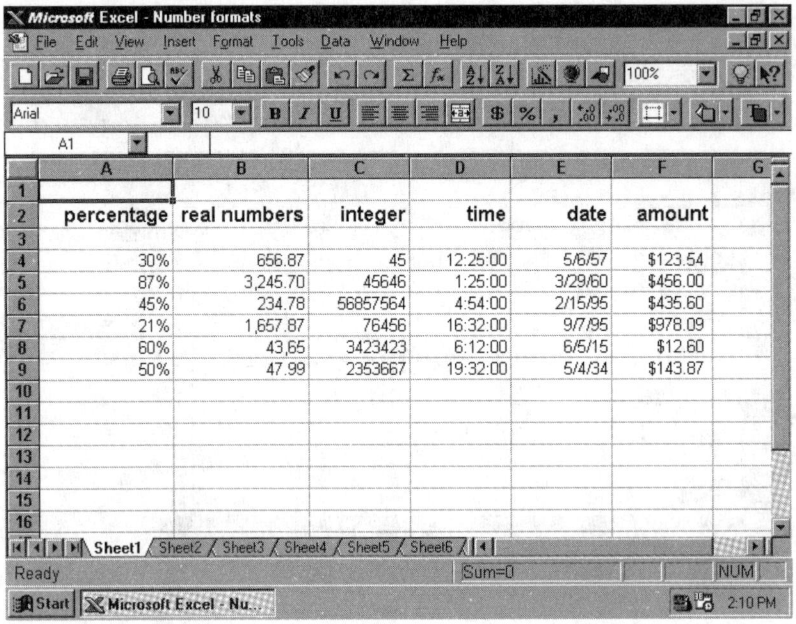

Figure 11-3

You can use many different number formats—integer, real, dollar, time, date, and more—in your spreadsheet

any number in that cell will automatically be preceded with a dollar sign.

Making Your Spreadsheet Look Good

Aside from helping you calculate and track your financial data, spreadsheets also let you format the data so it is attractive and easy to read. You can change typefaces, center text, shade parts of the spreadsheet, use color, include titles, and even give your spreadsheet a 3-D look. There are a number of characteristics of your spreadsheet that you can customize to draw attention to the most important information.

Tip: If the text you enter in your cell is longer than the display allows, it will appear shortened. The text is there, but the cell is more like a window—there's more information there, you just can't see it. To adjust this, spreadsheets have an automatic sizing or "best fit" option that will change the size of any selected cells, rows, or columns to allow for a full display. Your entries will then be much easier to read.

Your spreadsheet can be formatted using preset templates that are offered with the program. If you aren't sure how to best lay out or format your spreadsheet, look for these automatic formatting features. With automatic formatting, you enter your data in

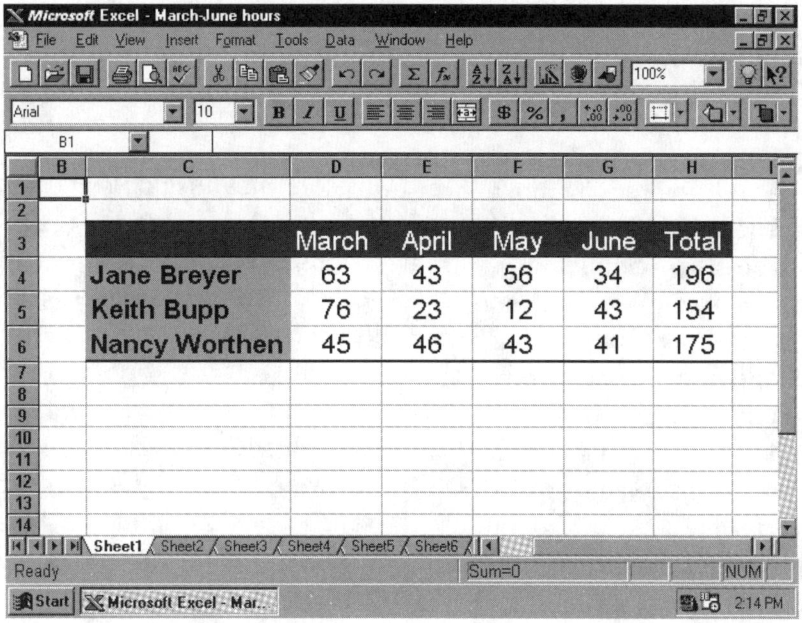

Figure 11-4
Templates help to make your spreadsheet professional looking and easy to read

the appropriate rows and columns and then select the most appropriate format from a list of possible formats. The program automatically gives your spreadsheet a polished, professional look, as shown in Figure 11-4.

Spreadsheet Calculations

Spreadsheets are especially valuable in performing calculations. A spreadsheet program is like having a ledger with a calculator built right into it. For example, if you have a "utilities" spreadsheet with electric bills in one column, gas bills in another,

water in another, and so on, you can assign a formula to a cell at the bottom of each column that calculates the total of your monthly payments by adding all of the corresponding cells together. The formula remains vigilant if you change any numbers in the column—say, for example, you mistakenly entered April's water charge for February and corrected the mistake a week later—the formula would automatically change the total as well. A formula assigned to a cell doesn't stop working; it remains with your spreadsheet until you change the formula or delete it.

Crime Stoppers: Know Your Formats

Can a numerical format really make that much difference? It sure can. Just ask your local bank president about the dangers of "salami slicing" or "sausage slicing," an embezzlement technique that strips a fractional amount from an entry and "loses it" to another account.

Here's how it works, and here's how your spreadsheet can do something similar.

You deposit a sum of money in your savings account and you record the number in your spreadsheet. Using your spreadsheet, you calculate the interest that your money earned. Let's say this quarter's interest was $123.45.08. Your spreadsheet records that, right?

Not exactly. Your spreadsheet calculates that, but your brain records something different. The number has what appears to be an extra decimal place. In our minds, we don't pay any attention to it. But a disreputable accountant might.

When interest rates are calculated, the numbers usually don't come out even.

Instead, they include some fractional amount, in this case, 8/100ths of a penny. If you choose the wrong format in your spreadsheet, you will never see the fractional amount.

OK, you aren't going to worry about a fraction of a cent on your own spreadsheet. Consider in a financial institution, however, where perhaps millions of such transactions are made each year. A crooked accountant "slices" the fractional amount off each interest calculation and directs the "slice" to a special account. Those fractions add up to a lot of money over time if they are all going to one place.

No one at home with a spreadsheet will miss much with those fractional amounts, but selecting the wrong format for a number can result in rounding off numbers in a way that can lead to more serious errors. When setting up spreadsheets and using formulas to calculate, be alert for similar number format mistakes and avoid "self-cooking books!"

Looking at Your Spreadsheet Differently

The ledger format that you get with a spreadsheet program can really help you see things you otherwise wouldn't be able to see in your numbers. Certainly, seeing things laid out so neatly helps. But a spreadsheet program's ability to reformat your numbers on the fly gives you the ability to see your numbers from several different views and to experiment and evaluate "what if" scenarios. "What if" we took that vacation? Or "what if" we sold the house and got an apartment? Of special importance in rearranging a spreadsheet is the ability to sort your data based on the criteria of your choice.

Sorting Information

Spreadsheets let you sort and reorganize your ledger in a variety of ways. Let's say you are helping with your organization's fundraising campaign and your spreadsheet includes a column of volunteers who collect contributions. Your spreadsheet program can sort all of the volunteers alphabetically for easier reference. If you want to sort based on a different criteria, say, based on who collected the most donations, you can sort on the dollar amount as well.

Spreadsheets go a step further, letting you sort on multiple criteria. Using the volunteer example from before, let's say you have a column of how many hours each volunteer has worked. A compound sort would first sort on their hours and then sort on the size of the contribution. In Figure 11–5, a volunteer organization sorts on the number of hours worked and the contributions the volunteers have solicited. Based on a little spreadsheet analysis, Joan Wilson didn't earn the most, but she was most effective; she worked less time than others and collected more than most.

Keeping Your Spreadsheets Organized

A single spreadsheet can contain 256 columns and thousands of rows (they don't all appear onscreen, but the scroll bars let you see how large the spreadsheet can be). To keep organized (and sane), you should definitely keep your spreadsheet size to a minimum. If you do have a lot of numbers to enter and the spreadsheet is getting too "spread out" and difficult to understand, you can break the spreadsheet into smaller spreadsheets and "link" them together. Linking lets you keep different segments of one large body of information on different spreadsheets. If you change values on one spreadsheet and the other spreadsheet has a formula that uses the values of that spreadsheet, the dependent values will automatically update.

For example, you create one spreadsheet to show contributions to your organization and another spreadsheet to show membership fees. Your budgeting spreadsheet is a third spreadsheet, but it is based on the contributions and membership fees compiled on the other two spreadsheets. When you link these spreadsheets and the contributions, dues, or membership fees fluctuate, the budgeting spreadsheet automatically changes to reflect the changes entered on the other spreadsheets. If you use linking when setting up your spreadsheets, your projects will be easier to understand.

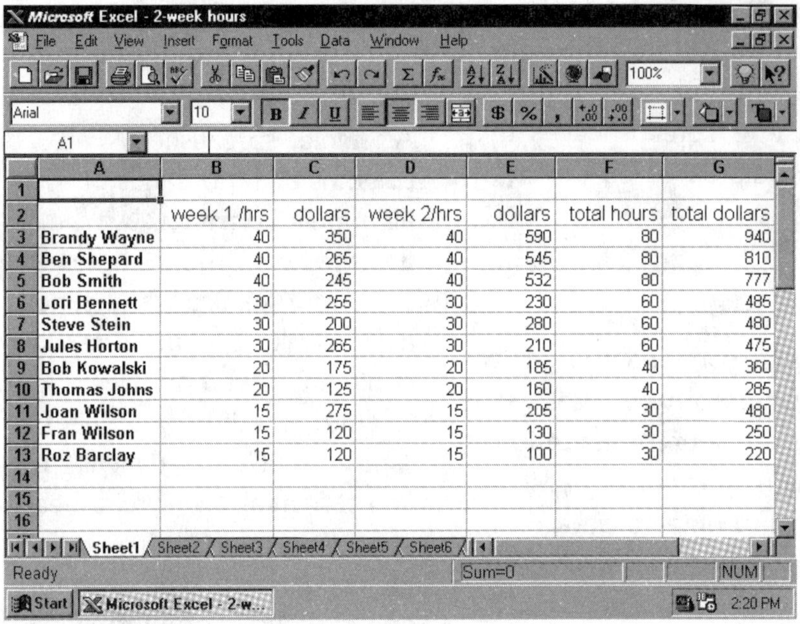

	A	B	C	D	E	F	G
1							
2		week 1 /hrs	dollars	week 2/hrs	dollars	total hours	total dollars
3	Brandy Wayne	40	350	40	590	80	940
4	Ben Shepard	40	265	40	545	80	810
5	Bob Smith	40	245	40	532	80	777
6	Lori Bennett	30	255	30	230	60	485
7	Steve Stein	30	200	30	280	60	480
8	Jules Horton	30	265	30	210	60	475
9	Bob Kowalski	20	175	20	185	40	360
10	Thomas Johns	20	125	20	160	40	285
11	Joan Wilson	15	275	15	205	30	480
12	Fran Wilson	15	120	15	130	30	250
13	Roz Barclay	15	120	15	100	30	220
14							
15							
16							

Figure 11–5

A compound sort lets you analyze your spreadsheet in some very complex ways

---

Golden Rule:

Keep your spreadsheets small and elegant. If you need to include a lot of data, find a way to logically categorize and divide the data and use links to keep everything understandable.

Linking a Spreadsheet to a Word Processing Document

Remarkably, linking also applies between different types of programs. You can, for example, cut and paste a spreadsheet or part of a spreadsheet into your word processing document. If you decide to go back to update or revise your spreadsheet, the numbers you pasted into your word processing document are automatically revised. That means if you write a letter or report that relies on (and uses) numbers from your spreadsheet, you never have to worry about them becoming out of date.

Note: When you incorporate a segment of spreadsheet into your word processing document, it only updates as long as the two documents—the spreadsheet document and the word processing document—are on the same machine and remain in the same folders or subdirectories.

Graphing Options

The ability to visualize or display numerical information is invaluable. One of the most impressive features of a spreadsheet program is its ability to turn your spreadsheets into graphs. With graphing, a spreadsheet program lets you select all or part of your data and instantly display it in graphical form, as shown in Figure 11–6.

Graphing doesn't require any manual drawing of any kind on your part. The program does all the work for you. You can graph your spreadsheet information in a number of different forms—line charts, pie charts, bar charts, and more—depending on the nature of the information. Figure 11–7 shows some of Microsoft Excel's graph options.

Any change in the data in a spreadsheet that has an associated graph affects the graph accordingly; you don't have to specify or "fudge" any changes with the graphics.

Macros: Automating the Whole Spreadsheet Process

A macro is a list of commands or functions that can be performed with a single keystroke or click of the mouse. The term itself may not be very descriptive, but macros

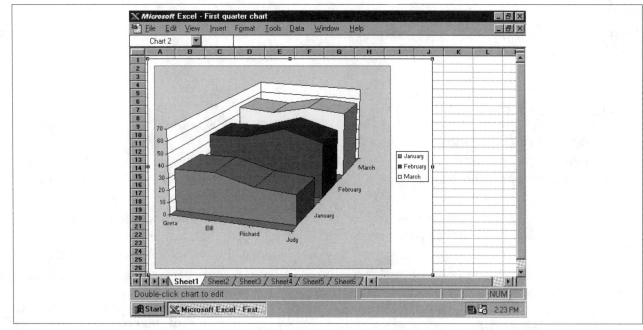

Figure 11–6

Seeing a graph of your spreadsheet can have tremendous impact

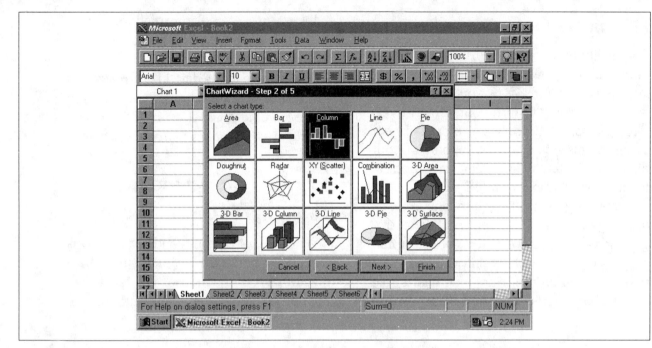

Figure 11–7
You can graph and regraph your spreadsheet in a myriad of different ways

represent a powerful feature that can save you a lot of time. Macros are also easy to create with the built-in macro recorder, accessible from the spreadsheet's menu bar.

A macro recorder is like a built-in stenographer that watches your actions and then plays them back upon request. When you activate the recorder, it watches, for example as you select a cell, change the typeface, enlarge the typeface, and then center the text. Press the macro recorder's Stop button to stop recording and you are prompted to name your new macro. Save

the macro by naming it and you can access it any time.

Tomorrow, when you are working on your spreadsheet and you need to reformat more cells as you did yesterday, you can pick the cells that need reformatting and then select your macro. Automatically, the contents of the cell get the new typeface, the typeface gets bigger, and the text is centered.

Note: **There is no limit to the number of macros you can create. The more macros you can create for yourself, the faster you'll be able to work.**

What's Available

Spreadsheets like Lotus 123 (PC), Microsoft Excel, and Novell's Quattro Pro (PC) are excellent programs that offer features a professional accountant can take full advantage of. Unless you are an accountant or you're running a business, you probably won't need anything with quite so much octane. If you don't need the power, or if you are new to spreadsheets and you'd like to work with one before spending a lot of money, you would probably do better to start with the spreadsheet provided in an integrated package like LotusWorks (PC) or ClarisWorks (PC/Mac). These products are scaled down versions of their more powerful siblings and afford you a lot of spreadsheet options without the premium price (see more on integrated software in Chapter 13).

Top Notch

- Lotus 123 (for IBM compatibles only), Lotus Development Corp., 1-800-343-5414. This is the granddaddy of the three top notch programs (street price: $340).
- Microsoft Excel (for IBM and Mac), Microsoft Corporation, 1-800-426-9400.

Currently the best selling spreadsheet program (street price: $300).

- Novell Quattro Pro (for IBM), Novell Corporation, 1-800-453-1267. Powerful spreadsheet program (street price: $300).

Great Deals (again)

The following products are inexpensive and include scaled down versions of high-end spreadsheet programs. They all cost about $100 or less and you get a lot more than just a spreadsheet. For more information, see Chapter 13, "Integrated Software Programs and Suites."

- ClarisWorks includes a decent spreadsheet program (street price: about $75 for PCs/$90 for the Mac).
- Microsoft Works (Mac and PC) includes a version of Microsoft Excel—with less horsepower (street price: $75).
- WordPerfect Works includes a scaled down version of Quattro Pro (street price: $75 for PC only).

CHAPTER

12

Database
Programs

Everybody uses databases, even people who have never touched a computer. A database is a storehouse of information that is broken down into categories and organized for easy access. The phone book is a database, your own personal address book is another.

Organizing Your Information: Database Programs

A database is a collection of information that can be searched quickly, based on some "criteria" like last name (in the white pages) or type of business or service (in the yellow pages). If you are looking for a way of organizing some body of information—a stamp collection, an address book, recipes or phone numbers—a database is the way to go.

What a Database Program Can Do for You

A database program lets you create a structure in which to store a large amount of information. You build this structure with two basic components, namely, fields and records. If you were to build a mailing list for an organization, for example, each index card would hold all of the pertinent information about each member—name, address, phone number, etc. Each card represents a record, so if you have 50 people in the organization, you have 50 records. Each piece of information on each card represents a field, so every record has a name field, a street address field, a city field, and so forth. Each record is made up of many fields.

You specify all of the fields that you need for each record, indicating where and how you want your record to appear on screen, thereby determining the design of your mailing list. You can create fields for different kinds of information—text-based information, numbers, pictures, and more.

Once the fields and the database structure are defined, you must conform to the layout; you can't save a picture where you are supposed to save a phone number, for example. A basic layout for a home inventory database is shown in Figure 12–1.

Alert: **Computer jargon can be as confounding as it is ambiguous; the terms** *database program* **or** *database manager* **can refer to the actual filing system that holds the information ("we'll check the database") or the program that is used to design and create the database ("I built my home inventory system with Microsoft Access.").**

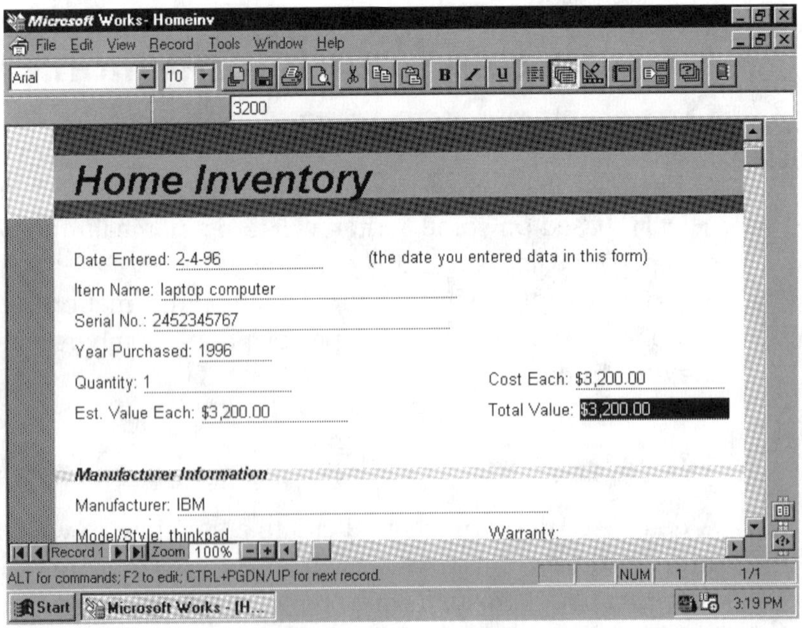

Figure 12–1

A database must be designed before you can use it

Finding and Retrieving Information Fast

Wouldn't it be great if everything was as well organized as the library card catalog? With a database, not only can things be well organized, you can get important information back a lot faster than you can find things at the library. In some quarters, finding information fast isn't a luxury, it's a requirement. In a hospital, for example, there are thousands of patients who are cared for in any given year. These patients all have important information associated with them and a number of hospital personnel may need access to it in different ways. Doctors in the emergency room may need access to a patient's medical history while someone in the accounting department may need the billing history on that same patient. A patient's name, address, social security number, insurance carrier, prescriptions, and allergies may all be included in the database. A database of this sort may take months, if not years, to create and fine-tune.

Nowadays, many businesses large and small use database programs for inventory control. In some bookstores, for example, inventory is tracked via a computer database. When you purchase a book and the person scans the bar code on the back with the magic wand at the counter, the database program automatically reduces the inventory number by one. When another customer calls to check if that same book is in stock, an employee can check the database to see if any copies are still in the store. Accurate inventory can really affect a company's bottom line.

For businesses, a database can be critical to the success or failure of the company. To ensure that the database is just right, a business must spend a large amount of time analyzing what the database must do *before* creating it. This is not a trivial task and requires computer or database programming skills. Many companies hire database developers or consultants to come in and design the database for them. If any part of the database is incorrectly designed or badly implemented, the company can suffer significant losses.

Unless you are running a business, you won't have to hire a database programmer, but you will have to think about what information is included in your database and how you plan to retrieve it.

It is possible to create less complex databases. Figure 12–2 shows some of the possible "pre-fab" databases that Microsoft Access will help you create with the help of "wizards." These wizards (as Microsoft calls them) take you step by step through the creation process and afford some customization along the way.

Flat File Versus Relational

When you start looking for a database program, you'll be confronted with a couple of confusing terms to denote two different kinds of database programs: flat file and relational.

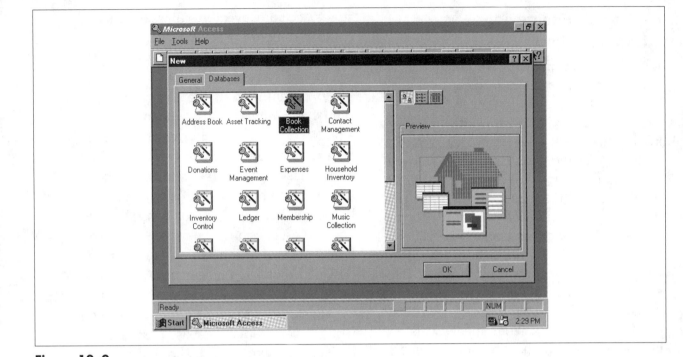

Figure 12–2

Some database programs will walk you through the creation of the more common databases

A computer sales representative may lead you to believe that this is really tricky stuff, but it really isn't. A flat file database is easily compared to a card file. In a flat file database in a doctor's office, for example, each person has a record (a card) in the database on which all of their information can be found. With a relational database, you can break all of the information up into the equivalent of several different cross reference card files; a patient's name and address appears only in the address card file, while his or her appointment history is in another card file. This can actually make your system run faster because it lets you access only the information you need at any given time *and* eliminates the need to continually input redundant information.

If you designed a flat file database to track customer orders, for example, you would enter the customer's name with each order he or she placed. That's OK for new customers, but for established customers, you are entering information that you've entered before. With a relational database, you can enter the customer's name and address *once* in the appropriate card file. When the regular customer places their next order, you don't have to enter their name and address information, you can just reference it in the other card file.

As simple as that may be, the distinction between flat file and relational can blur, with some flat file databases allowing for some cross referencing. In addition, it's not always clear—at least to nonexperts—when one of these types of databases is preferable over the other.

What a Database Can't Do for You

As mentioned earlier, some programs will walk you through the creation of basic databases so you can create one in very short time. If you are building a more complex database, you'll need to do some work. So, unless you're willing to invest the time, don't set unreasonable expectations for yourself. Before you start building the database, you must figure out what you expect the database to do for you.

Once you have actually created your database, your database needs to be *populated*—filled with information. Depending on the amount of information, this can be a very tedious and time-consuming job. Someone has to sit and type the information in manually. If the information is not well organized or if the inputter's typing skills are not good, this can take an extra long time. Regardless, it has to be done and

unless you are bringing your information in from another database program, your database can't do it for you; you will have to do all of the work.

Your work is still not done—even after you have entered all of your records. Databases need constant attention and maintenance; records must be updated, new features need to be added, and problems need to be fixed as they crop up. As you learn more, your database will improve proportionately.

Tools for Designing a Database

Some databases include a programming language you can use to build your database, but unless yours is a major project involving thousands of records, it's overkill. Other programs, like Claris FileMaker Pro, are somewhat easier programs, but you'll still have to do some learning. Some, like the scaled down versions that appear in integrated software packages, are simple and straightforward.

If you'd like to create a database for your recipes, stamp or coin collection, FileMaker Pro, Microsoft Access, or Lotus Approach may be ideal for you. These programs offer a lot of power and they are better suited to nonprogrammers. A word of caution, however: "better suited" is not synonymous with easy. Figure 12–3 shows a sample FileMaker Pro screen.

What's Available

Professional-level database tools are both costly and cumbersome, and they require a professional to pilot them. Your best bet is to stick with a mid-range or entry level—novice—program.

Mid-range Tools

Here are some mid-range tools that provide significant power and a learning curve that can be challenging but not necessarily daunting. With these programs, you can dedicate as much time as you want to learning one of the products but still be able to produce a respectable database without ignoring your social life.

- **Access** (Microsoft) has become one of the most popular database programs available. It is powerful enough for just about any task, but basic enough to let you learn how to use it. For PC compatibles only. (Microsoft: 800-426-9400.) Street price: $320.

- **Approach** (Lotus Development) is not as popular as the other products, but it does provide all the tools necessary to build a good database. For PC only. (Lotus Development: 800-343-5414.) Street price: $100.

- **FileMaker Pro** (Claris Corp.) was one of the first databases tailored to the nonprofessional. Like Access, it is powerful but relatively straightforward to learn. For Mac and PC. (Claris Corp. 800-544-8554.) Street price: $120.

The Bargains

Again, if you are looking for something that will work fast and doesn't have a steep learning curve associated with it, check out the integrated programs (described in further detail in Chapter 13):

ClarisWorks (for Macintosh only)

Microsoft Works (for Mac and PC)

Novell's PerfectWorks (for PC compatibles only)

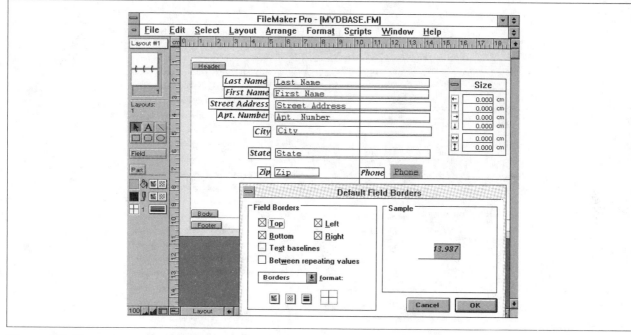

Figure 12–3

Building a database can be a demanding—and rewarding—task

Alert: **Database programming requires a lot of patience, a lot of skill, and an organized mind. If you're an orderly person to begin with, your organizational skills will pay off in a big way when creating and designing a database.**

Contacts Databases

A contacts database or personal information manager—PIM (rhymes with "Tim")—is a predesigned database that lets you track people: friends, family, business asso-ciates, and colleagues. With a contacts database, you don't have to design anything because the database is built for you. You just need to enter the information that is relevant to you. You can view the information in a number of different ways, as if you could display your phone book based on last name, company, street address, or ZIP code. Figure 12–4 shows a typical view of a contacts database.

Note: **A contacts database was so named because it was origi-nally intended for professional people who had to track their profes-sional *contacts*.**

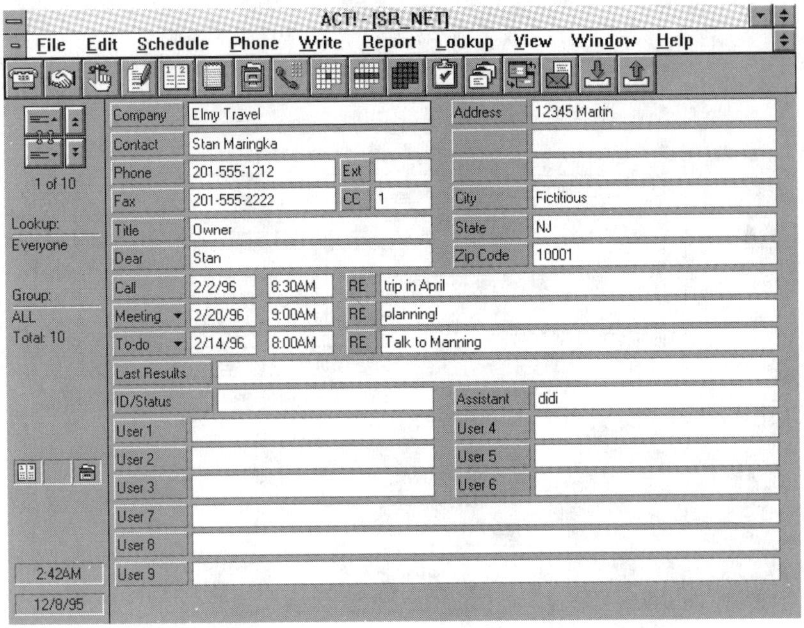

Figure 12–4

A contacts database can really help keep you organized

The distinction between a contacts database and a PIM are pretty blurry. A PIM is like a contacts database with additional calendar and event scheduling features. PIMs are more like super-organizational databases that let you track more than just names and addresses. The more sophisticated of these programs cross reference your address book with your appointment calendar, so when you schedule Tuesday's lunch with Jim, the program prompts you with a list of all the Jims in your database to make sure it knows—and you know—which one you are supposed to meet. If it's a new Jim, you can then enter contact information specific to him.

Tip: **Ever get charged for a long distance call to a number you don't recognize? (A certain brother who shall remain nameless—*Eric*—calls the number to see who it is!) If it's in your PIM, it's easy to track down. Open the PIM and do a search on the number. In seconds, you'll have searched your entire phone list and found the mystery person or establishment.**

What's Available

Some PIMs are quite expensive (over $300) and offer all sorts of bells and whistles more suited to a corporate executive. For those of us who are a little more down to earth, $100 will get a great product. Here are a few of the programs available:

- **ACT!** (Symantec: 1-800-441-7234)—they call it a contacts manager—is for the more serious minded. Street price: $175. For Mac or PC.

- **Claris Organizer** (for Mac only) is extremely powerful and a great deal with a street price of $50 (1-800-544-8554).

- **Expresso For Windows** (Berkeley Systems) is cheap but good at $70, and comes with a sense of humor (1-800-877-5535).

- **Lotus Organizer** (Lotus Development) is a good product for PCs only. Street price: $100 (1-800-343-5414).

Making Your PIM Portable

Of course, most of us don't want to have to turn on the computer just to get Auntie Em's address. Any good PIM or contacts database has printing options that allow you to print your address book, phone list or appointment calendar virtually any way you want. (Some PIM developers even include address books with their software that you can put the printed pages in.)

Profile:
Greta B. Lipson

Project/Activity

Creating a database to track book publishing projects

Project Start Date

1994

Hardware/Software Used

Apple Centris 610
PowerBook 100
8MB RAM (4MB and RAM Doubler Software)
Hewlett Packard DeskWriter
Microsoft Works
Microsoft WORD

Contact

Greta B. Lipson
c/o SeniorNet Profiles
1 Kearney
San Francisco, CA 94108

Getting Organized

Her office is crammed with books on child development, education theory, and teaching strategies, not to mention the piles and piles of children's books. She has authored and co-authored nearly twenty books herself that have been published by several different publishing houses.

Who

Greta Lipson retired recently after many years as an associate professor of Education at the University of Michigan. Honored by Michigan's Association of Governing Boards as a distinguished faculty member for her extraordinary contributions to Michigan higher education, she remains kinetic, writing books for elementary and secondary level educators.

Married for over 50 years and the mother of three boys ("they're all grown men, but who's counting?!"), Greta and her husband Bill moved back to Detroit, Michigan after the war. "Those were tough, tough years, but we managed," says Greta. "Bill worked like a dog, opened a successful restaurant, and I earned my doctoral degree in education by going to night school with him watching the kids. My Bill has always been there for me and I always admired his self-confidence. He has always been supportive—he was a feminist before there was ever a term to describe such a person."

Greta and Bill enjoy an extremely active social life, seeing plays, concerts, and visiting with friends and family. "My sister and most of the kids live fairly close by, so our calendar is pretty booked up—there's not a whole lot of time for me to be online—even though my son and many of our friends keep trying to get us into it."

What

Greta's professional writing career has continued unabated for about twenty years. "I'm at the point where I can't keep track of the projects," she says. "I've avoided it for some time, but I realized late last year that I was in desperate need of some sort of database management system."

Greta got started building a database in 1994, and the project has demanded a lot of planning. The database must track a lot of information related to many different projects. "Every book I've written has a different editorial staff," says Greta. "Publishers come and go, different editors are assigned, new co-authors appear, the royalty statements need to be tracked—and then there are all of the proposals. I really want to include the book covers in the database, as well." One of Greta's books appears in Figure 12–5.

Working with the database in Microsoft Works, Greta is enthusiastic that the project will continue to evolve. "We keep tweaking and tweaking," she says. "Eventually you just have to accept what

the database can and can't be—I'm just really excited to have some organization in my office."

Thoughts On Computing

"I've been writing professionally for a long time," says Greta Lipson, "and since I got a computer I could understand, it has proven to be the best productivity tool of all times."

It wasn't always that way. For many years, Greta relied on a manual typewriter and then several generations of electric typewriters. "I had been using an electric typewriter and I kept trading up to more advanced models," she says. "By the time I got rid of that thing, I felt like it needed mud flaps and a rear view mirror!"

The truth is, Greta's maiden computing voyage was a bad one. "My husband, Bill, and I aren't technically inclined (Bill still fixes everything in the house with Scotch tape!) and I was afraid of the technology. My first computer was an old DOS machine and I couldn't make any sense out of it. Even with plenty of help from the family, it stood largely unused—for years. When my son tossed his "old" Mac SE computer on my desk in 1990, I expected to ignore it, but I was hooked. I bought a laptop two months later so I could work up at Lake Huron, where we love our summer outings and I can work by the water."

Some advice? "The bottom line is, you need to persevere—and find the option that's right for you. I had one computer that didn't help me, but this one helps so much that I got a laptop version, too. It feels good to be productive and keep track of so much. It's the ultimate efficiency expert."

Greta's final observation? "Our social life is everything to us and we're still mobile enough to take advantage of it, so we don't feel the need to spend much time online. But most of our friends are older than us and they can't get around like they used to. These are people with vital minds who are now faced with various physical limitations. But with the computer they can transcend their limitations. The computer has become their intellectual lifeline. It's not just about having a shoulder there— it's about continued intellectual growth— It's all very inspiring."

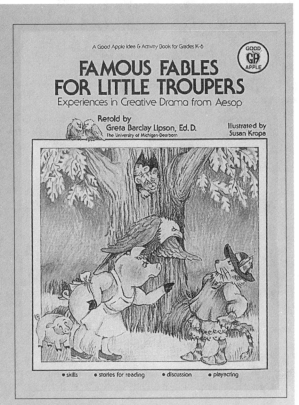

Figure 12–5

The cover of the first book Greta wrote—on her personal computer

CHAPTER
13

Integrated Software
Programs
and Suites

You probably got a computer (or you'll get one) expecting to do a few different things: a little writing, a little accounting, and a little organizing. You aren't planning on any epic literary projects, so you don't need a deluxe word processor; you aren't planning on doing General Motor's payroll, so you don't need an atom-powered spreadsheet program; and you don't have as much stuff in the garage or storage room as they have at WalMart or Home Depot, so organizing won't require a top of the line database program. You need some of everything, something that provides a little of the most used programs; namely, an integrated software program.

Of course, you may also want the creme de la creme of software. Your small business has taken off and you need it all: a dynamite word processor, spreadsheet, and database. If that describes you and your needs, you'll want to get an "office" or "suite" set of products. An office or suite product offers all of the most powerful programs at a very attractive price.

Integrated Software/Your Software Swiss Army Knife

An integrated software program is like the software version of a Swiss army knife: it's built to do a little of everything and as long as you have one, you'll be prepared for just about every small job. These programs give you a little of several different kinds of programs. In any given integrated package, you are likely to get a scaled down word processor, spreadsheet, database, and telecommunications program (for going online). Some integrated programs may give you a drawing and/or graphics program as well. Each piece of the integrated program is called a *module*. The modules are full-featured but somewhat stripped versions of the full-blown professional programs that the companies offer. Figure 13–1 shows the opening screen of Microsoft Works, Microsoft's integrated software package—word processing, spreadsheet, database, and communications capabilities are all included. Integrated programs are ideal in many ways: inexpensive, comprehensive, small in size, and easy to use.

Tip: **Many computer makers offer integrated software programs "free" when you buy their computers. When buying a new computer, check whether such a program is included.**

What Integrated Software Can Do for You

For most users, integrated software is just what the doctor ordered. Integrated programs offer more help in getting things done, with more canned forms and templates, and with the reduced number of features, the programs are easier to learn. They're also very inexpensive.

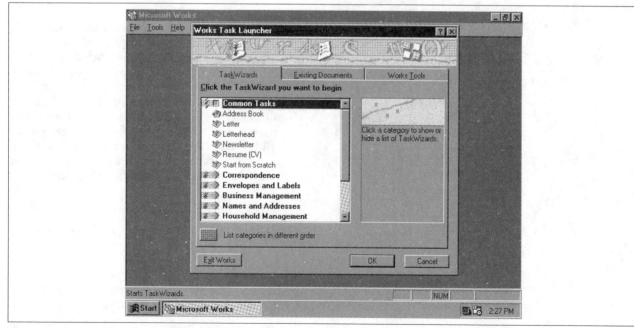

Figure 13–1

Microsoft Works is an integrated software package

What's Available

Here are some integrated software products to consider:

- **ClarisWorks** (Mac and PC compatibles) (Claris Corporation: 1-800-544-8554) provides word processing (ClarisWrite), database, spreadsheet, graphics (ClarisDraw), and communications, and they offer handholding throughout document creation so that you are guaranteed good-looking documents. They are out to impress (street price: $90 Windows, $130 Mac).

- **Microsoft Works** (Microsoft Corporation: 1-800-426-9400) offers a formidable program with modules based on MS Word (word processing), MS Access (database) and MS Excel (spreadsheet). A telecommunications module is also included—and the Mac version has even more. Microsoft Wizards, Microsoft's way of gently stepping you through the creation of a document, are especially helpful (street price: $100/PC and Mac).

- Novell's **PerfectWorks** (Novell, Inc.: 1-800-451-5151) includes six modules: drawing, painting, spreadsheet, telecommunications, database, and word processor (based on WordPerfect)—street price: $110/Windows only.

Integrated software programs are especially good introductory tools because each module is a lot less intimidating. You may not have any interest in a database at first—maybe you wanted an integrated program for the inexpensive word processor—but since you get all of the other programs, you can experiment with them, learn how to use them, and perhaps discover some computer tricks you never knew about. At any rate, if you never use a couple of the modules, say telecommunications and spreadsheets, you still have a great deal. And if you discover that your needs outgrow one of the modules—say you would like to write a James Michener-sized novel, you can always buy the more powerful software and you still have the other modules to use.

Tip: **The modules you find in an integrated package look and function just like their more powerful siblings. If you like a certain module in your integrated software program but you need more features, consider upgrading with the same software company: the more advanced version of the program will be just like the program you are used to using—with more features— so you won't have to relearn any commands.**

Good Things in Small Packages

Integrated software programs offer a couple of other significant advantages. All of the modules are accessed through one icon, so you don't have to navigate all around your computer (or through folders or subdirectories or program groups) to find the database or the spreadsheet or word processing modules. Integrated software programs also occupy far less disk storage space than their full-featured counterparts. If you have limited storage space—or if you plan on using a laptop that has less hard disk storage space—an integrated program is the perfect choice.

A Quick Look at the Modules

Integrated software programs from different companies vary quite a bit. ClarisWorks and Microsoft Works include clip art and Novell's PerfectWorks offers drawing and painting modules. Versions of the program from the same company can differ dramatically as well. Microsoft Works for PC compatibles does not include a graphics module, but the Mac version does. The Mac version also has an address book and a good appointment scheduler/calendar. When a version is updated, it can also change significantly, so be aware of the version *number* you are getting.

What Integrated Software Can't Do for You

To fit in such a small [disk drive] space and be so inexpensive, each module offers a reduced set of features. A word processor module, for example, won't offer a table of contents feature, an index generator, or many of the other features you would want when creating a long document or book. A spreadsheet module will not include all of the sophisticated graphing features you find in the full-priced version. So, if you need all of the bells and whistles that the high-end version of a program has to offer, you'll have to get the high-end version.

The Big Bundles

There's another kind of package deal available, often referred to as a "suite" of products, an "office" bundle, or, not surprisingly, an "office suite." If you need more than one high-end office product, say a professional-level word processor *and* spreadsheet, and the ones you want all come from the same software company, you can get them bundled together for a comparatively low price.

Lotus, Novell, and Microsoft all offer such bundles. These product bundles are really the best way to go—*if* you need more than one of the high-end versions. When you purchase a bundle, you will probably pay half of what you would normally pay if you bought these products separately. There is usually a product included in the set that you don't expect to use, but like the integrated programs, if you have it, you can learn about what it can do. When you get everything so cheap, you can think of the unused program as a freebie.

Alert: **Watch the version numbers on all of the products that you get in a professional bundle. Be sure that all of the programs are the most current.**

What's Available

The professional bundles are a good deal for power users; they are much cheaper, but they aren't cheap. There are three big competitors.

- **Office/Office Professional**, from Microsoft Corporation (1-800-426-9400) comes with MS Word (word processor), MS Excel (spreadsheet), MS PowerPoint (a presentation graphics program), and MS Mail, an office e-mail program (street price: $500). Office Professional includes MS Access (the database program) and MS Scheduler (street price: $600).

- Novell's **PerfectOffice** (Novell, Inc.: 1-800-453-1267) includes WordPerfect (word processor), Quattro Pro (spreadsheet), Presentations (presentation graphics), and InfoCentral (a personal information manager). By adding another $200 to the $600 price tag, you also get Paradox (a relational database program) and software development tools. Be prepared for a lot of program: PerfectOffice is perfectly *huge*, requiring 84MB of storage space!

- **SmartSuite** is another from Lotus Development Corporation (1-800-343-5414). This contains Lotus 123 (spreadsheet), WordPro (a word processor, formerly called AmiPro), Approach (database), and Lotus Freelance Graphics, plus Organizer (PIM) for a list price of about $800. This is smaller than PerfectOffice and only requires about 30MB to install on your hard disk (street price: $400).

What do the big companies gain by offering these big bundles? These companies are looking to turn you into a dedicated customer, loyal to the products in their line. By getting you to use their products, they expect to make more money when you upgrade each product. If they get you to buy their products exclusively (like you do with a bundle), they are closer to achieving their goals.

Personal Finance

Personal finances are just that: personal. And though everyone's situation is unique, everyone has pretty much the same plan: to exercise minimum financial risk while obtaining the maximum financial gain—and always maintaining maximum security. On top of ensuring financial stability and success, everybody has to document his or her finances on a series of hieroglyphic tax forms in time to pay taxes. That's not always so easy to do.

Managing your finances requires planning, and lots of it. There are many software programs and electronic services available that can help out immensely. Many of the programs assume that you are new to the subject matter and will walk you through all of the steps needed to complete the task at hand. Others, like software for tracking your mutual funds or stock investments, are not designed so much as tutorials, but as tools to help manage your assets more effectively. Whatever aspects of personal finance you are interested in, you won't find a single program to cover all of your financial chores. Instead, there is a variety of programs that can ably provide assistance in different areas.

Many people who have *not* used these programs often ask whether the programs are really beneficial. The answer is a field-tested *yes*. The most popular of the programs are easy to use and for the time you put into learning them, the return on your investment is very high. The software programs described here can help with a diverse range of financial tasks and have proven to be quite helpful to the *millions* who have adopted them.

What Personal Finance Software Can Do for You

There are many different aspects to personal finance: savings, taxes, wills, and investments; as well as the mechanics of budgeting, checking, and bill paying. All of these can be made much easier with the right tasks software program.

Budgeting

The purpose of budgeting is to figure out where all of your money is going and to ensure that it is going where you want it to go—when you want it to go there. Although your spending habits are probably well established, the right software can automate much of the budgeting process and help you identify things about your spending habits that aren't otherwise obvious to you. You provide budget profile information and the right program can track your budget with vigilance and let you know when you stray. Budgeting software can also alert you to hidden and not-so-hidden trends in your spending.

Paying Your Bills and Balancing Your Checkbook

Does anyone take pleasure in balancing a checkbook? Maintaining your checking account balance and reconciling your checkbook can take an inordinate amount of time; either you use a calculator or you do the math manually on a notepad. Either way, the more checks you write, the longer it takes, and the more errors you—and your bank—are prone to make. When you do make a mistake, you must start over, find the mistake, and correct it. In the event you have done *your* math right and still can't get the numbers to reconcile, you must call your bank to track down their mistake. It's a lot of time spent doing something you can give to your computer to do—if you have the right software, that is.

Checkbook software has several other less obvious advantages. If you think about it, the checkbook ledger you are used to writing in is not especially "user friendly." You must enter detailed numeric information in a very narrow ruled space, requiring a manual dexterity—and hawk-like vision—that not everyone over 50 (or under 50, for that matter) has. Replacing or supplementing your checkbook with a software version of a checkbook can rid you of these difficulties.

Quicken

Quicken, from Intuit Software (1-800-624-8742), is the most successful product of its kind and one of the most successful software products of all time. It helps you with all aspects of budgeting, including tax planning, financial planning, forecasting, budgeting, and more. If you can buy only one personal finance software program, Quicken is the most versatile.

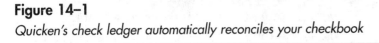

Figure 14-1

Quicken's check ledger automatically reconciles your checkbook

Quicken is especially popular for its check ledger, as shown in Figure 14–1. The check ledger reconciles an entry as you enter the specifics of the check.

Quicken and Budgeting

To streamline the task of budgeting, Quicken lets you define spending categories that your checks can then be assigned to. Say, for example, you want to track all household expenses versus medical expenses. Each (related) check you write is automatically placed in the appropriate category for later analysis. If you want to break down the categories further, say expenses

based on particular medical specialists, Quicken also lets you do that.

Tip: **Quicken's Category feature is especially helpful come tax time: you can print a report on exactly how much you spent on what and give that to your accountant (or use it yourself) for itemizing and figuring out your deductions.**

Quicken's automatic ledger capabilities are certainly not limited to your checking account. You can set up credit card accounts, savings accounts, and investment accounts, and when you enter a debit or credit, the debits/credits/totals are automatically calculated for you.

Quicken lets you generate a variety of reports at any time so you can see exactly *what* you are spending your money on and *how much* of it you are spending. Quicken lets you automatically create a graph to see a breakdown of your monthly expenses versus your monthly income. If you see from your report, for example, that your long distance phone bills are accounting for too much of your monthly budget, you can then adjust things accordingly.

From the graphs, you'll be able to see where you need to make some budget cuts. Quicken displays how well you are keeping to your budget and shows clearly what areas need adjusting. If you have multiple accounts that you want to track together, Quicken accommodates this by letting you *link* accounts; multiple accounts are all a part of your budget and the balance in one can affect another.

To be really thorough, you can create monthly or quarterly budget reports based on your current expenses and earnings. These kinds of reports are easy to design; Quicken prompts you for relevant information—like an interviewer—and asks you for the categories you wish to place your expenditures under.

Quicken and Printing Checks

A good personal finance package can also print checks for you. In fact, with Quicken's check printing option and windowed business envelopes, you print your check so that you don't even have to address the envelope; the addressee's name and address are aligned with the cellophane window. In concert, these features can make your day-to-day financial chores a lot easier.

Quicken and Paying Bills Electronically

The only thing worse than having to pay all of those monthly bills is *forgetting* to pay those monthly bills. If you want to save yourself the cost of envelopes, you can get an online payment service, like CheckFree. With CheckFree (1-800-877-8021) and Quicken, you specify where the remittance should be sent, how much it's for, and when you want it to be sent. With the push of a button, the payment is made from your desktop. The service carries with it a $9.95 monthly service fee for 20 checks. When you look at how many bills you pay in a month—credit cards, gas and electric bills, telephone, home insurance, life insurance, mortgage payment, water bill—you may easily have fifteen or twenty that go out monthly. When you look at the cost of stamps, envelopes, and the time you spend addressing everything, you can actually save time and money by paying bills online.

Quicken's Financial Calendar

One very good feature: Quicken has also included a Financial Calendar to remind you of important billing dates. Mortgage payments, condominium maintenance fees, rent, and other "perennials," are always due on the same day of the month, and with Quicken's built-in Financial Calendar, you get a pop-up message to inform you that a bill (or bills) is due. This may not sound like an exciting feature, but that's only because financial "alarm clocks" are new for most of us. The financial calendar can prevent those moments when you realize you are a week late with a critical payment.

Alert: **Financial calendars are a real boon, but they only work if you are using your computer on a very regular basis—turning it on at least once a day. If you aren't turning on the computer regularly, the financial calendar can't remind you that you need to pay your bill on the day you didn't turn on your computer!**

Quicken offers a tremendous number of additional features. If you have mutual funds or you trade stock, Quicken can help you set up and track your portfolio. (Updating is not automatic, unless you subscribe to an additional service.)

Getting Help with Your Taxes

With so many taxpayers frustrated by impossible-to-follow tax forms, you may have predicted that someone would create a program to assist in doing your taxes. You were right. Several companies smelled success in this market, and just about every year, at least one of the companies gives away their tax software for free—or for the cost of postage and handling. If you want to just try out the software to see if it's right for you, find the free product and get a copy.

Their strategy is simple: you get their software free this year, and you'll be more likely to buy *their* product *next* year. Since the tax forms are revised every year, you have to buy a new version of whatever program you are going to use each year, and because you have already used their program for this year's tax return, they feel you'll pay for it next year. Regardless of what choice you make next year, you can learn about a product without spending a lot of money.

Who Uses Tax Software?

Tax software can help just about anyone who has to file, and it's of special benefit to those people who have complicated tax returns that require lots of different forms.

The best of these programs support around 100 different forms, so you can expect to find the forms you need. Most important, these tools are not intended necessarily for accounting professionals, but for lay people. To make the software easy to use, the programs let you fill in your forms via an "interview" process. As shown in Figure 14–2, the program walks you through the forms, asks you questions, and prompts you for the necessary information.

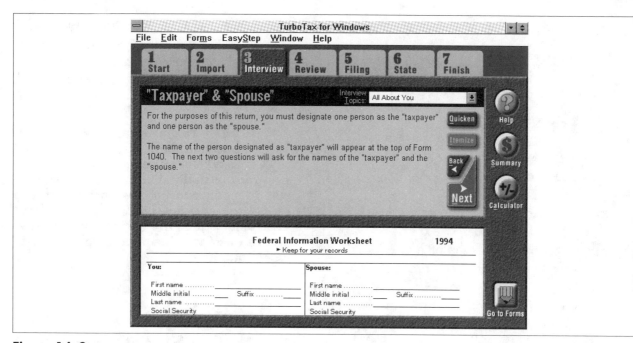

Figure 14–2

TurboTax lets you walk through the filing process

You type in the information and it automatically does the math and formatting. In addition, IRS techno-speak is translated in simple terms so you won't miss the meaning of convoluted instructions. Some of the programs also suggest possible deductions that you may have missed. The better programs also allow you to enter information in "shoe box mode"—if you happen to be among the less organized—it helps you sort your receipts into the right categories. Many of the programs also offer modules for doing your state returns as well.

Since this is such a lucrative market, there are a number of competitors with very good products, including Computer Associates' Simply Tax, H&R Block's Kiplinger's TaxCut, and Intuit's TurboTax and MacinTax.

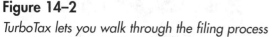 *Alert:* **Don't be confused by the names of these products. Several of the products have changed hands and some of the products have the same names. If you see a product with the right name but from a different company, check to see if the product is really the one you want.**

Finally, tax programs do not assume any responsibility for your filing. You are ultimately responsible for your filing (and any mistakes that may occur). For peace of mind, you can use a program to go through

Will I Get Audited?

A tax audit is everybody's nightmare. Tax preparation software makes things easier for you, but will the IRS look upon you more kindly? Are they less inclined to audit you? Are they more inclined to audit you, or does using tax software not make a difference one way or the other?

In the long run, they are probably less likely to audit, but not specifically because you are using a tax preparation program. First, when you use software, your tax return is neat, clear, and easy to read (you print the completed form on your laser printer and it is identical in every way to the forms provided by the IRS). IRS auditors also know that with tax software the computer did the math, not a human who was rushing to get the return done at the last minute. That means there are fewer errors for them to worry about. Finally, tax software alerts you (while you complete the forms) of those things in your tax form that are likely to attract IRS attention—you can fix these problems before you send in your form.

your taxes and then take the return to an accountant to see just how good a job you did. You'll certainly understand the procedure a lot better and next year's returns will be easier.

Tip: **Tax programs let you output just about any tax form you'll need for filing; a tax software program virtually eliminates the need to run to your nearby post office (or IRS office) to get a missing form. If you have ever panicked at the last minute because you're missing a form, you won't have to worry any longer.**

Managing Your Portfolio: StreetSmart 2.0

Some brokerage houses provide various electronic services to help you better manage your resources. In order to take advantage of these, however, you must have an account with the firm. Charles Schwab and Fidelity Bank have both introduced products that address your investment needs.

Charles Schwab's flagship software program, StreetSmart, gives you the ability to manage your portfolio from your home. With StreetSmart, you can trade stocks, options, mutual funds and bonds; display position views; and get quotes and market indicators—all from your PC. Figure 14–3 shows a StreetSmart portfolio report screen.

StreetSmart also provides access to a number of research options, including Reuters Money Network and Dow Jones News Service, Standard and Poor's Money-

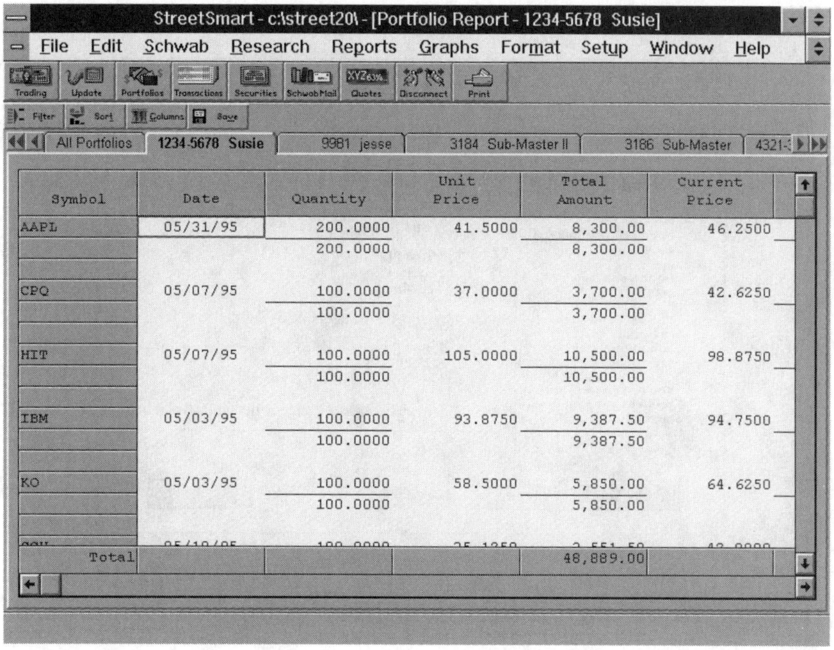

Figure 14–3
One of the several different views that StreetSmart's portfolio report screen can provide

scope, and Company Reports. StreetSmart also provides you with a regularly updated mutual fund performance guide.

StreetSmart is available only to Schwab customers for $60, but the price fluctuates. If you already have an account with Schwab, there may be a reduced price or giveaway promotion to take advantage of.

Estate Planning

If you are concerned about estate planning, Living Trust Maker (Nolo Press) lets you build a revocable living trust. This allows you to leave property to loved ones or family members in the event of your death while avoiding probate.

You may have thought that you needed a lawyer to make a trust, but you don't. Although you may want to confirm your documents with your attorney, Living Trust Maker walks you through the document creation process step by step, prompting you for information and explaining the significance of each section in gentle yet straightforward terms. Figure 14–4 shows you one of the Living Trust Maker screens. The manual includes a legal guide to living trusts, so you'll learn the basics (and not so

```
┌─────────────────────────────────────────────────────────┐
│ ─              Living Trust Maker                   ▼ ▲ │
│ File  Edit  Help  Window                                │
│   ┌─────────────────────────────────────────────────┐   │
│   │ ─                 RIOS.TRS                    ▼ │   │
│   │                                                 │   │
│   │  TRUST DOCUMENT FOR INDIVIDUAL: CHECKLIST       │   │
│   │                                                 │   │
│   │  Here are the        √ ○ 1. Your State          │   │
│   │  elements of a trust                            │   │
│   │  document.           √ ○ 2. Your Name           │   │
│   │  Go through them in    ◉ 3. Trustees            │   │
│   │  order.                                         │   │
│   │                        ○ 4. Property To Be Put in Trust │
│   │  You will come back                             │   │
│   │  to this list after    ○ 5. Beneficiaries of Trust Property │
│   │  completing each                                │   │
│   │  part.                 ○ 6. Residuary Beneficiaries │   │
│   │  You can go back to    ○ 7. Property Management for Beneficiaries │
│   │  previous parts at                              │   │
│   │  any time.             ○ Display/Print Trust Document │   │
│   │                                                 │   │
│   │  ┌──────────────────┐        ┌──────────────┐   │   │
│   │  │ What Each Part Does │      │     OK       │   │   │
│   │  └──────────────────┘        └──────────────┘   │   │
│   └─────────────────────────────────────────────────┘   │
└─────────────────────────────────────────────────────────┘
```

Figure 14–4

Living Trust Maker walks you through the process of creating a legal document via an interview process

basics) on your own time. If your lawyer charges too much, this will reduce those fees significantly, because you can go through much of the material yourself, without his or her clock ticking.

Alert: **Even though these documents may be legally binding, it would still be a good idea to review the documents with your attorney to make sure you have covered all of the bases.**

Note: **There are some things Living Trust Maker cannot provide: Living Trust Maker cannot create a "marital life estate trust" or A-B trust (designed to save on estate taxes).**

Creating a Will

As litigious as American society has become, it may also come as a surprise that you can create a perfectly acceptable will without paying for the services of an attorney. With Nolo Press' WillMaker (Figure 14–5), the process of creating a will is easy, straightforward, and educational. Like Living Trust Maker, WillMaker walks you step by step through the process. The software has its limits, however; it tells you what you can't specify or do in your will as well as what you can do and what you must do.

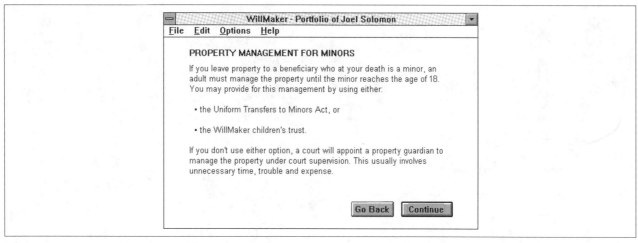

Figure 14–5

WillMaker's documentation has been prepared by attorneys, so you are getting legal advice, without having an attorney present

What's Available

There are a number of products available, as outlined below. Pricing and ownership of these products continues to change, however, so be aware that the name of the product you are looking for might be slightly different.

Budgeting/Checking Account Products	Street Price	Maker	Phone Number
Managing Your Money	$35.00	MECA Software	1-800-537-9993
Quicken	$40.00	Intuit	1-800-624-8742
Microsoft Money	$25.00	Microsoft	1-800-426-9400
Tax Software Products			
Kiplinger's TaxCut	$30.00	H&R Block	1-800-288-6352
TurboTax	$45.00	Intuit	1-800-756-1040
MacinTax for the Mac	$60.00	Intuit	1-800-756-1040
Simply Tax	$60.00	Computer Associates	1-800-808-6000
Will, Estate, and Trust Products			
WillMaker	$40.00	Nolo Press	1-800-992-6656
Living Trust Maker	$50.00	Nolo Press	1-800-992-6656

Profile:
Hazel Phillips

Project/Activity

Small Business bookkeeping and tax return preparation.

Project Start Date

1989

Hardware/Software Used

IBM PS/2
Printer
TurboTax

Contact

Hazel Phillips
c/o SeniorNet Profiles
1 Kearney
San Francisco, CA 94108

Immaculate Tax Returns

Hazel Phillips used to do tax returns by hand as a source of income. After taking a computer course at Stephen F. Austin State University, Hazel learned about TurboTax and several other tax preparation and finance programs. Things have not been the same since for Hazel Phillips.

Who

In 1987, after working for 25 years as a personnel manager for a business forms company, Hazel retired to an even busier schedule. Her hobby of collecting antique spoons and Hummel figurines and plates makes her a regular at antique shops and flea-market type stores, and her nine grandchildren keep her plenty busy. Her husband, Carroll, has a flourishing neon-sign business, for which Hazel helps take care of invoicing and finances. "You need to start up something in the morning," says Hazel. "I like to start my computer up and Carroll likes to start the store up. He loves it and I love the computer."

What

After Hazel's course at the university, she was hooked. "The professor told us about TurboTax and since learning how to use it, I'll never go back to doing returns manually." She now prepares her and Carroll's tax returns and, as a gift, she also prepares tax forms for family members and friends.

A friend of Hazel's kept telling her about Quicken and other personal finance software. "I didn't think it could make that big a difference," she says, "but I'm a big fan now—it's so accurate." Hazel uses Quicken for balancing her checkbook and doing other finance chores. I can't believe how long I went without it—you must try it—you'll really be impressed."

Hazel's computer education hasn't stopped with just personal finance and tax software, however. "You have to keep learning," she says with conviction, "so I've been taking classes through SeniorNet here in Nacogdoches—we just had a class on online communications and the Internet; they got me out there surfing the Web (see Part III of this book for more information). I love it, but I don't have the time to really invest—the folks down here doing the Internet stuff are up there for hours, every day and there are so many things to pursue."

Hazel also is a firm believer in giving back to the community. Aside from volunteering at the local SeniorNet Learning (she taught a word processing course) she is an active community volunteer, helping to distribute food to the needy at the Harvest House. "We help to feed over 200 families, and we provided 270 turkey dinners for Thanksgiving this year. It's really important work."

Thoughts on Computing

Hazel is modest about her accomplishments. "I'm not really smart, like some of these folks, but learning about computers has just been great. You can learn so

much and it makes so many things so much easier. It's not that easy for me but I'm really anxious to take more classes and learn more—I want to learn about genealogy and I really want to prepare a family cookbook."

Hazel is also very interested in getting a new computer. "My computer is very old and a lot of the new programs won't even run on it. I'm trying to convince Carroll that I really do need a new machine. Hopefully when he sees this in print, he'll come around!"

Art, Music, and Multimedia

As a tool of communication, the computer has become invaluable. As a tool of self-expression, the computer is also—surprisingly—proving itself invaluable. Computer technology has helped open new avenues to anyone and everyone with a creative streak, providing new and extraordinary ways to artistically communicate feelings, ideas, and opinions.

Music and Sound

For many years, a computer was meant to be a scientist's, engineer's, or writer's *silent* partner. The only noise that you were supposed to hear come out of your computer was the beep to tell you that something wasn't quite right or to let you know the computer had completed its task. Maybe Jules Verne and his peers could see the utility of a talking robot, but most computer professionals could not foresee the importance of computers in the world of sound and music.

That all changed in 1984 when the first Apple Macintosh was introduced with sound capabilities. Whenever you turned on a Mac, you didn't get a chirp, you got melodious sounds, and as the technology advanced, so did the quality of sound and the audio capabilities of the computer.

Now, more than ten years later, computers are in the hands of everyday people who enjoy using them to make sound. With more and more people interested in exploring these audio options, most computer makers are including advanced sound capabilities with the

201

machines they make. There are many programs that use sound—virtually *every* CD-ROM includes sound in some way—and if you don't have the appropriate hardware (typically a sound card and some sort of speakers or headphones), then you won't be able to hear what the computer has to aurally offer.

The Utility of Sound

For the most part, sound is used in programs and CD-ROMs intended for the home (as opposed to the office). Nowadays, sound is used with a computer for system messages (as substitutes for "beeps" or alarm clock warnings, for instance), games, music software, CD-ROMS, and voice recognition programs (where the computer performs a task based on your spoken command). As an educational aid, sound-capable computers are proving themselves to be invaluable. There is nothing better than being able to hear what the foreign language you are studying actually sounds

like; to hear the musical instrument, animal, or bird you are studying; or listen to an orator deliver a highly charged speech. Although many of these uses would be considered intrusive or disruptive in an office or corporate setting (it's hard to concentrate if ten people in a room are all trying to listen to different things playing at once), sound is becoming more commonplace in the office as well. For example, scheduling programs can (quietly) alert an employee of an impending meeting with one sound while the arrival of an online message is signaled with a different and distinctive sound.

Fun with Sounds

Probably the easiest way to start experimenting with sounds is to listen to the ones that come with your computer. In Windows 3.1, the easiest way to find these is through the Control Panel and the Sound option (*not* the Sound Mapper). On the Macintosh, these options are also in the Control Panel, listed as Sound. The Sound dialog box in Windows 3.1 is shown in Figure 15–1. (In Windows 95, the equivalent dialog box, Sound Properties, is still accessed through the Control Panel. It has a few more options—and more sounds—and the event list appears above the sound display, but it works in the same fashion.)

If you have a PC-compatible computer but you don't have a sound card, you can't take advantage of any of these sound options and all of the options in this window are grayed out. If you do have a sound card, then you can have some fun.

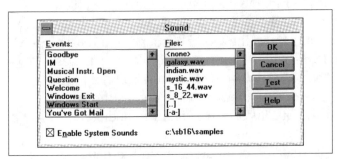

Figure 15–1

The Sound dialog box in Windows 3.1 is accessible through the Control Panel

In Figure 15–1, the left side displays the different actions or events that can have sounds associated with them. When you click on an item in the event list on the left, the highlight on the right side will move to the sound that will be heard when the action on the left occurs.

For example, when you have a sound card, you probably hear a sound every time you start your Windows computer. This is listed in the left column as "Windows Start." When you click on that, you will see the sound in the right window that is played as Windows 3.1 starts up. To change the Windows 3.1 startup sound, click on any of the other sounds. On a PC, there is a test button so that you can hear what the sound sounds like. On the Mac, you double-click the Sound Control Panel and the list of sounds appears. You hear the sound when you click on the sound's name.

Where Do the Sounds Come from?

Both IBM- and Mac-compatible computers come with only a few recorded sounds, but there are millions of sounds that people make available that you can obtain with relative ease. There are a number of different sound compilations that you can buy, including sound effects, instrumental sounds (flutes, pianos oboes, etc.), and sounds from famous television shows or movies. (Science fiction shows that feature distinctive sounds—Star Trek's "transporter," "phaser," and "communicator" sounds—are very popular collections.) Before spending any money, though, you should check

out what's available through your nearby user group or through your online service. On America Online and CompuServe, for example, you'll find plenty to keep you occupied in the Music and Sound Forums.

You should know that sounds can require a lot of disk storage space, depending on the length and clarity of the sound; a long "recording" takes up more space, and higher fidelity sound demands even more. If you want to download a lot of these via a network, you should have a fast modem, otherwise you'll spend more time downloading the files and that means more online charges.

Alert: **PC and Mac sounds are not compatible. Macs and PCs record and store sound in different formats, so you cannot play back the basic sounds on both machines.**

PC as a Tape Recorder

As odd as it may seem, any IBM compatible with a sound card (and any Macintosh) can perform the same functions as a tape recorder, but in many ways the computer is a more effective tool than a tape recorder. Many computers come with a microphone so you can experiment with the sound capabilities right out of the box. If your computer is sound ready (it has a sound card) and you want to experiment but you don't have a microphone, you can get a cheap one from your local electronics store. (These typically require a *miniplug*, a small male plug that plugs into your PC sound card jack or the back of your Mac.)

Recording your own sounds can really be a lot of fun; you can create talking greeting cards, talking letters to friends, and with the right software, your computer can play any of your custom sounds back at any time—like your grandson's "night gramma" message when you turn off your computer.

How to Make Your Own Sounds

Once you have a microphone, you can record sounds onto your computer. If you're wondering where the sounds are being stored, they are actually being recorded onto your hard drive! There is no tape per se; the storage space on your drive acts as your blank tape.

In order to record sound onto your hard disk, you must run a small audio recording program. Most computers with sound cards (and sound cards that you buy separately) come with such a program. When you run the program, it appears onscreen as a tape recorder with tape recorder buttons (called *transport controls* in professional parlance), but instead of pushing the buttons with your fingers, you use the mouse. Some programs will display recording levels—meter readings to alert you to distortion in your recording. When you speak into the microphone, watch the levels and adjust them accordingly to guarantee a good recording.

A computer with a sound card should also include sound editing software so that you can edit whatever you record—in much the same way they do in a professional studio. Figure 15–2 shows a sentence captured

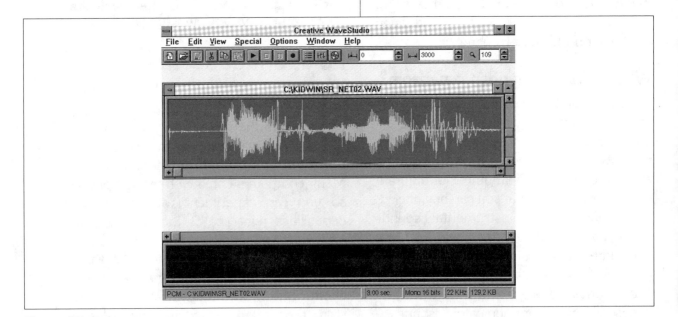

Figure 15–2

What the words "Hello From SeniorNet" look like in Creative Labs' WaveStudio

in Creative Labs' Creative WaveStudio—"Hello From SeniorNet!" When you click on the Play button to hear the sound, a line moves across the wave (like the bouncing red ball along lyrics) so you can identify how the wave form corresponds to the words. In this example, each set of peaks is a word.

With sound editing software, you can cut out words, play sounds or sentences in reverse, add reverb and echo, fade in and out, and perform a host of other tricks. These features are really fun to play with and you'll really learn a lot about how sound works.

Alert: **Interested in making a collection of sounds to sell to other audio fans? Like everything else in computing, there are copyright issues to be addressed, so before you decide to sell a diskette with the "Theme From Spartacus," make sure your recording falls within the category of public domain—i.e., no one owns the music or sound. Many of the originators of these sounds expect to see some sort of royalty or residual for the use of these sound clips. Recording things for personal use on your own machine? Everybody does this, so don't feel too guilty about it.**

Music and Computers

Computer science is a science and music is an art, so computers and music may seem like strange bedfellows, but really they aren't. Whether you are a musician or just a lover of music, computers can help

broaden your appreciation of the art, help you learn more, and even accompany you in your next performance.

There are many different ways to enjoy music; those people lucky enough to have learned an instrument may take pleasure in performing. If you didn't have the opportunity in your earlier years, perhaps you'll take pleasure in learning an instrument now. Perhaps you simply enjoy listening to good music. You'll find plenty of support and opportunity to experience all of these—with your computer's help.

Music Appreciation

Music appreciation can come in many forms with a PC. If you never bought an audio CD player (the device that made the phonograph obsolete!), but you got a CD-ROM drive with your computer, congratulations! You have an audio CD player built right into your computer.

Alert: **If you buy self-powered speakers for your CD-ROM (or if they come as part of a package deal), don't be too surprised if you also get a buzzing or hissing accompaniment. Many of these "multimedia speakers" are low priced and the quality is less than stellar.**

To use your CD-ROM drive to play audio CDs, you'll need a small program to turn on the CD player to play the songs, but this should have come with your computer, sound card, or your CD-ROM drive. Now, with speakers or headphones, you can listen to Vivaldi, the Beatles, Sinatra, or any of your favorite artists.

What's Available

The products mentioned here are really just the tip of the iceberg. If you'd like to hear about other products, you should do additional research. To get you started, here are four companies that offer a wide range of music products.

Opcode Systems (1-800-557-2633)—Opcode is responsible for perhaps the most impressive array of professional music software programs available. They also produce some fine products for beginners. Mostly Mac-based, they have quietly begun producing products for PC compatibles.

Passport Designs (1-800-443-3210)—Passport Designs produces products for both Mac and PC computers. Most of the products are MIDI-based; others are for digital audio.

PG Music (1-800-268-6272)—The makers of Band-in-a-Box, PG Music has a number of products available, including a $29, full-featured sequencer for Windows as well as a $50 collection of over 400 well-executed classical piano favorites. (The Pianist, Volumes 1 and 2.)

Voyetra Technologies (1-800-233-9377)—Voyetra makes a wide range of inexpensive software programs for PC compatibles. Many of their products have been included with different sound cards, so you may already have one or more of their products.

 Note: If you aren't into audio CDs yet, you will be amazed at the selection available. Many older artists whose LPs and tapes have been discontinued or were out of print are being reissued on CD and they sound divine. You might be surprised to find that CDs are more expensive than LPs, so consider buying your selections, when possible, at a used CD store. Used CDs are a much safer bet than used records since there is no vinyl to scratch and the sound quality doesn't degrade over time.

Music CD-ROMs

If you are interested in learning more about a particular piece of music or about a composer, a number of exceptional CD-ROMs are available for musicians and nonmusicians alike. The Voyager Company has produced several such CD-ROMs as part of their Companion Series (distributed by Microsoft). These CD-ROMs focus on particular composers and include passages with images and historical background surrounding the piece or passage. There are CD-ROMs on Stravinsky's *Rite Of Spring*, Mozart's *Dissonant Quartet*, Beethoven's *Ninth Symphony*, and Schubert's *Trout Quintet* among others.

In a somewhat different vein, but no less inspired, Microsoft's "Musical Instruments" is a wonderful guide to virtually all things plucked, bowed, blown, or struck. Figure 15–3 shows one of the screens from this program. This CD-ROM is a guide to the universe of musical instruments. Featuring instruments from around the world, they are each beautifully photographed with a description and explanation of how the instrument is played. Each instrument is also accompanied by a note or phrase played on the instrument itself. The CD-ROM also includes explorations of several different genres of music from gamelan to orchestral to rock and roll.

Learning to Compose and to Play Music

If you are more of a hands-on person and you're interested in learning to compose or play music, the computer may prove to be

the best instructor you could hope for: you learn at your own pace and you don't get badgered when you don't practice! There's a remarkable number of diverse tools that can help you learn. Here's a look at a few different options.

Learning to Play

If you are interested in learning to play music—specifically if you'd like to learn to play songs and improvise, Band-in-a-Box (PG Music, 1-800-268-6272) is the program for you. Band-in-a-Box is like the old Music Minus One records, where the only people recorded were the *other*

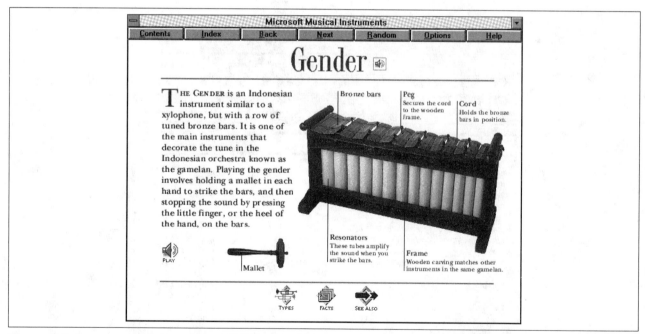

Figure 15–3

Musical Instruments from Microsoft—an interactive walk through a musical instrument museum—but no museum has a collection like this

instrumentalists—your instrument was missing so you could play along with the recording, and solo as well. With Band-in-a-Box, the program can play hundreds of tunes the way *you* want to play them. You select the tune, you set the tempo (you can change the tempo during the tune and, unlike changing the record player's speed, the pitch doesn't change). You can select the key and you can change instrumental sounds. You can even change the "groove" (bossa nova, cha cha, swing, two step). If you want, you can play "My Funny Valentine" with a Caribbean flavor or "Black Orpheus" with a string quartet! Figure 15–4 shows the playalong screen.

When you select a tune in Band-in-a-Box, the screen displays all the chord changes. When the tune starts, a marker shows you where you are in the tune, so following along is a breeze. This is learning by doing and you don't need to get two or three other musicians together to do it. (Band-in-a-Box is one of the best selling music products available.) Be sure to check the hardware requirements for the product—

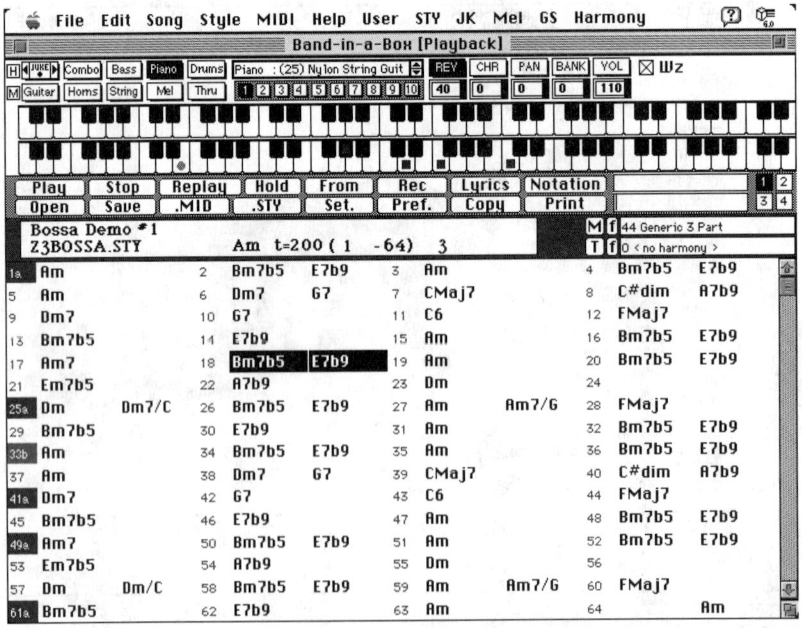

Figure 15–4

Band-in-a-Box lets you play along with all sorts of tunes—at any tempo you choose and in any style

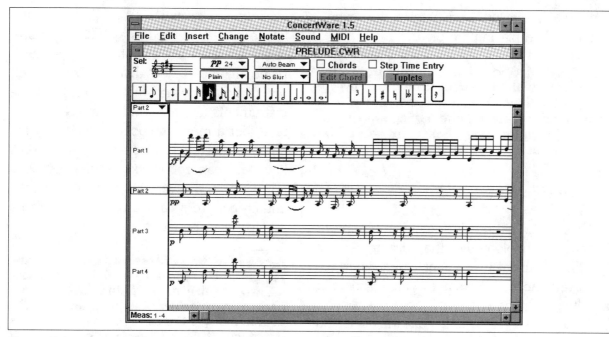

Figure 15–5

With a program like ConcertWare, you can compose and arrange with up to 16 instruments at a time

you'll need a MIDI interface (explained next) and a MIDI-compatible sound card or synthesizer that includes drum sounds.

Arranging and Composing

If you want to try your hand at arranging or composing, there are programs especially for you. These programs are like the musical version of word processors, and they let you manipulate music in much the same way. You enter your music on staves with your computer keyboard and mouse or with a MIDI keyboard (described later in this section). Figure 15–5 shows a screen from Jump Software's ConcertWare that lets you compose and arrange with up to 16 differ-

ent instruments. You can cut, copy, and paste passages; transpose; use dynamics; repeat passages; and much more.

One rather impressive feature (albeit common) of these programs is that you can designate whatever instrument you want for any part and change the instrument (or mute it) at any time. This lets you experiment with limitless variations and voicings; perhaps that vibraphone should be a marimba—push a button and try it out. Like it? Leave it. Don't like it? Click again and the vibraphone is back. In addition, when you write a piece of music or compose a score, these programs will play the music back for you and actually use your markings—including dynamics, for example—when playing the piece.

> *Alert:* **Some music programs will give you a little bit of everything. If you are interested in a particular feature—like having your notation program play back your score—be sure to ask before buying.**

MIDI

One of the big breakthroughs in computer music technology was the development of MIDI—musical instrument digital interface (pronounced to rhyme with "Kiddie"). Although it is confusing as an acronym, MIDI can be easy use. In part, MIDI lets you capture your performance without actually recording the sound. It records only the things you *did* in performance: which notes were played, the tempo, and the dynamics. If you play the MIDI recording back into a MIDI synthesizer (these have many sounds stored in them), it will play your performance identically—using the sounds that are on the synthesizer. MIDI works as if you are creating a player piano's piano roll every time you perform.

> *Note:* **MIDI files are much smaller than audio ("tape recorded") files. A 1-minute high-quality audio recording may require over 5MB of disk space. One minute of a MIDI file may require less than 1Kb!**

If you want to create a MIDI file with a keyboard, you need a MIDI-compatible music keyboard—you can get cheap ones at Target or Kmart. True, the computer keyboard can be used as a music keyboard, but you won't be able to "play it" as a piano. If you play a different instrument, you can explore the MIDI options for those instruments (drums, wind instruments, guitars), but a music keyboard is certainly the easiest route. Even a small 40-note MIDI keyboard can sound exquisite, resembling anything and everything from majestic church bells to a cathedral pipe organ to a muted jazz trumpet.

> *Note:* **Unless indicated on the MIDI synthesizer, Macintosh users require a MIDI interface to connect a synthesizer to the Mac. For PC users, many PC sound cards include an interface. If your PC sound card doesn't have one, you might want to purchase a MIDI interface.**

Some of the most impressive music software programs are MIDI-based, and it's easy to see why—with a minimum hardware investment, you get great sound and lots of options; when you use a MIDI notation program and play back your work, the instruments can sound live. When you record a MIDI performance, you can edit the MIDI file instantly, altering virtually every aspect of the piece.

What's a Sequencer?

One of the most popular types of MIDI programs is called the *sequencer*. A sequencer has an interface that looks similar to an unwound piano roll, as shown in Figure 15–6, but it allows you to compose for

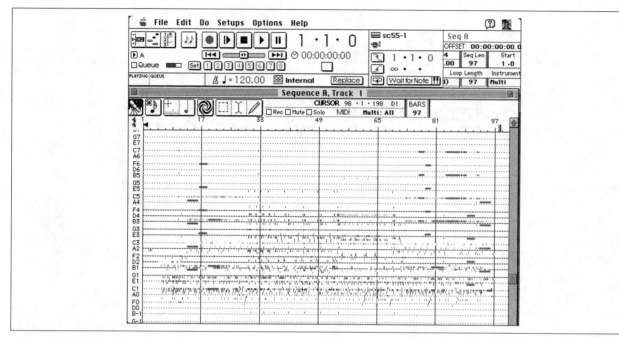

Figure 15–6

A MIDI sequencer screen—powerful but not intuitive

many instruments and perform all sorts of wild editing tricks. Although it's impossible to tell in black and white, there are six different instrument tracks shown in the figure. Each instrument is assigned a different color so you can more easily discern the different musical parts. You can change keys; transpose sections; and cut, copy, and paste passages and parts (like you would words with a word processor). With advanced sequencers, you can even mix MIDI parts with recorded passages.

One of the magical things about MIDI is altering tempo: unlike a standard audio recording (or recording stored on your hard drive), MIDI lets you speed up a performance without altering the pitch—(If you speed up an audio recording, say from 33 rpm to 78, everyone sounds like a singing chipmunk). MIDI is how Band-in-a-Box lets you change tempo without changing pitch.

The biggest problem with sequencers is that the interface can be especially challenging. In addition, there are so many of them on the market that you really need to do a lot of research to find the one that's best or most manageable for you. There are some very inexpensive sequencers around, and there are also high falootin' sequencers that retail for as much as $1,000!

A Musical Field Trip

Have you been in a music store lately? Well, the corner music store doesn't look quite the same anymore. Some of the instruments resemble science experiments gone awry. Some of the pianos look like you should land a lunar module with them instead of play music on them. In fact, many MIDI-based instruments are hybrids. Yamaha's Disclavier is an acoustic piano with a floppy drive and MIDI capabilities built in. Yamaha's KX1 is a small strap-on keyboard that has a neck, like a stringed instrument. Some instruments have a pitch bend wheel, a small wheel that bends the pitch of the instrument as you turn the wheel. Now, keyboard players can "bend a note" the way Benny Goodman could, sliding gradually from one note to the next without stopping.

To get a glimpse of what this new technology can do, find a big music store that sells computer software and pay them a visit. The clerks in these stores are often young, impatient, and very interested in selling, so tell them you *only* have $1,000 to spend and let them show you some stuff. (OK, it's a bit of a fib to say you are spending money when you aren't, but it may be hard to get their attention otherwise.)

You definitely want to hear what these keyboards sound like. All of the synthesizers have headphone jacks, so have them give you a set of headphones (so you won't disturb the other customers) and check out some of the sounds. Most synths let you step through all of their sounds with the push of a button, so it's not too difficult. Even if you have never played an instrument before, pushing a single key on a music keyboard and hearing the equivalent of the Mormon Tabernacle Choir is both inspiring and hilarious. You'll be amazed at how good *you* sound—even if you don't know how to play music!

Playing MIDI Clips

If you snoop around in any of the online music forums or at any user group meetings, you'll probably notice or hear about MIDI clips or MIDI files. These are MIDI song files that you can use as you would a player piano's piano roll. You load it into your computer and with a MIDI player, you can hear the song using the sounds available with your MIDI sound card or synthesizer.

Alert: Sometimes MIDI files will use different instruments than you expect them to, resulting in a cacophony instead of a symphony. To ensure that your MIDI files play properly, look for those that were created specifically for your particular synthesizer or sound card, or that use the General MIDI standard.

What Are MIDI Patch Files?

There are also other files that you may stumble onto, namely MIDI patch files or just MIDI patches. Unlike the sound files that you use on your computer—Johnny Weismuller's ape call or the sound of breaking glass—you can't listen to a MIDI patch as you would other sound files. These files represent setups sound that you load into a particular MIDI synthesizer.

These sounds are created by "sound designers," people who instead of becoming instrument designers like Stradivarius, have learned how to shape and create unique sounds with a computer and synthesizer. They can sit at a computer (or a synthesizer) and sculpt a sound—adjust all the physical characteristics by turning knobs and switches and clicking on the mouse—and then distribute those sounds to musicians. You say you want to use a sound that's a cross between a piano and a Schnauzer? How about a cross between a tuba and a cello? Anything and everything is possible, and there are libraries of such sounds available from small independent sound companies, who often advertise in the back of music magazines.

Where to Hide a 50-Voice Choir?

Electronics is making remarkable inroads into the world of music performance. At a recent performance of Tchaikovsky's *Nutcracker* by the San Francisco Ballet, the orchestra performed wonderfully, along with the 50-voice choir that sang in the snow scene. But wait a minute...there was no choir on stage and they certainly weren't in the orchestra pit. Although you heard the choir perform with the orchestra, none of the members of that choir were on the premises.

Welcome to the world of *sampling*. Sampling technologies allow a musician to prerecord a sound or note—in the chorale case, perhaps a vowel "oooooo"—store it in the computer or keyboard's memory, and then play the single note back at different pitches as a melody. Unlike a prerecorded passage, a sampling keyboard is played like any other keyboard, so the sampled part—in this case, a choir—can be perfectly incorporated into the performance.

Music and Computers:
Just a Few Words

There is a lot of language surrounding music and sound on a computer. Again, this isn't rocket science, but without the words, the subject matter may become impenetrable. Here are some terms and explanations.

8-bit/16-bit sound A descriptive characteristic of digital sound quality. Eight-bit sound describes lower resolution sound and 16-bit is required for high-quality sound. As a comparison, telephone sound suffers from low-quality, 4-bit sound.

CD-quality sound High-fidelity sound characterized by 16-bit resolution and sampling rate of 44.1 or 48 kHz.

DAT Short for digital audio tape. The cassette tape equivalent of a CD.

Digital audio Audio recorded and processed without analog (reel-to-reel) tape. Digital audio is easier to edit and does not degrade from the editing process, as does analog tape.

General MIDI The latest version of the MIDI standard (see MIDI). All General MIDI equipment uses the same index of musical sounds so that your MIDI piano concerto doesn't play back with a ukulele or other unintended sound.

MIDI Musical instrument digital interface. The protocol that lets specially designed musical instruments communicate with computers and other technologies.

Sampler A device used to digitally record a sound. Samplers record directly to a hard drive. A sampling keyboard lets you record the sound and use the sample as the keyboard's sound.

Sampling rate The frequency at which a sound is sampled.

Sequencer A popular music program that lets you record a performance and store it as a MIDI file.

Sound module A music synthesizer that provides all of the sounds and characteristics of a synthesizer, without the keyboard. Sound modules are much cheaper than their synthesizer counterparts. If you already own a synthesizer but you hear a new one you really want, you can buy the sound module, plug it into your existing keyboard, and use your original keyboard to play the sound module.

Synthesizer An electronic keyboard that lets you manipulate electronic (and sampled) sounds and use those sounds in performance.

Note: **Sound designers create and shape sounds for other musicians to use on their synthesizers. On some CDs, these people may be referred to as synthesizer programmers—they program a synthesizer to create just the right sounds for a particular artist.**

Want to Find Out More?

The bookshelves are loaded with computer magazines, and while many of them are good, you may want to go to more of a specialty magazine for information on music-related technologies.

Two good choices are *Electronic Musician* (published by Mix Publishing in Emeryville, CA) and *Keyboard Magazine* (from Miller Freeman Publishers, San Mateo, CA). They are usually aimed at a fairly savvy audience, but it's eye opening to skim the magazines and see what this stuff looks like. *EM* is usually more gear and technology oriented with reviews and tutorials. *Keyboard Magazine* also includes gear and technology reviews, but it has more interviews, personality pieces, and human/music interest information. (Does Oscar Peterson use electronics?—Did Ben Webster's pianist abandon the acoustic piano for a synthesizer?—yes.) Since rock and popular music have embraced this new technology, most of the profiles, however, are slanted to younger musicians.

Computer Graphics

Like the introduction of photography, it has taken many years to establish computer graphics as a serious medium of expression. Over the years, though, it has matured in remarkable ways, taking on the hallmark of a serious and artistic art form.

Like music programs, the range of computer graphics software is exceptionally diverse. Some programs are used to create animations and special effects or enhance color, others are used to manipulate photographic images, and still others are used to render scenic landscapes. Some programs are intended for designers, some for fine artists, others for photographers. If you aren't an artist but you do appreciate fine art, there are CD-ROMs of great collections.

Art Appreciation

If you do appreciate fine art, The Microsoft Art Gallery on CD-ROM gives you a chance to visit London's National Gallery without leaving your home. Audio tracks provide narration and background on the paintings, on the artists who rendered them, and more. Another CD-ROM, American Visions from Eden Interactive, includes over 200 works by American artists. This collection includes both paintings and sculptures.

Although it's hard to classify, Art Spiegelman's Pulitzer Prize winning *The*

Complete Maus (Voyager), is a unique artistic work. Originally a two-volume comic book, *Maus* is an emotionally moving allegory based on Spiegelman's father's experience in Nazi Germany's death camps. The CD-ROM includes observations and background on how the comic was conceived.

Clip Art

Clip art, examples of which appear in Figure 15–7, are small graphic images that you can use to enhance your document or picture. Clip art is available from a wide range of sources. Many desktop publishing programs include free clip art, and there are huge collections you can buy on CD-ROM. Clip artists normally specify that you can use any of their images freely in your documents or publications—except to resell them as your own clip art.

Images Online

When you travel online, you will discover an infinite array of photographs and computer graphics available free. These are classed by type, by archive, and/or by artist, so you'll know where to get what. You are always welcome to download these images, but remember that graphics files tend to be quite large, so depending on the speed of

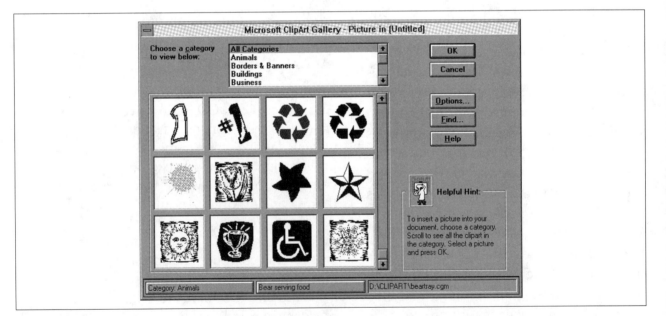

Figure 15–7

Clip art can help you better communicate your thoughts and feelings

your modem, a single file may take a very long time to download.

There are also CD-ROM collections of computer art and photographs. Corel has a remarkably extensive collection of such CDs, and they are always adding to it. CD-ROMs range in price, so shop around and don't buy until you find the set of images you are really most interested in—at the price you can afford.

Fractals

Probably sooner than later, you will come upon graphic images referred to as fractals. These are rather startling images, usually color images, that have an organic appearance to them, as shown in Figure 15–8.

Discovered by IBM fellow Minot Mandelbrot, fractals are the graphical representations of a class of mathematical equation. The images are generated by plugging a couple of numbers into the equation and then letting the computer graph the results. You'll find freeware and shareware programs around that let you create your own fractals, and experimenting can be a lot of fun. Mandelbrot images can get very complicated, and some of the programs build animated clips where you get to watch the image evolve and change.

Learning to Draw

People who don't recognize the value of computer graphics usually cite the stylized look of such images. How can a computer

Figure 15–8

Fractals are elegant and their beauty reveals a mathematical underpinning

that generates these same images help to teach the fundamentals of art? The answer: Very well. Two programs, in particular, stand out: Dabbler and Sketcher, from Fractal Design Software. These are inexpensive programs that simulate natural media—watercolors, pens, chalk, ink crayons. They allow you to select different paper types or canvas types, which behave differently depending on the type of "ink" or "paint" you are applying. Figure 15–9 shows an example of the kind of image that can be created with Sketcher—and used in one of the program's tutorials.

Aside from creating astonishing looking images (without the stains on your clothes, furniture, and carpeting), the Dabbler

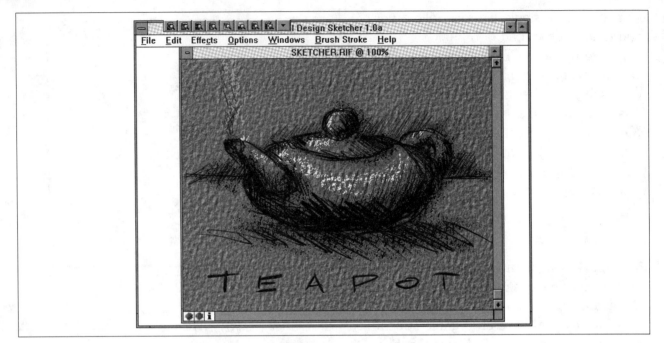

Figure 15–9

A sketcher's dream come true—software that simulates chalk, scratchboard, and other noncolor "natural media"

manual includes the *Walter Foster Learn How To Draw Guide* that you will find in many art supply stores. Sketcher, the black and white alternative to Dabbler, is a gray scale program—256 shades of gray—and this can look like charcoals, pen and ink, pencils, and other materials that appear in shades of gray.

These programs let you use your mouse as your paintbrush, but a mouse is not pressure sensitive—it doesn't respond to a lighter touch, like a pencil does. If you really want a treat, get a digitizing pad and stylus (described in Chapter 8). Designed like a pen, the stylus and tablet *do* interpret pres-

sure and touch, and your pictures will reflect this added expressive element.

Paint Packages

A great many of the graphics programs available allow you to create some very good looking art in a very short time, although a masterpiece will require time and talent. If you want to use your IBM compatible to explore this world without too much expense, try CorelDRAW! 3 or 4. These are inexpensive and older versions of CorelDRAW! 6, the latest and greatest product from Corel. Paint packages give you a diverse set of tools that can really stimulate your imagination. Figure 15–10 shows the kind of graphics that can be generated with a paint package.

Field Trip #2: SIGGRAPH

DisneyWorld is good. Laser Light shows are good. Great America is good. SIGGRAPH is unbelievable! SIGGRAPH is the Special Interest Group/Graphics of the Association of Computing Machinery (ACM). This conference, which changes location each year, features the cutting edge in all visual technologies. Will you be in over your head? Will you be overwhelmed? Without a doubt, but walking from booth to booth and taking in the visual feast will surely astound. There are courses, seminars, and lectures, but these are expensive, require registration fees, and are usually for advanced users. But you aren't going for that; go to experience the exhibit floor as sales reps hawk their wares and show you animations and visuals the likes of which you have never seen before. There is also a gallery (open to the public) of the latest in computer art.

The real highlight of SIGGRAPH is the SIGGRAPH Theater, a two-hour extravaganza featuring the best computer graphics from around the world, assembled especially for this show. For the price of admission, you'll be treated to some wondrous works (some may leave you a little confused) with thousands of other graphics enthusiasts cheering (and booing) their faves. Be sure to get your ticket for this first

Figure 15–10

"Tools" let you use a "spray can," effortlessly generate complex geometric shapes, automatically alter perspective, and provide a host of other features

because they sell out fast. For show and SIGGRAPH membership information, call ACM at (212) 626-0500.

Presentation Software

If you want to produce your own computer-based slide show/multimedia presentation, start with a presentation program such as Microsoft PowerPoint or Adobe Persuasion. These programs will walk you step by step through the process of building a computer slide show, replete with sound, graphics, and text.

These programs are ideally suited for businesspeople and marketing representatives who must visit clients and try to pitch ideas or products to them. With a presentation program loaded on a laptop, the representative can benefit from having a high-quality slide show, customized to that

Computer Graphics: Just a Few Words

The language of the computer imaging crowd is different from the other crowds. Here is some of the lingo, demystified.

8/24/32-bit color 8-, 24- or 32-bit color defines the color range possible with a particular computer or graphics program. Eight-bit color defines a color range with up to 256 colors, 24- and 32-bit color defines a range of over 16 million colors.

Bitmapped graphic A graphic that's assembled as a collection of dots. Bitmapped graphics, unlike PostScript graphics, aren't scaleable; if you enlarge the image, it becomes rough and unattractive.

Gradient A smooth and gradual transition from one color, say black, to another, for example, white.

Gray scale The use of multiple shades of gray—usually 256—to create an attractive, noncolor image.

Object oriented An image made up of components that can be individually selected and edited without affecting other parts of the image.

Palette The range of colors used in an image.

PostScript A language that lets you draw high-quality images that can be printed at any size with equally clear results.

Radiosity (pronounced ray-dee-oss-itty, like "curiosity") A means of rendering an image created with solid modeling software to provide the most realistic image possible.

Ray tracing A type of rendering that calculates reflections and light intensities to create very realistic images.

Rendering The coloring and shading of an image by the computer.

particular client, without slides and an overhead projector.

Using Your Own Art Work

If you have some art work that you created without a computer and you really want to use or manipulate it with your computer, you'll need to use a scanner. As outlined in Chapter 8, scanners let you digitize your photos or art. Once scanned, you can open them in your favorite graphics package and edit them in unique ways.

Storing Your Photos on CD-ROM

If you'd like to use personal photos on your computer, but you don't have access to a scanner, you can get photos "developed" on CD-ROM as well as on regular photographic paper. When you send your film to Kodak for developing, in addition to prints, you can get your photographs on Kodak's PhotoCD. This option is inexpensive—about $10 per roll—the image quality is great, you can always use the images on your computer, and the images are preserved and won't be damaged. All you need to do is specify on your Kodak film pouch the computer format you require: PC or Macintosh.

Advanced Graphics Programs

There are a lot of programs available that get a lot of press and that you will hear a lot about. These programs allow a trained artist to create some exceptional work, but they are costly and they require experience with graphics and a lot of effort.

PostScript: Tools for the Graphic Designer

PostScript-based illustration programs have brought deliverance for digital artists looking for precision in their work. PostScript is a language that describes an image, so when an artist draws, the image is "transcribed" as a list of commands, such as "draw circle" and "draw rectangle." To print a PostScript file, the commands are sent to a "PostScript compatible" printer that can decipher the instructions and reproduce the image. One big advantage with a PostScript image is that very complex elements in the image can easily be changed. Also, since many fonts are PostScript fonts, it is the easiest way to create graphics that incorporate text as part of the image. These programs, Adobe Illustrator and MacroMedia's Freehand, for example, are expensive and require more work to master, but they are indispensable tools found in every professional graphics and design studio.

Image Manipulation

A computer graphics artist can produce photographic-like images that you may not be able to distinguish from a real photo. Not only can computers generate images that appear to be real, computer programs let you manipulate real images so they appear to be unreal—or at least so that they include unreal elements.

Probably the single most popular program of this sort is Adobe Photoshop, a photo enhancement program that has really come to define the genre. What does Photoshop do? Imagine having all of the benefits and options of a darkroom sans the chemicals and costly supplies—built into your computer. With Photoshop and similar programs, you can alter the contrast of an image, create duotones, alter the color composition, manipulate elements of a photograph as if you were recreating the image, and attach "filters" to your virtual camera. Photoshop's filters exceed the capabilities of lenses and filters that you would normally use with a camera; color filters, wide angle, fish eye, and telephoto options are available, but there are also special effects that let you simulate motion blur, and other filters to simulate special paper and chemical processes. What's even more impressive is that these filters and lenses can be used to alter a photo *after* it has been developed, without affecting the negative or "print" in any way.

Who uses a program like Photoshop? The artists in every newspaper and magazine art department. They use Photoshop (or a similar program) to compose their graphics. Many magazine cover images—like the *Times* much publicized O.J. Simpson mug shot—are edited or retouched with Photoshop before being printed.

What About All of that Stuff on TV and in the Movies?

The special effects on TV and in the movies are really not much different than what you can do at home on your computer—just more so. There are all sorts of special effects programs available, such as KPT Bryce (about $130, by HSC Software Corp., 805-566-6200), a program that creates stunning landscapes that look strikingly similar to photographs from Bryce

Canyon or other equally majestic national parks—as shown in Figure 15–11. As is the case with any graphics software, the more complicated the image you want to create, the longer it takes your computer to render it for you. A simple image in Bryce can take a Pentium-based machine or Apple PowerMac over eight hours to render.

 Alert: **The results of any modeling program can easily entice you into buying it, but be forewarned: even with a powerful machine, the software can easily take a few hours to render a single picture.**

Solid Modeling and Rendering

When credit cards dance in unison or locomotives metamorphose into race cars, you are seeing the magic of computer graphics.

The images and special effects are painstakingly produced using solid modeling software. This is the software that lets you build three-dimensional shapes and objects. The software can even calculate how the light from a lamp will change the appearance of the room, calculating and casting shadows and reflections. If you move the lamp? The software automatically recalculates how the shadows and reflections should change. Figure 15–12 shows an image created with Infini-D, which is a 3-D solid modeling software from Specular International, Inc. (The color image was reduced to black and white for use in this book.)

These images require a tremendous amount of calculations by your computer. For special effects on television and in

Figure 15–11

KPT Bryce creates magnificent landscapes—in slightly less time than it took Mother Nature!

Figure 15–12

An image that was created with Specular's Infini-D, a 3D solid modeling program

movies, the software is often commercially available, but the pros run it on superfast machines or they break up the picture into little pieces, have several machines work on it—a technique referred to as "network rendering"—and automatically reassembling the pieces upon completion.

What's Available

Computer graphics benefits from many companies producing remarkable programs. To get a better sense of what's available, you'll have to do more homework. In the meantime, here are some of the most impressive and popular programs:

For the Pros or Aspiring Pros

Adobe Photoshop for Mac and PC (Adobe Systems, Inc. 800-833-6687)—The premiere image-editing program (street price: $600).
Fractal Design's Painter for Mac and PC (Fractal Design Corp. 800-297-2665)—A remarkably powerful program for fine artists and designers (street price: $340).
Macromedia's Freehand for Mac and PC (Macromedia, Inc. 800-945-4061)—A *professional* PostScript illustration program (street price: $400).

Great Deals

If you want to learn about art and computer graphics, you can jump in without paying a small ransom for software. Here are lower-cost options that still provide a lot of power.
CorelDRAW! 3.0 for PC compatibles only (Corel Corp. 800-772-6735)—A powerful entry-level multipurpose graphics program; it's an old version of the PC's leading graphics program (street price: $65).
Fractal Design's Dabbler/Sketcher for Mac and PC (Fractal Design Corp. 800-297-2665)—Dabbler is a scaled down version of Painter and Sketcher is a gray scale version of Painter (street price: $50).

Anatomy Lesson:
Computer Graphics Image

With all of the different computer graphics tools available, it's hard to tell what parts of an image have been altered and which ones have not. This image has several components, each showing what different programs allow you to do. Have you seen these effects used in newspapers, magazines, or television?

1 Many programs let you open a scanned image that you can then manipulate or paint on to your heart's content.

2 Sections of a photograph can be "airbrushed" out—flaws, blemishes, and any imperfections can be removed without a trace. This image had a bad scratch that crossed this woman's cheek.

3 PostScript fonts can be enlarged without *jaggies*.

4 This text is an enlarged bitmapped font. Notice that it looks rough and jagged—it has *jaggies*—compared to the surrounding text.

5 The title is given depth by creating a blurred shadow behind it.

6 Special effects "filters" can distort or enhance an image—a Photoshop trademark. A ripple effect was created here with a single mouse click.

7 Multiple images can be layered and processed individually or as a single picture. Here, the ocean surf provides a backdrop and additional images are altered in separate layers.

8 Gradient Fills let you fill a space with a color that smoothly transitions into another color.

9 An image can be processed with several different effects—natural media effects are produced here with Fractal Design's Painter program.

Profile:
Nathan Zabarsky

Project/Activity

Creating computer based multimedia slide shows that incorporate, music, art, and poetry.

Start Date

1994

Hardware/Software Used

Pentium-based PC (100MHz)
24MB RAM
Prosonus 16 Sound Card
Adobe Photoshop, Fractal Design
  Dabbler
Kai's Power Tools, Convolver (HSC)
Image Pals

Contact

Nathan Zabarsky
c/o SeniorNet Profiles
1 Kearney
San Francisco, CA 94108

Artistic Vision

Nathan Zabarsky has a vision to share. Having worked in the creative arts for so many years, the fruit of his labor—and that of his peers—easily covers his apartment interior, acting as a guide to his inner view.

Who

Nathan Zabarsky is an artist. In his youth he attended The Music and Arts High School and subsequently studied art at Columbia University and The Art Students League in New York City. "I started as a painter," says Nathan, "but to get by I made frames in a picture frame shop. My boss was a photographer and one day he took me on a shoot. From that day on, I was hooked."

Nathan's love affair with photography blossomed. As a freelance photographer, his images graced the pages of such prestigious magazines as *Smithsonian* and *National Wildlife*, and his work has been exhibited all over the country. Then came the move to California where Nathan worked for the Department of Water resources, capturing the construction of the Oroville Dam on film, from start to finish. From that assignment, Nathan came to appreciate the natural beauty of the West.

Unfortunately, Nathan's ability to travel the backroads was curtailed when

he developed spinal disabilities. He can only stand for short periods of time and spends much of his time in a hospital bed. The pain prevents him from pursuing photography—at least as he once did.

What

For a person as creative as Nathan, the physical limits placed on his ability to express himself were nearly unbearable. "Those were very dark times for me," said Nathan, "but I was 'rescued' by a very good friend who introduced me to computing and computer graphics. He saved my life as an artist."

Nathan has become quite prolific with hundreds of images generated and/or manipulated with software. "The computer hasn't altered the creative process, it has allowed me to come back to it."

Nathan's latest project: a collection of 16th and 17th century haiku verses set to music and sound. "I'm using MIDI and audio for this," a passionate Nathan explains. "I love baroque music, I love haiku, and I love being able to visually present and express myself."

Thoughts on Computing

"I wish I had more computer equipment because computer graphics and sound are very demanding of the hardware. But more important, I'm thankful I have the ability to express myself and even more thankful for the options provided in the world of computer graphics." Advice? "Explore, explore, explore," says Nathan, laughing. "A computer is no substitute for craft or creativity, but it sure offers some great opportunities to anyone interested enough to have a look. I can't recommend it enough!"

Note: **If you are interested in seeing computer graphics compilations, ask in your local video rental store. Watch the newspapers as well for any of the animation film festivals or the "Tourney (Tournament) of Animation." Tourneys typically publish what animations are included and which ones were computer generated.**

You can also purchase "The Mind's Eye," a collection of computer graphics clips available through Radio Shack Stores (about $15). If you care to join ACM's SIG-GRAPH, you can get videos culled from each year's conference through them as well.

What Is Multimedia and What Can I Do with It?

Multimedia is used as a catchall term to describe any program that incorporates some combination of sound, music, written text, pictures, animation, and video. To use these things in combination typically demands a more powerful machine with some extras on it. Multimedia does require a sound card and it does require a CD-ROM drive, and that usually means that you will need a couple of speakers as well.

To accommodate the additional requirements demanded for multimedia, Apple produced the "AV" series of computers—for "audio visual." These machines include built-in features for high-quality audio and video. PC compatible manufacturers build machines that satisfy the MPC—multimedia PC—standard. PCs that meet these standards are considered multimedia machines.

Alert: **The MPC standard has evolved over the years. Many older machines that carry the MPC label do not meet the newer MPC criteria. If you want a PC compatible that will offer current multimedia capabilities, don't depend solely on the MPC sticker as your indicator.**

The programs that allow you to create multimedia presentations include Apple's HyperCard, Asymetrix Toolbook, and Macromedia's Director. Of these, Hyper-Card is the least expensive (and probably the easiest to use). Director is quite difficult to learn and costs over $700.

With multimedia tools and an authoring program (like HyperCard or Director), you can create your own programs. You can build a slide show with a soundtrack and voice-overs. These programs let you incorporate MIDI files and short video clips as well. Many software and hardware companies use these programs to create self-running demos about their products—you click on the demo and it walks you through the company's product.

For the most part, multimedia is (for now, at least) easier to appreciate as an audience member. For a sense of what you can really expect, see Chapter 16, "Educational and Do-It-Yourself Software," to see what sorts of multimedia products developers are creating.

Educational and Do-It-Yourself Software

"It's what you learn after you know it all that counts."

—John Wooden

 Education? Do-It-Yourself? Learning about any computer hardware or software is certainly educational, but nine times out of ten it's a computer science education you're getting. If you want to learn about a particular subject or discipline, you should explore the world of educational software and do-it-yourself software.

Although some of these programs may have a high entertainment value, they are intended specifically to educate or help you perform some task on your own. The vast majority of these programs are CD-ROM-based since a CD-ROM is the only affordable way for a company to give you graphics, sound, animation, and lots of text on a single diskette.

> *Tip:* **Keep your eyes peeled for special "bundles"— hardware products that include CD-ROMs "free" as a promotion. Creative Labs, for example, has been selling a multimedia kit—CD-ROM drive, speakers, and sound card— bundled with 18 or 24 "free" software titles. The bundle has included best selling educational, reference CDs (encyclopedias, dictionaries, etc.), and a variety of other useful programs.**

What Can Educational Software Do for Me?

If ever there was an area of software that has peaks and valleys, educational software is it. The first generation of educational and instructional CD-ROM software has appeared, and like defining a

230

body of literature in the first years after Gutenburg's press, the ideas and potential are very exciting, but it's a free-for-all. No one knows how these products will develop over the coming years.

For computer nerds, there is certainly a contradiction here: The computer industry needs educators and nontechnical people to help guide the development of products so they are truly educational. At the same time, educators versed in traditional learning methods do not understand the potential for this new medium. The bottom line is that no one fully understands what people can and can't use. Remember, computer marketers were touting the wonders of multimedia in 1987, a good five years before it started to really take hold. Is there a formula for what works? If you know it, every computer company CEO and multimedia hotshot would love to be your friend.

As unclear as the path may be, there are many people with keen intuition and the radar of a bat who have successfully pursued and birthed some remarkable products. Keeping that in mind, you will find a number of innovative products out there that can help you learn everything from anatomy to Zydeco music.

 Tip: **Watch for CD-ROM guidebooks that offer overviews of available products. These guidebooks give brief summaries of CD-ROMs and their contents. Could anyone possibly review all of these products and assess them objectively? Not likely, but these resource guides tell you at least what's available in different categories of**

interest. Getting the yearly updates of these types of books will keep you informed.

Books: A Depth of Personality

Anyone who is a lover of books may mourn the quick acceptance of CD-ROMs. Do CD-ROMs signal the death knell for books? How can a CD-ROM offer the same comfort as a book? A book's worn and dog-eared pages offer us a poignant record of the times when we needed or wanted to read a particular passage. The scent that a book acquires over time, the stains on various pages, and the freezing of the moment—an outdated encyclopedia tells us when we purchased it and why. Books are a reflection of our children and ourselves. It's all part of the life of a book, and (true enough) lost when you use a CD-ROM. The whole idea of curling up with a good book hardly translates when you think of the harsh glow of the computer's display. You can grab a book anytime and read it anywhere; the dining room table, the bus, on the patio, on the beach, or by the fire. With these sorts of memories, is it possible to find anything good about a CD-ROM?

CD-ROM: A New Generation—and a New Personality

Time does march on. Books are glorious and will remain glorious, and will not soon be replaced by any technology. CD-ROMs mark a new generation, however—a technology that has the capability of offering certain advantages over books. Photography, after all, did not eclipse drawing, coming instead to represent another medium. CD-ROMs have a lot to offer, and we should take advantage of what they offer.

For example, CD-ROM reference titles offer several features and advantages over their papyrus-based siblings. A cornucopia of images, sounds, animations, and video clips is enough to engage anyone—especially youngsters—old enough to click a mouse button. Transliterations in a dictionary come alive because you can hear what a word sounds like just by clicking on it. Language tutorials take on new meaning with native speakers coaching you. Want to learn about the Mt. St. Helens eruption up close? You can do more than read about it; you can watch part of it. And what about Javanese Gamelan Music? All you have to do is click on a button and you can hear a Gamelan orchestra.

Perhaps you have a nice library that you have acquired over the years. Are you supposed to replace it with costly CD-ROMs? No, not really. CD-ROMs are, however, a meaningful extension to any library (many public libraries, in fact, now have computers and have extended their own resources with CD-ROMs). The next time you are planning on taking a course, learning a language, or studying a subject that carries a history with it, look at your CD-ROM options.

The World of Reference

Dictionaries, encyclopedias, thesauruses, collections of famous quotations, and almanacs are standard references that everyone can use, and they often prove invaluable—to anyone who can afford them. Even if you can afford such a compendium and you finally invest in an encyclopedia, for example, the books quickly become outdated. Nowadays, virtually every kind of reference work you can imagine is available on CD-ROM, and compared to their paper counterparts they are very affordable. In some ways, CD-ROMs are superior to their printed predecessors.

Some Nice Reference Features

It's hard to use a CD-ROM reference as you do a book. For example, if you are hit with a flash of inspiration while working in the kitchen—say you want to look up a word—your computer must be on and your CD-ROM dictionary must be loaded. That's hardly conducive to freewheeling thought and spontaneous creative bursts!

But CD-ROM references aren't supposed to be used like books per se. Instead, CD-ROMs are intended to help you when you are working on the computer, when you are at work writing your essay or letter *with a word processor*. If an idea comes in the kitchen, then a reference book is easier.

With that in mind, CD-ROM references have been designed for use while you are using some other program—like a word processor. Regardless of the program you are using, a small toolbar is displayed onscreen that gives you access to the reference books at all times. For example, while writing a short story with your word processor, you want to find a euphemism for "disobedient." You type **disobedient**, highlight it, click on the thesaurus icon, and launch the thesaurus. The thesaurus sees the word you've highlighted and automatically displays alternatives for you. When you have found the best word for the passage (say, "mischievous"), click on the thesaurus entry you prefer and it automatically appears in your text, replacing the original word you typed.

The same basic procedure applies when using the dictionary, the book of quotes, or some other reference. If you need to find the definition of a word, you can type it in your document, highlight the word, click on the dictionary icon, and the definition appears for you onscreen.

Note: **Many word processors include thesaurus and dictionary features, but these are not very complete. The reference toolbar bypasses these options and gives you access to a superior CD-ROM reference.**

Dictionaries

There are several different CD-ROM dictionaries, each providing slightly different features—including price. *Random House*

Unabridged Electronic Dictionary is excellent, as is *The American Heritage Dictionary Of The English Language.* Figure 16–1 shows the definition screen from *The American Heritage Dictionary.* This dictionary—a part of Microsoft Bookshelf (described later in this chapter)— lets you look up any word, pronounces the word for you, provides illustrations and graphics where applicable, and even offers an occasional short video and extended audio clip. Elements of the definition appear in colored or highlighted text. When clicked, additional information regarding the highlighted text appears. Clicking on a Latin prefix or suffix, for example, provides supplementary information on the origin and meaning of the prefix or suffix.

If you require "the best" and money is no object, then *The Oxford English Dictionary* is *the* CD-ROM for you. This work of art contains over 600,000 entries, including everything from the print version. The CD-ROM, however, lets you search for information in ways you wouldn't dream of, and the searches are faster and more thorough than humanly possible. Terms are cross-referenced so you can find multiple uses of a word within the dictionary. The drawback? The CD-ROM costs $895! That's a lot for a dictionary, and especially high when you consider how inexpensive a CD-ROM is to produce versus the paper version (Oxford University Press, 1-800-334-4249). Again, it's a lot of money; but if you need it, you need it. This one is strictly for those folks who need the best!

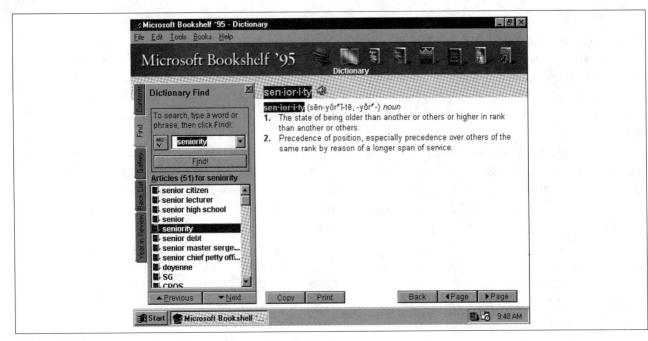

Figure 16–1

Definition screen from The American Heritage Dictionary

The Reference Deal of the Year

If you are a lover of good reference books, you probably have at least one thesaurus, one dictionary, one almanac, and so forth. Does that mean you will have to spend several hundred dollars to obtain all of those references on CD-ROM? No, thanks to Microsoft Bookshelf. Microsoft Bookshelf combines eight different books in one CD-ROM. For $100, you get a national ZIP code and Post Office directory, *The American Heritage Dictionary, Roget's Thesaurus, The Columbia Dictionary of Quotations, The Concise Columbia Encyclopedia, Hammond World Atlas, The People's Chronology,* and *The Funk and Wagnall's World Almanac and Book Of Facts. The Funk and Wagnall's Almanac,* shown in Figure 16–2, lets you enter a term and then provides a list of different locations in the book where the term is used. Granted, you can't take this almanac to bed, but on a sleepless night you can spend a lot of time in front of your computer "thumbing" through the almanac's contents.

When you install Bookshelf, a special access toolbar—a row of icons—appears

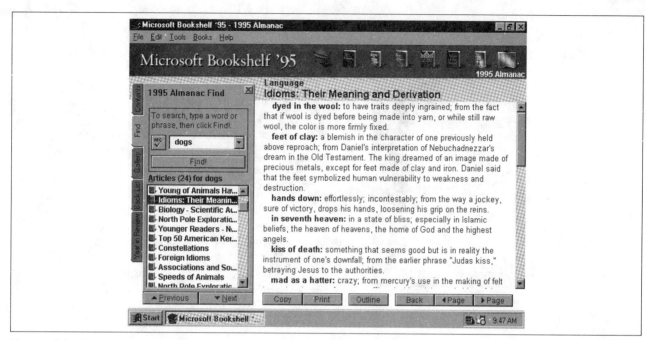

Figure 16–2

The World Almanac *from Funk and Wagnalls is part of Microsoft Bookshelf*

onscreen with buttons representing each of the reference works provided. You can customize the toolbar to include or exclude whichever reference titles you do (or don't) use and you can change the size of the toolbar to suit your visual requirements. You can also keep it anywhere you want onscreen and move it or close it at anytime. For $100, it's a very difficult deal to beat.

Encyclopedias

Large reference works, like encyclopedias that cover a diverse range of topics and are organized alphabetically, are well suited to the CD-ROM format. Special search tools let you find information on any topic instantaneously, and with *hypertext links*—a built-in feature that lets you click on a word and jump to related information—learning becomes even more gratifying.

Compton's *Interactive Encyclopedia*, Grolier's *Multimedia Encyclopedia*, and Microsoft's *Encarta* are excellent CD-ROM encyclopedias that include animation, video clips, and sound. To get a sense of what these digital tomes have to offer, Figure 16–3 shows a search screen from Microsoft's *Encarta 95*.

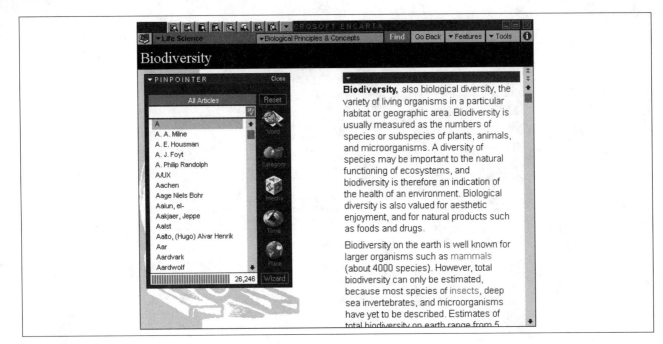

Figure 16–3
Microsoft's Encarta: *you can traverse search menus and learn and discover at every entry point*

Alert: **Some content for some of these reference books is based on publishing deals that the software company can make with other publishers or "content providers." If the software publisher can get rights to include the *New York Times* news archives, for example, you'll have a great news section. If they can only license content from a lesser source, the final product suffers. The *Encarta*, for example, defines "jazz" based almost exclusively on artists who recorded for a single record label.**

For publishers, a CD-ROM reference provides several production advantages. For example, CD-ROMs are easier to update. CD-ROMs don't require "page proofing" to guard against typesetting errors. The information is stored electronically, so the print cycles—sending the books to the printer and proofing for accuracy—take far less time. With less time devoted to production, more time and resources can be dedicated to the actual reference work.

Also, publishers can more easily revise editions and offer the revisions at very affordable prices. In days gone by, the cost of printing alone made revisions prohibitive. For the consumer, there was no such thing as an upgrade; your next set of encyclopedias was still to be over $1,000.

The Writing on the Wall

Every publisher of reference materials must now confront the new technology and rise to face the challenge. If they don't, they face the same fate that Encyclopedia Britannica met.

In 1994, Encyclopedia Britannica, the publisher of the reference perennial, encountered an increasing number of CD-ROM-based competitors. The installed base of CD-ROM-based computers was skyrocketing and every reference book publisher was making forays into the new technology.

Publishers saw the proverbial handwriting on the wall. Consumer response to CD-based encyclopedias has been overwhelming, in large part because of what they offer over the print editions. CD-based encyclopedias sell for anywhere from $50 to $350. The *Encyclopedia Britannica* in its printed form was selling for about $1,500. A CD-ROM is wafer thin and can be carried in a purse. The *Encyclopedia* took up an enormous amount of shelf space (you could buy a special bookcase for it!) and the whole set weighed about a hundred pounds. A CD-ROM weighs a couple of ounces. Finding information on a CD-ROM is child's play; a simple word search gives every occurrence of the word across all volumes.

According to *Forbes Magazine*, Brittanica had a very healthy sales force of over 2,300 representatives, but they feared any change in the sales structure. A Brittanica sales representative would earn over $300 on each sale and a CD-ROM precluded any such commission. They successfully fought and won the battle to keep new technology away; Britannica did not create a Britannica CD-ROM.

The Britannica sales force won the battle but lost the war. In 1991, Britannica began losing money and lost more than half of their sales team. How obstinate was the company? Very. Britannica owned Compton's, who successfully produced a CD-ROM encyclopedia in 1989. When Britannica started losing money, they sold the Compton's CD-ROM division to support the failing encyclopedia division.

They have since seen the light, albeit dimly. Britannica released a CD-ROM version of the *Encyclopedia Britannica Macropaedia and Micropaedia* along with *Merriam Webster's Collegiate Dictionary* on one CD-ROM. But the suggested retail price is an especially high $1,000 and the CD-ROM can't be used without a special hardware key (a dongle) that you attach to your parallel port. No one else forces end users to do this.

Finally, publishers had to negotiate the purchase of ever-more-expensive paper for printing *and* secure warehouse space to house the inventory. CD-ROM publishing avoids both of these issues entirely.

Atlases, Road Maps, and More

There are many producers of CD-ROM atlases and road maps. Microsoft, Electronic Arts, Broderbund, Rand McNally, Mindscape, and a number of other companies offer various products ranging from road maps to world atlases to 3-D globes. If you enjoy traveling, these CD-ROMs can be a real asset to your library.

Tip: **If you have a favorite magazine and it is taking up more space in your home than you can comfortably spare, call the publisher. They may have reduced the entire library of their magazines down to a single CD-ROM. If available, you can get rid of the attic full of magazines and find any article in any issue in an instant—by searching the CD-ROM.**

The Bible

You might think that this would be the first title *ever* produced on CD-ROM. You might also think that there would be versions too numerous to list here, but competing versions are only beginning to appear. Even without a lot of competition, however, Compton's *Multimedia Bible* CD-ROM of the King James Version has an excellent interface and includes readings by James Earl Jones. It also includes animated sections and explanations and interpretations of various passages. (Compton's New Media: 619-929-2500.)

The Arts

There are some remarkable products for learning about the arts, several of which were outlined in Chapter 15, "Art, Music, and Multimedia." *Discovering Music*, from Voyetra Technologies (1-800-233-9377) offers a smorgasbord of many different musical programs. The CD-ROM includes a musical word processor (for composing and arranging); a notation program (for printing music); a "jammer" (for playing along with more popular forms of music, such as reggae and hip hop); a "recording station" replete with a 10-track recording console; and finally, the "Music Conservatory," a look at major composers and their works, lessons in music theory, music history, and a music glossary.

Cinema

Interested in movies? There are several cinema compendiums on CD-ROM. These include video clips or excerpts from some movies and lots of interesting movie facts. Microsoft's *Cinemania* is an impressive product worth checking out, with hundreds of still shots, short clips, film bios, and more. This CD-ROM is actually a digital compendium that includes Leonard Maltin's *Movie and Video Guide*, Roger Ebert's *Video Companion*, Pauline Kael's *5001 Nights at the Movies* (Holt and Company), Ephraim Katz' *The Film Encyclopedia* (HarperCollins), and more. With *Cinemania*, you can find out details about thousands of movies and the people who created them. Figure 16–4 shows an expanded search feature of *Cinemania*.

Photography

Every November, someone in the family brings a new Instamatic camera to Thanksgiving dinner and takes photos. And every Thanksgiving the new Instamatic camera fails to work quite right—flashing and not flashing unexpectedly, giving Uncle Morty glowing Zombie eyes, and generating enough glare off of his bald pate to ruin the picture's exposure.

If you aren't satisfied with the photographs you (or a relative) are taking and you'd like to learn about the art of taking good photographs, consider *Understanding Exposure: How to Shoot Great Photos* from DiAMAR Interactive (1-800-234-2627). This is an ideal medium for teaching the relationship between film speed, aperture, lens types, and light. Photography pro Bryan Peterson offers

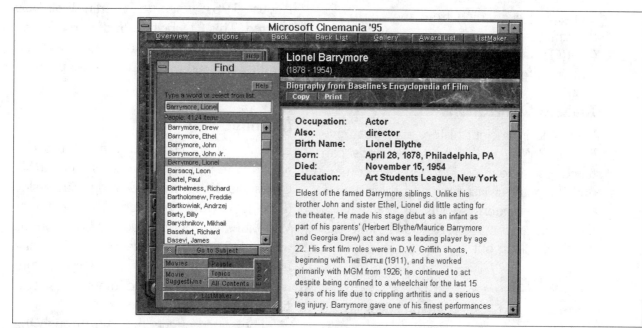

Figure 16–4

With Cinemania, *you can find out everything you ever wanted to know about famous actors, directors, and the movies they made*

in-depth tutorials and a fabulous photolab: You change various settings on your camera and see the change take place onscreen. You can experiment and learn how best to take certain shots—without using film!

Tip: **Keep your eyes open for the issue of your favorite computer magazines that feature a listing of top CD-ROM picks. New—and valuable— CD-ROMs are released every day and magazines report on them on an ongoing basis.**

History

CD-ROMs have also been used to great effect to teach and explore history. Examining everything from the "birth" of the universe to present-day world history, CD-ROMs offer history lovers an in-depth look at different historical periods.

Ancient Civilizations

Interested in ancient history and great civilizations? Microsoft's *Ancient Lands* can teach you about ancient Greek, Roman, and Egyptian civilizations and their contributions to modern society. If you have a taste for ancient history, you'll find this worth checking out.

World War II

Cartoonist Art Spiegelmann decided to document his father's experience as a prisoner in Nazi Germany's death camps. The result was the Pulitzer Prize-winning graphic novel, *Maus*, a cartoon novel depicting Jews and other victims of the Holocaust as mice and their Nazi perpetrators as cats. Voyager (1-800-446-2001) has released a CD-ROM version, *The Complete Maus*. The CD-ROM includes background information and insights into how the book was realized. Is it art? Literature? History? It is all those things, and then some.

The Cold War

If you're interested in a different view of post-war Germany, *Seven Days in August*, a compelling historical CD-ROM, is available from Time Warner Interactive. *Seven Days in August* recounts the week in August 1961 when the Berlin Wall was erected. This CD includes radio broadcasts, speeches, news clips, and video clips documenting this sad event and the people who were affected by it.

Maritime History

Even if you aren't that interested in a history of the sea, *Stowaway! Incredible Cross Sections* from Dorling Kindersley (212-213-4800), will make you a convert. With hundreds of richly detailed illustrations and animations, you'll learn all about life aboard an 18th century warship. Figure 16–5 shows one of the many cross-sectional views of the ship.

The sound effects that run through the entire CD really give you the sense of being aboard ship and the pop-up screens and animations give you a very real—some-

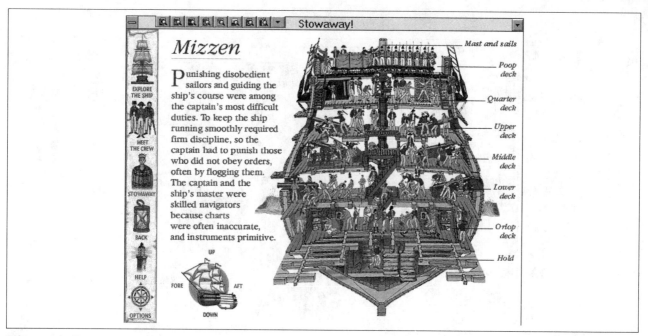

Figure 16–5

The complexity and attention to detail in Stowaway! will pique anyone's curiosity about 18th century seamen

times too real—sense of what these men had to endure.

The Human Body and Pharmacology

It used to be that only medical students could get access to the kinds of texts required to learn the intimate details and intricacies of the human body. Now, anyone can get the equivalent of these volumes, and more, on a CD-ROM. Medical CD-ROMs provide vivid detail of virtually any and every aspect of the human body. Animated Dissection of Anatomy for Medicine (A.D.A.M.) is the layperson's ver-

sion of software that A.D.A.M., Inc. has been providing to healthcare students and professionals for many years. Their medical illustrations are superlative, and their humor makes it an easy ride. Another excellent anatomy guide is *The Ultimate Human Body* (Dorling Kindersley), as shown in Figure 16–6.

Physicians often seem pained when patients quote from the *Physician's Desk Reference*, the compendium of pharmacological agents and their associated side effects. "If people knew the side effects of drugs, they would never take them," goes the logic. You can decide for yourself with *Pharmassist* (SoftKey: 1-800-377-6567),

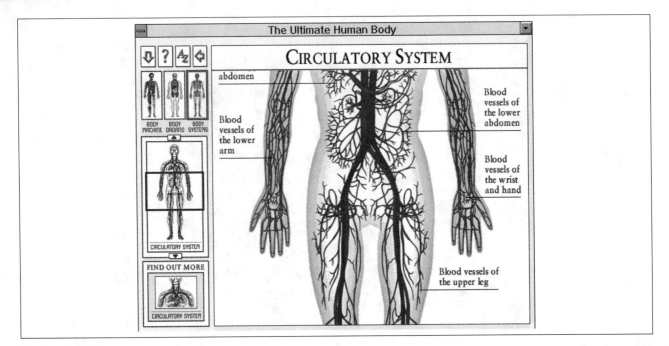

Figure 16-6

The Ultimate Human Body *(Dorling Kindersley)* provides informative and revealing views of the human form. This figure shows a segment of the circulatory system

a computer guide to pharmaceuticals. For about $45, this program provides information on drug interactions, side effects, first aid, and other important information.

Science and Technology

For many people familiar with his book, David Macaulay's *The Way Things Work* is a masterpiece of technical communication. The book, a compendium of machines, inventions, and scientific principles, is elaborately illustrated and succeeds in pulling the reader into what would otherwise be a set of dull lessons on, well, how things work.

If you've read the book, you'll love the CD! The Workshop screen from which you navigate is shown in Figure 16-7. The lessons and demonstrations include animations and voice-overs that succeed in a way the book cannot. With the help of the Great Woolly Mammoth, a cartoon of the prehistoric beast who assists in explanations and demonstrations, complex technical concepts are delivered in simple, engaging terms. And there are quirky surprises: The Historical Timeline for the Silicon Age (1941-1984) includes the smoke detector (1941), the amplifier (1947), the photocopier (1948), the microprocessor (1971), and the salad spinner (1972). The salad

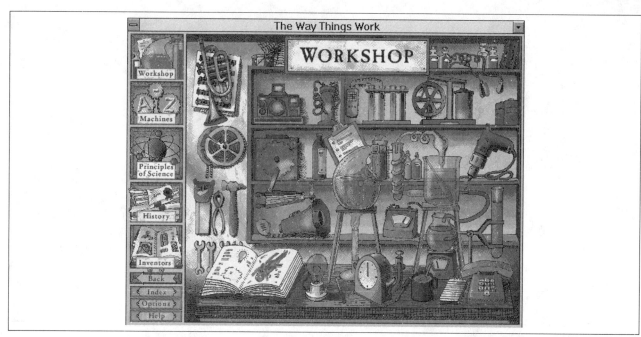

Figure 16–7

David Macaulay's inspiring The Way Things Work *comes to life in an equally inspiring multimedia rendition. This is the common man's multimedia guide to physics and machines*

spinner?! Without a nod or a wink, an explanation of centrifugal force and the gear ratios of the salad spinner is provided. It is, after all, technology of the Silicon Age.

Do-It-Yourself: Special Gifts for Special People

You've probably seen people wearing custom T-shirts or special buttons, or drinking from coffee mugs that are initialized or personalized in some way. Wouldn't it be great if you could design these sorts of things on your computer and then give them away as gifts? Welcome to *Gift Maker* (Maxis: 1-

800-336-2946). With *Gift Maker*, you can create an impressive assortment of personalized gifts for people and have those gifts sent right to their door.

To create a personalized gift with *Gift Maker*, you select the item from a list of items (T-shirt, duffel bag, pennant, etc.). The item shows up onscreen and you can then "compose" your design on top of it. Figure 16–8 shows a design for an apron.

You can include text and graphics, and you can use photographs as well (although there is an added fee for each photo). Once you have completed your gift design, you can save the information to disk and put the diskette in the mailer with your check

Figure 16–8
Gift Maker *lets you design custom gifts for friends and family*

or money order (Maxis recently set up a modem service so you can modem your order in for faster service).

The following is a partial list of the items that you can create (and prices, at the time this book was printed):

Item	Price
Apron	$16.95
Baseball cap	$11.95
Wall clock	$19.95
Mug	$11.95
Oven mitt	$14.95
T-shirt	$15.95
Coasters (set of 4)	$23.95

Congressional Budget Simulator

Here's a surefire way to find out what our Representatives in Congress are really up to. *Uncle Sam's Budget Balancer* from Banner Blue Software is based on the current year's federal budget and it includes over 360 budgetary options researched by the Congressional Budget Office. The simulation lets you try your hand at balancing the federal budget using the exact same numbers and variables the House of Representatives works with. This is strictly a text-based program—no fancy graphics, no sound—except perhaps your own moaning and groaning when you see how immense and convoluted the Federal Budget and the associated problems are.

Note: **Banner Blue includes this program—gratis—with its other programs. It is also available free of charge on various online services.**

Genealogy: Creating a Family Tree

Where do you come from? Do your children know the family ancestry? Will your grandchildren have any record of your lineage—and in turn, their own?

Tracing your family tree can be an arduous task requiring hours of research and the detective skills of Sherlock Holmes. Tracing your tree and providing it to your family is as lasting a gift as it is thoughtful.

To help make your job easier, there are genealogy programs available, most notably *Family Tree Maker* from Banner Blue Software. This CD-ROM product provides a family finder index with over 115 *million* names so that you can find relatives who were missing from your tree. Figure 16–9 shows a part of a family tree created with *Family Tree Maker.*

Banner Blue also has more than 45 CDs of birth, death, and marriage certificates

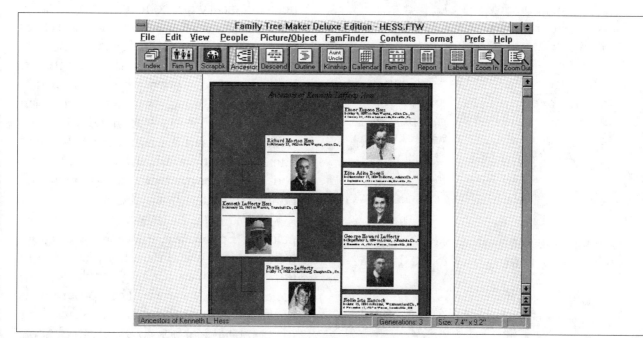

Figure 16–9

Family Tree Maker *lets you import scanned photos or Kodak's PhotoCD images. Once imported, your family tree can really take on a lot of personality*

The World Family Tree Project

The Mormons pride themselves in tracing their family trees, but what about tracing a world family tree? Ambitious as it seems, Blue Banner software is currently soliciting for electronic family trees that it hopes to eventually quilt together to produce the ultimate genealogical map.

Banner Blue hopes to collect the trees of *Family Tree Maker* users, connect them where possible, and then put the collection on a CD-ROM through which you can track and trace and connect other family branches and members. If you're interested in providing your tree and there is any confidential information or information of a private nature, Banner Blue recommends that you "edit" the tree before submitting it.

(that's thousands of megabytes) and census information going back to the 1700s.

Creating a Family Album

Creating a family album or set of family albums is one project that is of interest to many people. What usually winds up happening, though? You have an enormous box of photos that you are keeping in the den, perhaps with letters mixed in. A shoe box holds love letters or personal correspondence that you have kept through the years. The attic holds a slew of other items, and your brain, which can only hold so much anyway, was filled to overflowing years ago.

If you want, you can take the time to sort all of those photos, letters, and memorabilia (which duty says you should do), and you can type your memories, thoughts, and feelings in a word processed journal. The problem is that the task is monumental and it's compounded by the fact that seemingly random events in our lives that are not connected logically *are* connected emotionally; the photos and the letters and the stories may appear in different albums and you can't possibly cross reference these things! Even if you do a good job with an album, your memory, which is no less quirky than anyone else's, decides to flood with new remembrances of the Summer of '44, right after you neatly finished that album. Now you have important new information and no way to update your album.

In this case, your procrastination has paid off. *Echo Lake*, a jewel of a program from Delrina, is an innovative piece of software that makes creating family or personal albums a joy. The program is packaged in what appears to be someone's memorabilia cigar box covered with National Park stickers, pine cones, acorns, and old photos. Like many great products, it defies category or a simple one-sentence explanation. Instead of trying to explain the program, here's a quick look inside.

When you start the program, you are in front of an onscreen (comfortable) desk in a cabin, presumably at Echo Lake, as shown in Figure 16–10. It's hard to resist the warmth of *Echo Lake*. It's quiet, the coffee on the desk is piping hot (you can see the steam rising when you run the program), and you'll feel like sharing your memories as they rise to the surface. The desk even includes a snow globe, those souvenir collectibles that you shake and watch the snow settle. (When you click on your snow globe in *Echo Lake*, the snow covers your screen.)

The desk includes all of the tools you'll need to create your albums. You can crank out a new book at any time, select the binding style that you want, and enter information in the album—journal style—any time you want. You don't have to worry about running out of space on a page because each entry expands to accommodate what you are writing. If you have a journal that you want to keep, but that's highly personal, click on the picture on the wall to access a wall safe. The wall safe requires a password, and you can keep whatever journals you want there. No one can get to those albums without your password.

Figure 16–10
The warmth of Echo Lake

Echo Lake lends itself to the actual way you remember things. To fill in journal entries, for example, you can display a tree trunk that is segmented into a number of different areas of life interest, as shown in Figure 16–11.

In this way, if you remember something next week that you want to include, you can just push another pin into the tree and write an associated entry.

But what about all of the images? The photographs? The memorabilia? At the top of the page there is a drawer labeled "MEDIA," shown in Figure 16–12. Also shown in this figure is a drawer of "PAGES,"

a list of memorabilia to signify important events. These pages include birth certificates that you can fill out, birthday cards, and ticket stubs with room to indicate that special evening you remember so well.

The MEDIA drawer lets you select pictures, sounds, notes, and different kinds of graphics to include with any given journal entry. If you have a scanner, you can scan your photos and incorporate them into your album that way. *Echo Lake* can also import images from a Kodak PhotoCD. If you already have stories, anecdotes, or other writings that you created with a word processor, you can also import them. The

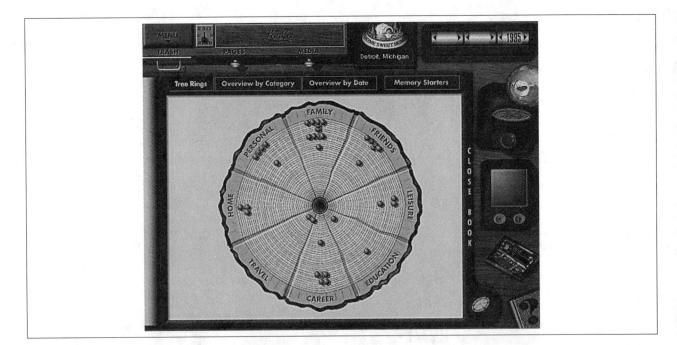

Figure 16–11

The tree trunk lets you push a pin in to mark a memory or journal entry. When you move your mouse across a pinhead, the title of your entry automatically appears

program offers a tremendous number of additional features to make the job of album creation as thought-provoking, reflective, and tender as it should be.

Echo Lake is also great for less epic projects. You can start out with an album about your weekend in the wine country—you'll learn a lot by working on a project you can complete in a short time—and keep the "life story" album as an ongoing project.

This black and white book can't convey the visual quality of this program—it's in color—but suffice it to say the program is lushly illustrated and really lets you capture the feeling of times gone by and the warmth of reminiscence.

 Note: **As a multimedia program that incorporates sound, pictures, animation, and photographs, *Echo Lake* can eat up a lot of memory and hard disk space. If you plan on undertaking a large album, make sure you have enough disk space to accommodate all of your sounds, pictures, and video.**

If You Can't Find It: Specialized References

Aside from all of the interesting educational and do-it-yourself titles available, you may be looking for something unique and off the

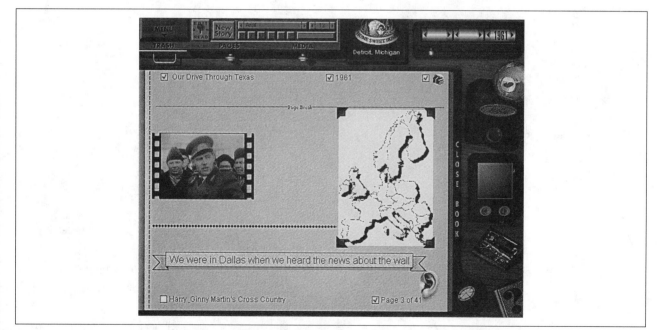

Figure 16–12

You can attach memorabilia to pages of your journal as well as sounds (here represented by a cassette tape), video clips (the video image is actually an excerpt from a newsreel on Kruschev), pictures, and word processed documents

Profile:
A. Langston Kerr

Project/Activity

Connecting seniors to the Internet, writing a manual to help guide them, and helping to integrate computer technology into Texas schools and libraries.

Project Start Date

1991

Hardware/Software Used

Compaq Prolinea (100MHz)
4MB RAM
Hewlett Packard 4P
Microsoft Works
Microsoft Publisher
Flatbed Scanner
CD-ROM

Contact

A. Langston Kerr
c/o SeniorNet Profiles
1 Kearney
San Francisco, CA 94108

Giving Through Education

He didn't lay his hands on a computer until 1991 and his home is on a lake in that part of Texas that America Online calls "too remote" for a connection with online services. But that didn't deter A. Langston Kerr, who, aside from now boasting online friends as far away as Australia, guided his entire community online, and helped put this "remote" community at the forefront of the digital revolution.

"They really teed me off 'cause they said we're so remote," he says, his indignation tinged with humor. "I said we'd get connected and I made my word good!"

Who

Like many seniors, A. Langston Kerr finds himself busier in retirement than when he was working. Born and raised in Texas, Mr. Kerr describes himself and his wife as 'outdoor people.' "We were raised in the country—we've lived in the country all our lives," he says warmly, "we even have a little lake right close to the yard." In retirement since 1986, Mr. Kerr was introduced to SeniorNet and was smitten by the organization, the technology, and the promise they seemed to hold.

Langston Kerr learned fast. After taking several computer classes and learning about computer communications, he forged a relationship with Dr. Lee Rayburn, the director of Stephen F. Austin University's Computing Center. His determination paid off and on January 5, 1993, when SeniorNet successfully sent its first e-mail message on the Internet. Subsequently, the University has been providing Internet access for the local SeniorNet community.

To ensure that seniors could really take advantage of their online access, Langston Kerr also began teaching courses to seniors on how to communicate via computer. When he's home, he and wife, Marie, sit together at the eight-foot-long knotty pine computer desk Mr. Kerr had custom built for their digital forays. They even send messages to one another while working at the desk!

What

The only thing A. Langston Kerr seems to like more than learning is sharing what he's learned. "There's never a time I have sat down and not learned something at my machine," he says. "It's amazing that way. But learning's not worth anything if you don't give back to the community. When you do, you really feel a sense of accomplishment and you know you've done some good. The pay is excellent like that."

Mr. Kerr has proven to be a natural wonder for seniors trying to learn about getting online. To make access as easy as possible, he even wrote a sixty-page man-

ual on accessing the Internet. "Getting on the Internet is easy, and I wanted to make it even easier," he says with pride.

Since then, it's been one continuous process of learning and exploring. Nominated to serve on the citizen's advisory committee of the Texas Telephone Association, Mr. Kerr lobbied successfully for the passage of House Bill 2128, providing extensive computer/telecommunications support for Texas educational institutions. "My wife Marie made every meeting with me," he says, "this bill makes Texas the country leader in telecommunications."

On Computing

A. Langston Kerr sees computers as an extraordinary educational tool. "This is really about education—teaching the young ones and the old. We want to remove fear from the older adults because anybody can learn to use computers. And kids soak up the stuff. My grandson, Danny Hartman, is ten and a half and he could type twenty words a minute on the computer before he could even write."

Does Mr. Kerr use his CD-ROM? "I sure do have one, but I use it to play my favorite Ray Price CDs while I'm learning how to use the Internet. There's so much out there to learn and so much to find. It's great!"

Anatomy Lesson: Genealogy

As more and more people look to trace their family histories, more genealogy programs—to help in the search for family roots—have become available. Banner Blue's *Family Tree Maker* is an extremely popular and well-designed program. *Family Tree Maker* makes the search for your lineage enjoyable and easy. Here's a deeper look at what this program has to offer.

1 The Index option gives you a listing of everyone in your family tree. You can click on any name in the index and go instantly to that person's Family Page.

2 You can create and edit a multimedia scrapbook for each person in your family tree. To create a scrapbook, click here. Scanned photos, images from Kodak's PhotoCD, and several other file formats can be included here. Sound and video clips can also be included in a scrapbook.

3 The Family Page lets you enter basic information about a family member. More detailed information about the person—medical history, nicknames, and more—can be entered on the More About Page, reached by clicking here. You can also customize 13 Fact fields on the More About Page to include information you think is most important.

4 Trying to organize the family for a picnic/reunion/get-together? How about a family newsletter or news update for the clan? The Labels option will automatically print labels with the current addresses of living relatives. You don't even have to address the envelopes or postcards yourself. *Family Tree Maker* does it for you.

5 The toolbar items—from Ancestors to Fam Grp—all automatically format the family tree information you have provided; you can view and print crisp and easy to read ancestor and descendant trees. The Calendar option collects birthdays and anniversaries from your family tree and builds a Birthday/Anniversary calendar for you. You can also create custom reports to get just the information you are interested in with the Report option.

6 Tabs on the Family Page let you jump between members of the immediate family.

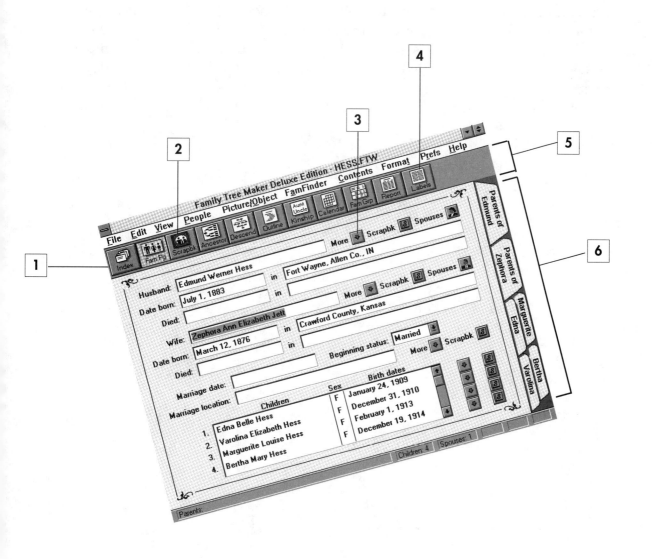

beaten path. For example, perhaps you are interested in a Spanish dictionary or a French dictionary. Better yet, perhaps you are interested in a dictionary of idiomatic expressions or computer terms. Many publishers are producing these works, but a limited demand for such products limits their availability (big chains may not carry them because they don't sell enough copies). To try and locate such a product, first call the publishers who you would expect would produce a book version and see if they can help. If not, try checking via an online service—it's the best way of asking around, since you are asking thousands of people around the country at the same time.

Entertainment and
Kid's Software

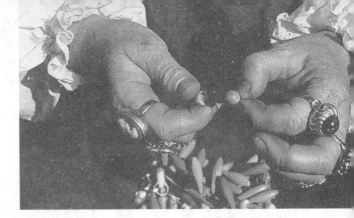

It's hard to imagine using something as powerful as a computer—the same thing that's used by scientists and engineers around the world—as a toy. Ironically, games and entertainment software have come to represent an enormous and popular segment of the computer industry. Once the domain of fading stars like Atari, the computer game industry now hosts challengers like Sony, LucasArts (George Lucas), and Disney. Many of the most popular games available today incorporate excellent audio and video special effects and require powerful home computers to work.

Not all game makers have the visibility of a company like Disney. Some companies haven't been around for very long and don't have many titles, but do have a best-selling game that has established them as "hot" in the industry. (If you have one game that sells in the millions, you're doing pretty well.) Others have been around for some time and don't have many hits, but have produced a lot of games. Still others are new and can only hope for hits.

It is certainly with some indulgence that parents get their kids a $2,000 Pentium computer or PowerMac to play the latest in video games. Computers, like hot rods in days gone by, are much the obsession of many kids.

Playing Games

Games for kids is one thing, but games for adults? Should you be doing this? Deciding on how you should spend your leisure time isn't really up for public discussion or debate; if you like to play games—pinochle, bridge, crosswords, poker, mah-jongg—you'll probably feel like you've found a little piece of heaven in the computer games section and you'll want to explore your options here. Even if you don't like to play games, though, you should take a quick look; you may find something here that really strikes a fancy you didn't know you had.

If you use a Windows machine, you get a couple of free games. *Minesweeper* is a fun strategy game that is easy to learn and not so easy to stop playing. Windows-based machines also have *Solitaire*, as shown in Figure 17-1.

If you want to see more, there are thousands of games available. If you're reluctant to look at games because you've heard or seen in the press that they are all obscenely violent, look again. There are lots of different categories for games, and the lion's share of the software—outside of the action genre—is based on concepts and goals other than vaporizing life forms. Here are some of the categories and the types of games you can expect to find.

Games from the Old School

If there's a game you have been playing for years, chances are it has been recreated in an

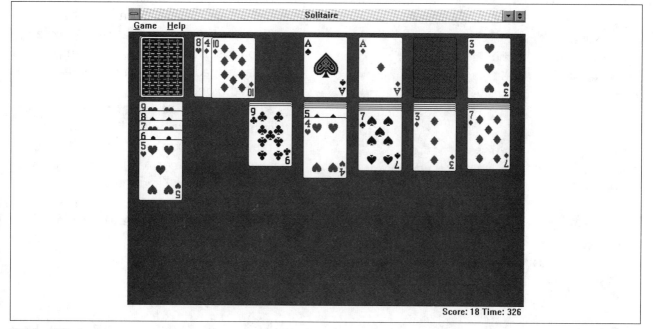

Figure 17-1
Solitaire *is easy to play and free—with a Windows-based computer*

The E- Game Business: It's No Game

Sure, a fast Pentium machine can offer some very impressive graphics and sounds for a game maven, but why spend all that money if you just want to play games? With Sega, Nintendo, Sony, and others, you can start in with some very sophisticated games for a lot less money.

Sega and Nintendo, fierce competitors in the games market, are each *multibillion* dollar industries. Sega and Nintendo make special purpose computers—game computers that sell for about $200. The games come on special proprietary cartridges. They feature good graphics and sound at a fraction of the cost of a good desktop computer. You might be prone to underestimate the size of these game companies or how successful they have been: These companies have a very sophisticated approach to the market, which accounts for their multibillion dollar sales figures.

In fact, you can't get past a cartoon or children's show (except on public television), or a comic book, without finding an ad for at least one of the games. Like everything else these days, games are marketed in much the same way as movies: There are tie-ins everywhere. In fact, *Mortal Kombat*, *Super Mario Brothers*, and other hit games have spun off movies.

electronic format—with some new wrinkles. *Chess*, *Go*, *Bridge*, *Monopoly*, and many more are available on diskette or CD-ROM.

Chess: A New Opponent— and Mentor

If you like chess or want to learn how to play, there are some very good chess software games. These games can be tailored to your particular skill level, so whether you're a great player or a novice, the computer games will still be worthy opponents.

Visually, computer chess games give you several options for play. The board can appear in a traditional format or as a 3-D game. Figure 17–2 shows a 3-D view in Mindscape's *The Chessmaster 4000*. For entertainment value, some of the games animate captures—some more violently than others. *BattleChess*, for example, has actually turned a basic chess game into an animated bloodbath.

The games flag illegal moves, let you take back that move you didn't *really* mean to make, and, if you want to take a break or get something to eat, let you save the game in progress. If you liked the way you played a game, you can save the game to see how it went. (To get a real sense of what *The Chessmaster* has to offer, see the anatomy lesson later in this chapter.)

Adventure Games

Adventure-type games have been very popular, intended more for the explorer/ puzzle-solving crowd. The standard scenario

Figure 17–2

Computer as chess player: A formidable opponent and excellent instructor

is that you find yourself in a castle/village/city/haunted house and you need to collect treasure and solve puzzles to find the secret of the game. Sometimes dragons, trolls, or other run-of-the-mill nemeses will "turn you to goo," but your demise in these games is never graphic like it is in many action games.

Be forewarned: Many of these games can be outrageously complex. *7th Guest* and its successor, *11th Hour* (Virgin Interactive Entertainment, Inc.), put you in a haunted mansion with the stuff bad dreams and Vincent Price movies are made of. You need to get to the attic, and your ability to "win" depends on finding clues in different parts of the house and solving some very difficult puzzles. *7th Guest* has a clever story line to help keep you glued to the game. If you like puzzles that seem impossible to solve, this may be just the thing to bang your head against!

Broderbund's *Myst* is one of the most challenging games and a work of art unto itself. The developers have created a mysterious island and an atmospheric adventure with painstakingly detailed art—and basically no directions! You must identify clues and what they mean to move through this mysterious island—and through time. Again, few directions are provided, so if you are the kind of person who gets frustrated

Anatomy of a Chess Game

It's a thinking person's game, so why not play chess against a computer?

Chess programs present a classic challenge to both chess masters and computer programmers. With so many strategic approaches, can a machine, calculating all the possibilities, compete with a bright, cunning, and temperamental human? The verdict is still out on who will ultimately win, but for most levels of play—including advanced—these games make for an excellent challenge.

1 In this match the board is viewed from above, but you can change to a 3-D view at any time. The chess pieces can reflect many different themes—from ancient Chinese characters to characters from the Middle Ages.

2 Menu options keep this game a challenge. You can save either completed games or incomplete games to return to later. You can redefine The Chessmaster's "personality" and change its strategy when playing against you. You can get advice on your next move. You can even look at a library of classic tournament games.

3 Specific windows let you monitor the action. The Game Status window gives you the amount of time spent in play and the last two moves by each player. You may be fast, but the computer is relentless. Here, the computer program—The Chessmaster—has completed 18 moves in about 21 seconds.

4 The Legal Moves window lets you look at all your options.

5 You can watch the computer think in the Thinking window. The Positions Seen field lets you know how many board positions The Chessmaster has checked. The Depth indicates how many moves ahead the computer is thinking.

6 The Captured Pieces window lets you see who has lost which pieces.

7 The Best Line window again lets you see what's on The Chessmaster's mind. This time it's the computer's best move, calculated immediately after its last move.

8 The Moves List lists every move you and The Chessmaster have made. Controls provided in the window let you play back all or part of the game at any speed.

9 Chess clocks track the time for each player. These clocks continue to track even if they are hidden.

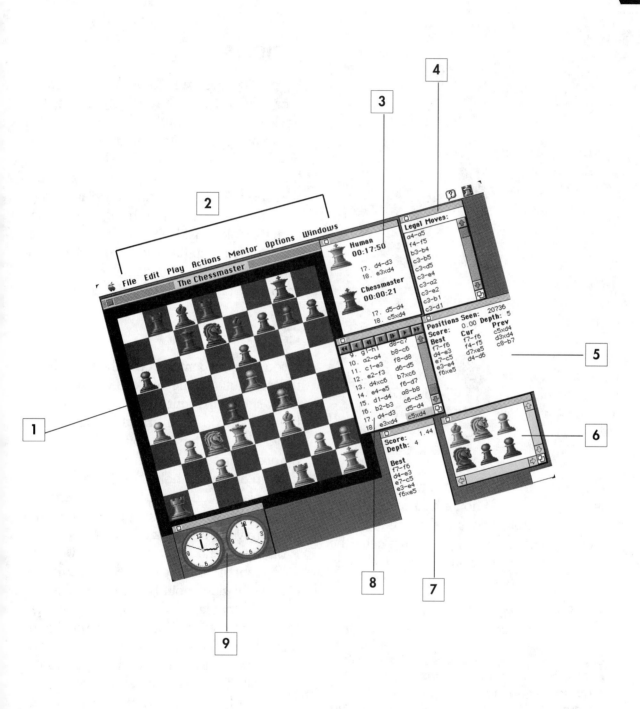

How to Create a Hit Game

Like a best selling novel, you can't just will a software program to become a hit.

One software company, Id Software, took a gamble by offering the first levels of their game, *Doom*, for free. Accessible through many different sources, you could play the game as long as you wanted, without paying anything. You could only move to the higher levels of the game, however, by purchasing the full product.

Id was counting on getting people hooked on the easier levels of the game. They succeeded. *Doom* ranks as one of the most successful games of 1994 and *Doom II* (the sequel) has proven even more successful.

with the AAA Trip Tik, stay away from this game; you'll spend hours hopelessly lost in the *Myst* before things make any sense. If you can hold on, and if you are excited by a challenge, you'll get sucked into the game and play for hours.

Tip: **Many adventure and action games come with few, if any, written rules or documentation. If getting started proves too frustrating, check out one of the many computer gaming magazines or books. You'll find strategies, tips, tricks, and "cheats" on how to reach higher levels of the game.**

Sports

If you like baseball, football, golf, tennis, race car driving, basketball, soccer, or hockey, then computing is really for you! There are games galore modeled after your favorite sports. If you're a baseball fan, there are games where you can assume a particular player's identity and play in various stadiums. There's no need to reminisce about Wrigley Field—it's back and you can play there! If you find race car driving to be thrilling, an Indy 500 game lets you race against other drivers—and the clock.

Golf

If you love the game of golf, then you'll love the computer game of golf. In Microsoft's *Golf*, shown in Figure 17–3, you can select the course you want and the level of play you'd like to attempt. You can even do a *fly-over*, an animated view of what you face on any given hole.

If playing onscreen isn't good enough for you and you're looking for something a bit more visceral, check out Sports Sciences' *Pro Swing* and *Tee V Golf* (1-800-860-4727, about $200 each). *Pro Swing* is a digital golf club about half the size of a regular club, that lets you play indoors, hooked to your computer. When you swing, a floor unit tells you how fast you hit the ball, how far it traveled, the angle, and the position of your ball. The golf club can actually act as any one of several different types of clubs, so you can pick the appropriate club for the

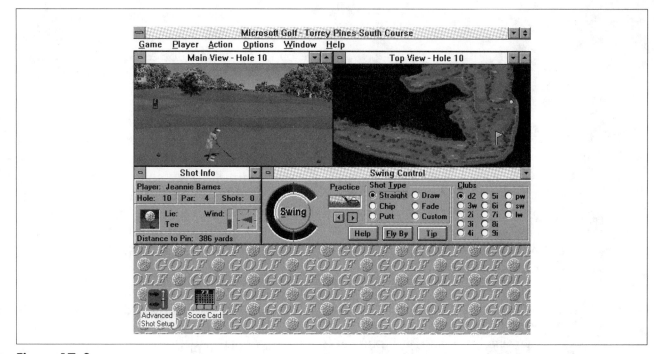

Figure 17–3
The game of Golf: On CD-ROM, it's easier on your feet than ever

particular shot. When you change clubs, the alignment of the head changes, requiring you to change your stance, as you would if you were on a real golf course. Like Microsoft's *Golf*, *Pro Swing* and *Tee V Golf* let you play multiple courses, but you'll have to come up with an extra $20 to add each new course. Playing this kind of virtual golf, though, will save you a bundle on greens fees. You can visit Pebble Beach, Torrey Pines, Mauna Loa, and many more. Flaws? At last report, putting is a problem: If the ball is aimed at the hole, you can't miss; the ball goes in, regardless of how much force you use.

Simulations

Simulation programs give you the opportunity to execute some task or practice a skill without suffering the consequences normally associated with the activity. Simulation programs give the user a greater appreciation for what is required to perform a particular task while actually teaching the fundamentals

Virtual Reality: A Reality?

Virtual reality is a technology whereby a computer projects you into an artificially created world. Wearing special gloves and stereoscopic goggles, you see a computer-generated version of the world projected through the goggles. The computer reads your physical movements and lets you interact with the environment you have selected.

If you've read any press accounts of virtual reality, you might think you could relive Cervantes' life by putting on a pair of goggles and holding a plastic sword in your hand. Marketing hype aside, the technology has a long way to go yet.

Although the technology may not be fully realized yet, there is enough of it available to allow people to have a little fun. Virtual reality centers—the very upscale video parlors of the day—let you experience video games that use some of this technology. Unfortunately, these games cost a lot of money to play—about a dollar per minute—so your options are limited; if not by the limited technology, then by the cost of using what is available.

of the task itself. Simulations, several of which are described here, are considered by many users to be as educational as they are entertaining.

Flight Simulators

For many years, pilots, astronauts, and other highly trained professionals have used *simulators,* special programs or chambers that simulate a cockpit or other complex environment, so they can improve reaction time and hone their skills. These simulators can cost hundreds of thousands of dollars, but low-cost versions are now available for use on home computers.

The most renowned of the lot is Microsoft's *Flight Simulator. Flight Simulator* (and like products) lets you experience a variety of flying conditions. There are several different types of aircraft available to train with and the control panels are accurate representations of what you'd find in the actual planes. Be forewarned that these programs are not trivial. Neophytes typically spend a whole lot of time crashing into the runway. Depending on your level of concentration and patience, simulators may prove to be more frustrating than entertaining—at least at first.

A Different Kind of Simulator

Aside from simulating flight, Maxis has created the Sim simulations, an entire family of innovative programs (yes, they are educational) based on urban planning, public policy, genetics, animals, and ants.

SimCity, for example, puts you in charge of an urban metropolis. Your city has all of the problems of any city: urban blight, industrial accidents, population shifts, and major changes in revenue streams. It's your job to run the city efficiently and keep it in the black—and livable. If you think this would be boring, think again; the Sim games have proved remarkably successful. Given the current healthcare debate, *SimHealth*, a simulation intended to give you an understanding of what is necessary to create and manage a national healthcare system, is especially timely.

Shoot-'em-Ups

Shoot-'em-ups are action games. If you read the papers these days, you may have the impression that these games should be X-rated. The theme of computer games may seem a bit unsettling: You [kill/punch/ kick/hit/blow up/chain saw/shoot, etc.] as many [aliens/zombies/kung fu guys/space-ships/humans/caterpillars/frogs, etc.] as you can before they visit the same fate upon you. Many of the most popular games— *Mortal Kombat*, *Doom,* and *Doom II*—are ultragory games of this ilk. The contents and themes of these games are such that labels appear on many of them to warn parents. The gore factor is high, but software developers argue that cartoons like *Tom & Jerry* were even more violent. It's up to you as an individual to decide.

The shoot-'em-ups hold a player's attention in part because the level of play

Field Trip

If you want to see what a lot of these games offer—and you don't mind being jostled by adolescent kids as they pump quarters into vending machines—check out a video arcade. These arcades offer many of the same games you can get on a computer—you just have to pay 25 or 50 cents per play. The games serve one purpose and only one purpose—they are games; they can't run word processing software or database programs or anything else. They have big graphic displays and audio speakers (to help intensify the game experience) and joysticks— no keyboards—built in. They are built extra sturdy; their target audience's enthusiasm would otherwise result in a lot of broken parts. You can try a game there and watch firsthand how the "pros" play. One word of advice: Take earplugs (or Kleenex) for your ears. The volume in some arcades can be uncomfortably loud.

becomes increasingly difficult as you progress through the game. A player who reaches the next level will be faced with more killer gerbils that can fly faster, suck more blood, and have more weapons at their disposal.

What's Available

There are thousands of games out there, and thousands more will appear. It's impossible to predict what you might like; that sweet, gentle friend of yours may like nothing more than to kill animated zombies on the computer screen all day. Decisions are rarely based on the rational or logical. Here's a list of some of the better established game companies with one or two of their more popular titles.

Company	Titles	Phone Number
Broderbund	Myst/Where in Time Is Carmen San Diego?	1-800-521-6263
Spectrum Holobyte	Tetris/Iron Helix	1-800-695-GAME
Accolade, Inc.	Hardball/Jack Nicklaus Golf	1-800-245-7744
Cyan, Inc.	Cosmic Osmo/Manhole	1-800-718-8887
Electronic Arts, Inc.	Wing Commander/PowerPoker	1-800-245-4525
LucasArts Entertainment	Rebel Assault/Tie Fighter/X-Wing	1-800-782-7927
Maxis	SimCity 2000/SimEarth	1-800-336-2947

Alert: **Many of these games expect you to use your home computer expressly for the game itself with nothing else running. They also expect your machine to be configured especially for the game. Don't be surprised if you go through installation for some of these games (like *Sea Wolf* and *Wing Commander*, for example), only to be told that you don't have enough memory. This is a common problem and the program developers explain in their manuals how to get around this inconvenience.**

As violent as some of these games are, the creators and players of these games are not without their moments of humor. For example, in *Doom II*, the characters are customizable. You don't have to go gunning just for the bad guys as defined by the developers. Instead, you can replace them with an enemy of your choice. One popular replacement has been Barney the Dinosaur, the purple dinosaur that preaches syrupy sweetness to little kids on TV (even the *New York Times* devoted an editorial to the phenomenon of parental "Barney Loathing"). In this customized version, parents and grandparents can experience some catharsis by eliminating Barney with a chain saw!

Children's Software

Everybody wants their kids and grandkids to have fun. And everybody wants their kids and grandkids to be smart. The computer software companies know exactly what you want and they try to push your buttons to get you to look at their products. It's not always easy for adults to spot a hit program, but don't take the company's word or listen to all their hype. Your kids or grandkids should be able to help, and programs that boast multiple awards for excellence should be noted.

When Kid's Stuff Isn't

Not all kid's software is good for all kids. If a child can't succeed at the game, if he or she can't execute the tasks necessary to move to the next level, or if the software keeps asking questions the child can't answer, then he or she will get frustrated, bored and (nine times out of ten) upset. To guard against a software mismatch (and a potential emotional meltdown), look for something that fits the child's abilities and corresponding stage of development. The software shouldn't set an unreasonable pace for the kid. The kid should set the pace.

Like anything oriented for children, you have to pay close attention to the intended age range. If you get something even slightly outside their range—their developmental range—it can spell disaster.

Try a game before you buy it. If it's for your children or grandchildren, try to get them on the game first to see how they like it. Most of these companies offer demo versions of their games for free or for the cost of shipping and handling.

> ## Golden Rule:
> For kid's software pay close attention to the age range recommended on the outside of the disk or CD-ROM. If it says 5-8, don't get it for a 3-year old. If the program is rated for your child/grandchild's age range but it seems to be out of the child's grasp, follow the kid's lead—the program's not for him/her.

Art for Kids

If you've ever tried to work with oil paint or charcoal, you discovered firsthand how challenging (and frustrating) fine art can be. If you've ever used finger paints, dabbled in water colors, or sculpted with Play-Doh, you know how expressive (and how much *fun*) art can be.

Kids know, too. To get their creative juices flowing—and to let them have fun akin to finger painting, there are paint programs for kids. These programs offer different onscreen paint tools—spray cans, pens, pencils, crayons—but they are presented so that the kids can really create and build things.

Kid paint systems include *stickers* or *stamps*, little pictures they affix to their onscreen page. Dinosaurs, animals, birds, and signs are all included. Even erasing a picture is part of the fun. *Kid Pix*, from Broderbund, offers multiple ways to erase a picture—one erasure is accompanied by the sound of a huge explosion! One section of Electronic Arts' *Art Center* lets kids select a "profession" and then dress the characters with different articles of clothing. Another feature lets kids "pour" paint into the different predefined segments of an image to create great pictures, as shown in Figure 17–4, which the kids can then print out.

Most features are accompanied by goofy sound effects—a defining feature of *Kid Pix*—that can be turned off (or disabled) if they become too distracting. For the most part, though, sound holds tremendous appeal for little kids.

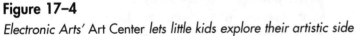 *Tip:* **Make sure the kid's software you buy has a money back guarantee. If the kid doesn't like it or you don't think it appropriate for your child, you should be able to return it.**

Much like books, these children's programs get much of their value from the guidance you can provide them with. Consider yourself a copilot and share the experience. When problems arise, you are there to help and when the little one is tickled by something, you get to share in their glee.

Figure 17–4

Electronic Arts' Art Center lets little kids explore their artistic side

Like television or movies, you'll also want to guard kids against programs that are unsuitable. You probably don't want a young child viewing a game in which graphic acts of violence are played out.

> *Note:* **Unlike television, children have the option to "replay" segments of a program over and over again. Clicking on a rock and seeing a crab pop out may have your little one in stitches—20 or 30 times in a row!**

Living Books

There are already some classic electronic works for children. The Living Books Series

(Broderbund) takes full advantage of sound, animation, and popular children's characters; they really capture the attention of children. The idea with living books is to offer a "book" onscreen. Here's how they work.

Just Grandma and Me is based on a book by the best-selling author, Mercer Mayer. The disk includes about ten "pages" or screens, each reflecting a page of the book. Each page, when loaded from the CD-ROM, is first read aloud to the child and then the child can, by clicking the mouse, explore other things on the page. Figure 17–5 shows one of the screens in *Just Grandma and Me*.

Figure 17–5

Broderbund's Living Book Series includes Just Grandma and Me—*a smash with little ones*

When the little one clicks on pictures in the book, the pictures come to life. Sometimes, clicking on the same object gets a different result, but little kids are always drawn in. What's under the rock? What's on the radio? Most everything the child clicks on pays off with animation, audio, and music.

In addition, the books are multilingual. *Just Grandma and Me* can switch from Spanish, English, and Japanese with a click of the mouse button.

Software Protection from the Little Ones

It's nerve-racking at times to have a kid on your computer. It only takes a second for them to format your drive or delete important files. To guard against lost or deleted files, you might want to check out Edmark's *Kid Desk* or Berkeley System's *Launch Pad*. These are *front ends*, programs that act as protection against children who might inadvertently wreak havoc on the contents of your drive.

Kid Desk and *Launch Pad*, as shown in Figure 17–6, give children who are using the computer access only to the files and programs that you allow them entry into. These programs can usually be configured to appear when the computer starts up. If you want to remove or avoid the program, in most cases, all you have to do is type in a password.

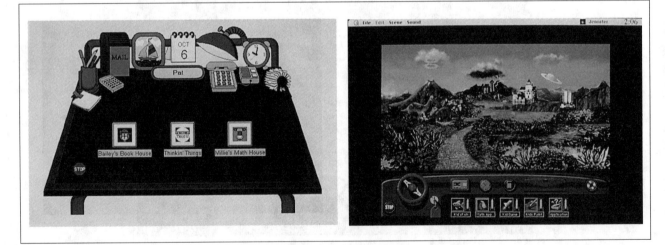

Figure 17–6

Kids have the freedom to go...where you'll allow them to go

What's Available

Like games, the number of products—good products—is too long to provide here. Instead, here are several of the best known kid's software companies and where you can reach them.

Company	Location	Phone Number
Broderbund	Novato, CA	1-800-521-6263
Davidson and Associates	Torrance, CA	1-800-545-7677
Edmark Corporation	Redmond, WA	1-800-426-0856
The Learning Company	Fremont, CA	1-800-852-2255

Utilities:
Making Computing
Easier

Your computer can be transformed in many ways to help you do many different things. As you work more on your computer and as the role of your computer expands, so will the need to more effectively manage the documents, images, audio clips, and other files you have created.

Utilities: Programs to Make Computing Easier

To maintain things, you'll want to keep your system software up to date, explore new programs that can help in the day-to-day operations of your computer, and learn about new solutions that are available to solve old problems.

Consider this example. You start a small company with a single filing cabinet for your records. As your company grows, more and more documents and records fill the filing cabinet. Soon, the filing cabinet becomes two filing cabinets. The company continues to grow, the filing continues to pile up, and you realize that you must hire an administrator to organize the contents, purge the unneeded files, and systematize things. As your company grows further, you look to organize and reorganize your records to allow for continued growth. If you didn't get the second filing cabinet, hire an administrator, and otherwise streamline operations, you couldn't have expanded successfully and your business would suffer.

You can look at your computer the same way. The more you use it, the more you need to organize and fine-tune things. As you work on new and interesting projects, you need to accommodate and organize all of the things you create as well as the tools—the programs—you use to create them. It's important that you keep up with all of the programs available to you, but there is another aspect to software—the side that lets you improve how you work on your computer and how you organize and reorganize. It's the side not of tools to build or create things (like word processors or spreadsheets), but of *utilities*—programs that ease the task of computing.

Since an operating system is supposed to let you manage the things you store on your computer, what are utilities there for? In many ways, utilities are there to address shortcomings in the operating system or to provide added functionality that a particular group of users may want.

For example, you are using Windows 3.1 and you want to find a file you created yesterday. You don't remember the exact name of the file, just that it had an extension of .fdr. You perform a hard drive search for all files ending with the .fdr extension. The search window brings up 80 files, but the files are not listed in chronological order. In fact, there is no way to view the search window chronologically. Not a big deal, right?

If you only needed to do this search once every nine months, you probably wouldn't think twice about it. But what if you had to do a similar search more often—three times a day, maybe—and you had to keep tracking down a single file from a list of 80 some-odd files? You would tire of manually combing through all the file names. You would want a search utility—a small program that would let you perform a particular kind of search that the operating system is not able to perform.

There is a wealth of utilities out there to help you improve your computer's performance—and make the job of computing easier for yourself. There are also utilities to get you out of some pretty tough jams—say you accidentally delete all of your financial records for the last two years, right before your appointment with the IRS. There's still hope—with the right utilities.

A Look at Different Utilities

Utilities are small programs that give added functionality to your computer or make computer housekeeping easier in some way. Many utilities are born of a creative person's need for something that the operating system doesn't provide. In fact, when a company designs a new version of an operating system, they look at popular utilities and determine if they should incorporate the "features" of particular utilities as part of the new version.

There's no easy way to classify utilities. Sometimes the more ingenious ones address problems that you didn't even realize you had. Here are a few important and ingenious utilities—and the needs that they address.

Disk Locking

If you haven't started already, you'll probably start storing some very personal information on your computer: financial records,
wills, trusts, a journey—things you don't
want prying eyes to access. Disk locking
utilities (like Norton's DiskLock from
Symantec, 1-800-441-7234, street price:
$100) let you turn your hard drive into a
safety deposit box. When a disk locking
program is installed on your hard drive and
you turn on your computer, you are immediately prompted for a password—your
password. No one can get past that screen
and gain access to the hard drive unless
they know the password. If your machine is
stolen, a locked disk is useless to the thief
and will have to be physically replaced (they
can't even erase it). But be careful; good
protection comes at a cost. If you lose your
password, there is no secret passage
through which you can regain access to
your hard drive. You won't be able to open
your hard drive, either. Disk locking programs also let you lock separate folders
(subdirectories).

Note: **Windows offers a very
diluted version of password protection. You—or anyone, for that
matter—can get around the protection in
Windows simply by turning off your
machine and then turning it on again.**

Screen Savers

Screen savers are programs that display an
image or animation on your screen when
you leave your computer on and don't use

it. Berkeley Systems (1-800-877-5535),
the company that really established the
screen saver market, offers lots of these,
and there are all sorts of screen saver
images available from other companies as
well. You can get a Star Trek collection,
cartoon collections such as Looney Tunes
(Bugs Bunny and company), Rocky and
Bullwinkle, and Walt Disney. When you
install your screen savers, you specify how
long the computer must be inactive before
switching the screen saver on.

Screen savers are certainly fun—and
fun to look at—but they aren't really utilities
in the true sense of the word: they don't do
anything for you. They do not, as some
people claim, protect your picture tube
from damage caused by displaying one
image for an extended period of time.

RAM Doubling Software

Everybody wants more RAM, but more
RAM is expensive and requires installation.
RAM doubling or RAM compression programs are a great alternative. These relatively new programs—like RAMDoubler
from Connectix Corp. (1-800-950-5880)—
trick your machine and your programs into
believing you have twice as much memory
as you really have (the program actually
compresses information in RAM so it only
takes up half as much RAM as normal). If
you have 8MB, the computer behaves as if
it has 16MB. If you have 16MB, it thinks it
has 32MB. RAM-doubling software offers
you a speed increase and the benefits of
having twice as much RAM—without buying

it. Priced at about $60, RAM-doubling software costs a fraction of a comparable RAM upgrade. What's more, these programs install with ease—you don't have to turn the program on or diddle with anything.

Disk Doubling

You may be in need of more hard disk space, but you may not want to spend the money on it just yet. Disk-doubling programs offer file compression—like a trash compactor—automatically storing your files and programs in a smaller space, and expanding them instantly when you access them. These programs are called doublers because you can store about twice as much data as you could on an "undoubled" drive. The most popular version of this utility is The Norton DiskDoubler (from Symantec, 1-800-441-7234, street price: $100) and Stacker for IBM compatibles (Stac Electronics, 1-800-522-7822, street price: $125).

Archival Compression

When you want to compress files down as small as possible, there is a form of compression beyond disk-doubling. Unlike disk-doubling programs that work to compress and decompress in an instant, these archival compression programs may take a little more time to squeeze, but the results can be remarkable. Depending on the type of file, it can be squashed to about 3 percent of its actual size. These programs, like WinZip, shown in Figure 18–1, (for IBM compatibles) and Stuffit (for Macintosh) are ideal for backing up files on a floppy. In Figure 18–1, the number in the Size category indicates the file size before compression. The number in the Packed column indicates the "zipped" size. The Ratio column tells you the reduction in size. Programs like WinZip are especially popular with people who send a lot of files on the Internet and across online services, because sending information online takes time and, typically, the more time you spend online, the more it costs. Sending smaller files results in lower online service charges (online services are covered in-depth in Part III).

WinZip is a shareware program available on virtually every online service that offers PC compatible utilities (you can also get it from any PC user group). The program is fully functional, but the creators request that you send in a registration fee of $29 for a single copy.

File Viewers and Image Readers

Many files can't be opened unless you have the same program that was used to create them. This is a very common problem with certain files (files created with non-mainstream programs, for example, that may be stored in an unconventional way). Other files may be damaged, and therefore unopenable. Special programs like CanOpener (Abbott Systems, 1-800-552-9157, street price: $110) let you open these files and see what's inside. CanOpener also lets you extract images or text from an otherwise unopenable document for use in another context.

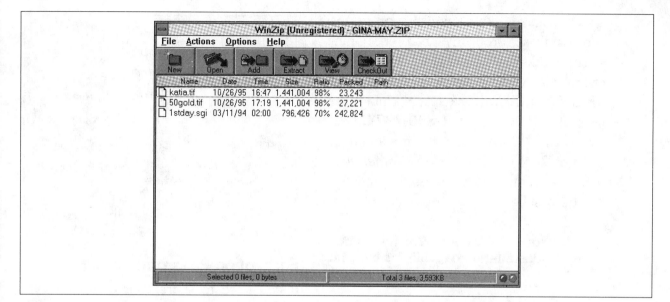

Figure 18–1

WinZip lets you compress your files for easy transmission and storage

 Alert: **File readers may open a file for you, but the formatting may be lost.**

Acrobat, a new program from Adobe Systems, Inc., lets you look at fully formatted pages—with text and graphics—without the need for a special application or program to view such files. Publishers can now create documents that mix text and graphics (creating the documents requires additional expensive software), and anyone with Acrobat Reader—it's available free on any online service—can read them.

Uninstallers (Uniquely PC)

When you install a program on a PC-compatible computer running Windows 3.1, it roots around on your drive, often burying files in multiple locations, altering system files to accommodate the new program, and inserting data and files in places you would never expect to find them. When you need to remove the program, however, there is no way to manually go through and find all of the files the program deposited on your drive. The result? You may be able to delete the files most obviously associated with the program, but there may be lots of other files (with cryptic names) that you'll never trace. The more programs you install on your computer and subsequently delete, the more unnecessary files you accumulate on your hard drive. The result is a hard drive filled with files that aren't useful and that slow down your system.

Uninstaller and similar programs address these problems head on. Uninstaller works backwards to remove programs from your system and reclaim all of the associated hard disk space. Uninstaller (Microhelp Software, 1-800-777-3322, street price: $65) requires a minimum of 4MB of RAM but *16MB is recommended*. It has been one of the best-selling utilities for the past year.

 Note: **Windows 95 has some uninstallation capabilities built in.**

Virus Checkers

You don't want a virus on your machine—or on your diskettes. No one is immune to viruses, but you can protect against them. Virus checkers quietly watch as programs load into RAM to make sure the other programs behave themselves. When suspicious activity is identified, the virus checker alerts you that something is awry and then—with your permission—can go about removing the problem. This is another kind of utility that has been successfully offered as shareware. Two of the most popular virus protection programs are Virus Scan (McAfee Associates, 1-800-866-6595, street price: $65) for PC compatibles and SAM (Symantec Anti Virus) for PCs and the Macintosh (Symantec, 1-800-441-7234, street price: $60). Virus Scan is available via online services, as are free SAM updates.

Golden Rule:

Keep your virus protection software current. New viruses are always popping up and old virus protection software won't recognize them. Virus protection updates are always made available via the online services, so it's best to get the most recent protection.

Encryption Programs

If you need to share your computer with others but you have confidential or personal information stored on it, you may want to try an encryption utility to scramble the contents of your personal files. With encryption, a person can open your file but the contents are completely unintelligible—unless they know the passcode. This sort of protection is especially important in, say, a doctor's office, where certain sections of a patient's records must remain confidential—perhaps only the physician should have access. In this case, an encryption program can be used to scramble the document. When an unwelcome reader views the document, they will see only gibberish onscreen. With the passcode, however, the document is fully readable and understandable.

One notable encryption program (PGP, short for "pretty good privacy") can be found free on the Internet and various online services, and there are several commercial versions of this program available.

National Security and the Clipper Chip

The United States government is very concerned with how its citizens use computers, especially how they try to scramble, encrypt, and otherwise conceal information. With encryption programs becoming increasingly sophisticated, the government wants to control encryption by creating a "master encryption" scheme that everyone could use—and to which they would have the key.

The fear is that with multiple encryption standards, the government cannot perform adequate surveillance on those considered dangerous. The Mafia would start encrypting their data and the government would be unable to break it. The Clipper Chip proposal calls for a special chip to be built into most computer-based electronic devices. In this way, you could encrypt everything, but in such a way that the government could always access your information. The government does not want criminals and terrorists encrypting communications so that the government can't decipher them. Even more important, the U.S. government doesn't want encryption tools exported to foreign countries (for fear that our espionage capabilities would be compromised).

Virtually everyone in the computer community has come out against this plan. One argument against it is that no encryption scheme is foolproof—especially one devised by government officials—and eventually hackers will find a way around it.

Utilities for Word Processors, DTP Programs, and More

There are also utility programs that are intended to enhance a particular program or address the shortcomings of particular programs. Microsoft Word, for example, provides very limited file management options; if you want to save a file in a yet-to-be-created folder, you must leave Word to do it. With utilities like Woody's Office Power Pack (Pinecliff International, $49.95, available online), you can do that and other Word "undo-ables."

Let's say you are creating a weekly 10-page newsletter with SS Gutenberg 4.0, a realistic-sounding but imaginary desktop publishing program. Due to the weird way the newsletter is assembled, you need the pages to be numbered sequentially from 1 to 5 and then backwards from 10 to 6. Gutenberg 4.0 can't do it for you automatically, but you find a utility that will let you define page numbering in Gutenberg 4.0 any way you want. This utility does not address a shortcoming of the operating system. Instead, it adds functionality to a particular program.

Remote Access Programs/Utilities

Remote access lets you use a nearby computer to access a machine that is far away—as if you are at the distant machine. Programs in this category, like Apple Remote Access (Apple, Inc., 1-800-776-2333, street price: $200) and Norton's PCAnywhere (Symantec, 1-800-441-7234, street price: $180) are great for telecommuting: the home-based staffer uses a modem and the remote access software to call the office machine. The office machine's modem accepts the call and the remote access software asks for the user's password and ID. If accepted, the user, sitting in the comfort of his or her home, now sees everything as if sitting at the office desk. In fact, the remote person can even send documents to the office printers and communicate with other people on the office network.

Undelete Utilities

You are working away on your computer. You have been diligently saving your work every three minutes over the last six hours. You have put an immense amount of energy into this project over the last few weeks. Your masterpiece is finally complete and you do what everyone inadvertently does at some point in their computing career: you delete the document. Uh oh. Your heart sinks, your shoulders sag, you wilt; unless you have an undelete utility like that provided with The Norton Utilities (Symantec, 1-800-441-7234, street price: $100). Properly installed and used correctly, undelete can bring back your file(s) intact and unharmed. When this fate befalls you, you will understand just how thankful people are for the utility.

Interestingly, this was one of the first "utilities" in the PC industry and is the centerpiece of the Norton Utilities, a collection of helpful and innovative system utilities. This single utility has been so popular that Windows 95 now offers a similar built-in feature.

File "Shredders"

A file shredder is the opposite of the undelete utility. A file shredding utility takes a file that you want to delete and *do not* want recovered and erases it completely from the drive. No recovery program—not the Norton Utilities or anything else—will bring it back. Perhaps not surprisingly, this utility is also one of the Norton Utilities; Symantec knows what's required to recover your files, and they also know how to prevent them from being recovered.

PC Exchange

There's nothing more aggravating than not being able to share documents with someone because one person uses a Mac and the other a PC. True, a floppy diskette can fit in both computers, but a Mac-formatted diskette—with files—will appear to be unformatted when put into a PC drive.

Apple has come up with an excellent utility—since built into System 7.5—called PC Exchange (Apple, Inc., 1-800-776-2333, street price: $70) that lets a Macintosh read a PC diskette. This is excellent for word processing documents created in cross-platform word processors like MS Word. When the PC diskette is put into the Macintosh drive, the diskette icon appears on the screen with the letters PC emblazoned on it. If you drag your Word for Windows documents from the diskette, you can open them from within Word—without a hitch. If you copy a document created with Microsoft Word for the Mac and put it on the PC diskette, you can open it in any PC compatible.

The Rest of the Story

There are zillions of other utilities—for using long file names in Windows 3.1, for creating virtual "post-its" to stick on your screen, for altering your display, for making the type on your screen look better, for improving search tools (to replace or enhance the "find" command your computer currently uses), and many more.

What's Available

Some companies specialize in utilities—but don't forget there's a world of shareware and freeware utilities available online and from user groups. Here are a few companies that produce utilities and development tools, and some of their more popular products.

Company	Utility	Function	Phone Number
Adobe Systems, Inc.	Adobe Acrobat, ATM	Display type	1-800-833-6687
Berkeley Systems	After Dark, The Screen Saver	Inactive screen	1-800-877-5535
Symantec, Inc.	Norton Utilities, DiskDoubler, DiskLock, Public Utilities	Disk and file management	1-800-441-7231
Niko Mak Computing	WinZip	File compression	1-203-429-3539
Stac Electronics	Stacker	Disk compression	1-800-522-7822
Aladdin Systems	Stuffit Deluxe	File compression	1-800-732-8881
Connectix	RamDoubler	Simulate doubled RAM	1-800-950-5880

You'll hear about some, and as you become more aware of the particular things you need, you'll learn to seek out others. The best sources for utilities (besides those sold commercially) are online services and user groups.

Development Tools

There is another class of software products that you'll no doubt hear about and see advertised. These are *development tools*— software programs and tools used by pro-grammers to create other programs. There are programming languages that you'll hear about such as C (pronounced "*see*") and C++ (pronounced "*see plus plus*") and *compilers*—special programs that convert the programmer's code into a language the computer can understand. There are also prototyping tools, such as Visual Basic and Visual C++, that let software developers quickly create working models or protoypes of products they may eventually build—similar to the way an automotive designer building model cars first.

PART III

Reaching Out: Online Resources

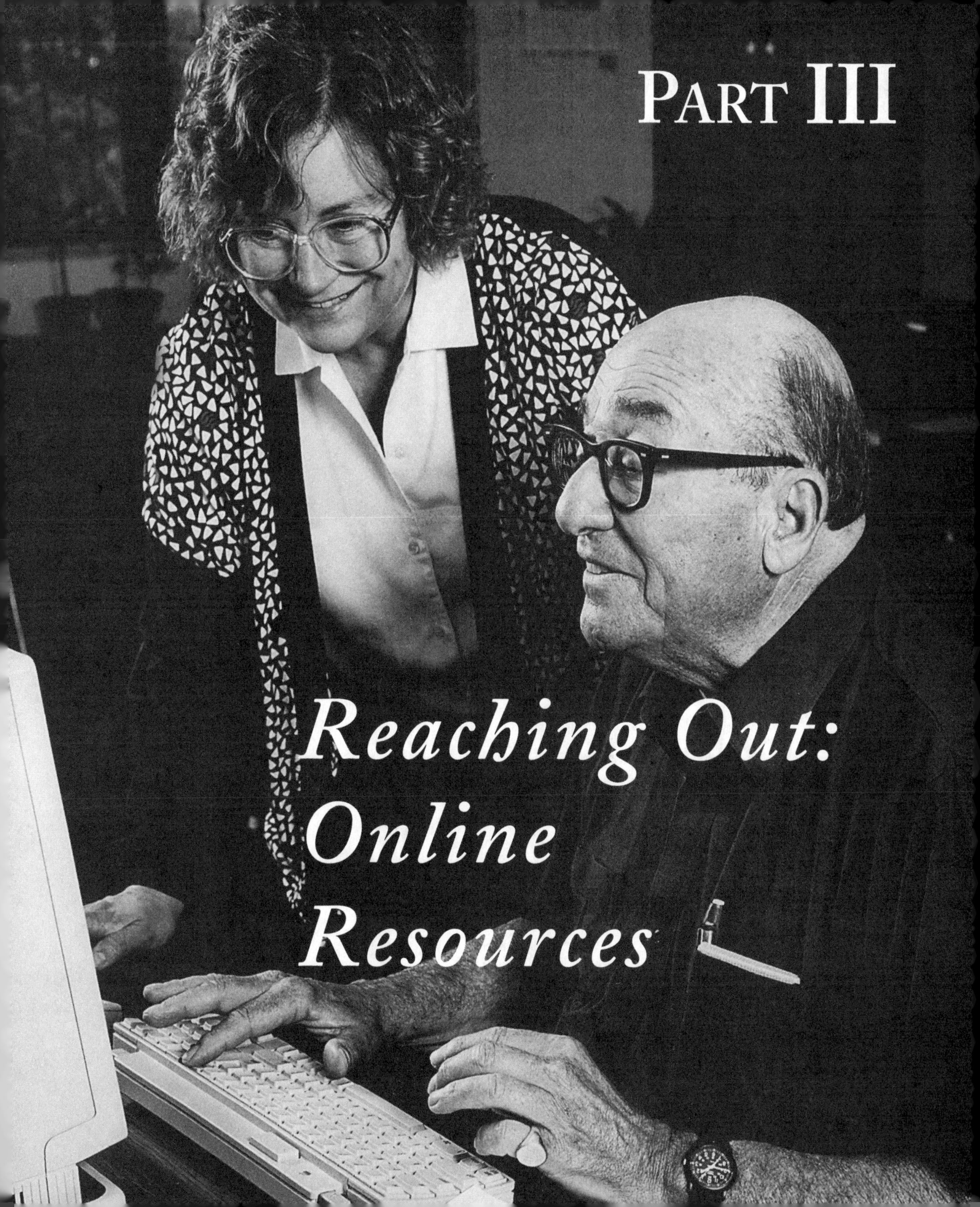

Getting Online—
What You'll Need

When Alexander Graham Bell invented the telephone, he never could have foreseen the burgeoning world of telecommunications. Talking to Watson was remarkable enough, but using phone lines to transmit moving pictures, still images, text, and more would seem the imaginings of an over-imaginative eccentric.

Welcome to the world of modern telecommunications! With a home computer, a modem, and a phone line, you can bring a world of resources into your home using the same phone line that then-Western Union President Orton mistook as a "toy."

This is no toy. True, you can use it to play games with people in other countries, but getting online means getting connected to a different community; a wired, international community where vital information can pass between individuals in an instant.

The computer has irrevocably changed the landscape of communications. Cable companies, telephone companies, and mass media companies like Time-Warner are all trying to predict the next step so they can be the first to offer new services to the communications-hungry masses. In the meantime, the online world awaits you. The requirements for getting access to the Internet and other online wonders are minimal. Here's what you need to get there now.

Requirements in a Nutshell

The basic requirements for getting online can just about fit in a nutshell. To get online, you'll need a computer, a phone line, and a modem. If you want to get to the Internet or one of the popular services like America Online (AOL), CompuServe, The Microsoft Network (MSN), or Prodigy (why else would you buy all this stuff?), you'll also need an "online account" or a "service provider" and their access software. A service provider acts as a facilitator, much like a long distance service does with your long distance calls.

Having the Right Kind of Phone Lines

First, the phone. If you don't have modular phone jacks and wall plugs—the kind where you can just slip the cord in or out of the phone or outlet—you need to contact the phone company and have the modular type installed.

If you already have a modular phone (and wall plug), then you're ready to go. Modems don't require special phone lines to work—they work fine on the same line you speak on.

If you find yourself online for extended periods of time, though, you may want to consider getting a separate line for your modem. When you are using your modem, you can't call other people or accept other phone calls, and, depending on your habits, that could really cramp your phone style.

Modems don't like to be interrupted. The slightest disturbance can break your connection—especially call waiting. If you have call waiting, you need to temporarily "suspend" it by entering *70 when you make your online modem connection. When you dial *70 before the number, any-

one calling your number will hear a busy signal. Having an online connection broken can be pretty irritating. If you are at the 55-minute mark of a 60-minute task, for example, you lose your connection and you must start the task over from the beginning. The computer doesn't know how to resurrect what you've done and you must start over from scratch.

> ### Golden Rule:
>
> If you have a second extension in your home, don't let anyone pick it up during an online session. If the extension is picked up, your modem connection will be broken.

Getting a Modem

If you don't already have a modem, then you'll need to get one. As discussed in Chapter 8, there are two different kinds: external (that sit on your desktop) and internal (that are installed in your computer). Either way you go, you should get the fastest modem available on the mass market, which is currently 28.8Kbps. These cost about $200, a little more for an external. You can find modems that are half as fast (14.4Kbps) for about $50, but if possible, go with the faster modem. It will save you time and money in online charges.

If you already have a modem (9,600 bps or below) and you spend a lot of time online—or you'd like to spend a lot of time online—try to get a faster modem. You may have already discovered that with a slow modem, the Internet experience proves especially aggravating, if not downright infuriating (you spend all of your time waiting for screens to appear), and your online bills may be unnecessarily high.

 Alert: **Sure, the 2,400-bps modem that you have from two or three years ago is still working just fine, but you are doing yourself a disservice by not upgrading; a faster modem leaves less room for problems online because you spend less time on any given task. A one-hour download with a 2,400-bps modem, for example, may take five minutes with a faster modem. A lot more can go wrong—like inadvertent disconnections—during these hour-long tasks.**

Putting Your Phone and Modem Together

To connect your modem, you'll only need the modem cable and a couple of telephone cords (all of the necessary cords and cables should be provided). One cord leads from your wall jack to the appropriate jack on the back of the modem (or the back of your computer, if you have an internal modem). The jacks are usually marked as "phone" and "line." The cord from the wall jack should lead to the modem jack labeled "line." The other cord should go from your phone to the modem. With this configuration, the telephone remains connected, so

you never have to disconnect the cables running to or from your modem or phone.

If you have an external modem, you need to connect it to the computer. You will need to attach one end of the modem cable to the modem and the other end to a communications port or serial port on the back of your computer. (Macintosh users have their modem port marked with a little picture of a telephone receiver.) You may have more than one serial port on your computer and you can use any one that's available.

Configuring Your Modem: Using Your Modem Manual

Once you've attached your modem, leave it alone. Aside from the basic setup instructions just provided, the real setup you have to do is with the telecommunications software (usually provided by your service provider). The software ensures that your modem can "talk" to the online service.

In the meantime, you may have noticed there is a lot of technical information in your modem manual. Making sense of your modem manual is a lot like making sense out of ancient Babylonian scrolls: you could probably do it if you had a couple hundred years of extra free time! Much of this information is addresses, telecommunications standards, interrupts, protocol, modem specifications, special scripting commands, and "strings"—commands that you can give to your modem. For the nonpower user, this information is nothing short of mind numbing (for some power users, too!)

High-Speed Phone Lines: Your Second Mortgage

Time is money! Big companies can't waste time waiting for information to come to them via *oh so slow* 28.8Kbps modems (the fastest commercial modems). Instead, they invest in ISDN systems— Integrated Services Digital Network—a high-speed communications network that allows for two 56Kbps or 64Kbps (depending on your state) transmission speeds—about five times the speed of a 28.8Kbps modem.

ISDN offers more than just speed; it offers simultaneous transmission of several kinds of information on the same line— voice, data, and fax, to name a few. For the Information Superhighway to realize its potential, ISDN—or something like it—will have to be available for the home as well. That's already starting to happen; new homes in California are regularly being equipped with ISDN lines.

There's also a new standard called T1 (pronounced "tee-one") that supports over 1Mbps. T1 lines are only cost-effective if used over three hours—this service can easily cost an astronomical $1,000 a month. Some bigwigs and high-profile computer nerds are getting T1 lines installed in their homes, but it's not for the masses—yet.

so don't feel bad if it doesn't make any sense to you.

Do Modems Break?

If you do have problems with your modem, don't just assume it's broken. The cable might be bad or the computer might incorrectly think it's connected to a different port. But, sad to say, modems can fail. They don't smoke, they don't explode and make a big noise, and they don't start whistling; they just stop working. Like any appliance, you may also wind up with a modem that proves dependable for years. There's no telling if you are going to be unlucky and get a short-lived modem, but you should definitely buy a name brand modem—like a Supra, or U.S. Robotics, for example—and send in your registration/warranty card to guard against the possibility of a breakdown.

Your New Phone Bill

After all of this talk about online charges, you are probably a bit concerned about what this "new technology business" is going to do to your phone bill. In most cases, using online services and the Internet shouldn't really impact your phone bill at all. The phone number that you dial for online access is provided by your online service and is typically a local number. The online service or service provider will bill you for service via your credit card (more on this in Chapter 21).

Online Services

Cyberspace is a much ballyhooed, oft criticized, frequently misunderstood world that is many things to many people. The term *cyberspace* was actually coined by William Gibson, the author of *Neuromancer*, to describe a world where people plug their minds into a computer network. Although getting online is not quite so dramatic as that, online services can provide you with entrée into the closest thing available.

Just what can you expect to find when you venture out with your modem? Like most everything, getting connected is what *you* make it; but, given what's available online, you can make it a life-changing experience.

Getting Online: Finding the Right Service

Online services have a lot to offer. The commercial services all offer e-mail, access to numerous electronic magazines, lots of information on computer hardware and software, travel information, games, shareware, freeware, and more. Services such as America Online, CompuServe, Prodigy, The Microsoft Network, and Apple's e-World all offer these options, but each online service offers them somewhat differently.

Alert: **The Microsoft Network requires Windows 95. If you don't have Windows 95 on your PC compatible, or if you are a Mac user, The Microsoft Network is not an option.**

Which Online Service to Choose?

Trying to figure out which online service to use isn't as confusing as it seems. There are two things you need to find:

1. Easy access to the resources, services, and information that are of greatest interest to you; and

2. A pricing schedule that is best tailored to the things you want to do online.

In some ways, choosing an online service is like selecting a long distance telephone service: you decide, based on your long distance habits, which service is the least expensive and can provide the most features. In the meantime, all of the services try to convince you to sign on with them by offering free incentives, ever-dropping rates and ever-changing (and frequently confusing) pricing schedules.

Online services succeed by providing a cornucopia of resources. To keep you coming back, those resources are updated constantly, with new contributors and new attractions. When a service fails to update and refresh materials and resources, subscribers lose interest, usage drops off, and the service fails.

Online services charge by the minute and though the hourly rate may not seem high, you can still run up a fairly big tab. On CompuServe, for example, there are additional charges that you can incur for accessing certain forums. To remain competitive, however, many of these surcharges are being eliminated or are being reduced significantly, but you can still expect to encounter them from time to time.

Your Final Decision... Can Change

Once you decide on an online service, you subscribe to that service and use it as much—or as little—as you wish. If you have any questions, you can always check out your billing (and usage) status online. The services always bill to whichever credit card you specify, so when you start your service and you see a mystery charge show up, you'll know what it's from.

At some point, you may discover that the online service you chose just isn't for you. In this case, call the service and cancel and your credit card billing should cease. Canceling one service doesn't mean you can't try another one. Online services are very much like long distance phone services in that regard: people are constantly abandoning one for the other, drawn by some feature offered by a competitor or pushed by some policy that, temporarily at least, upsets them. If you have trouble getting through on a voice line, cancel your service via the online service itself.

 Note: **Having one service does not preclude subscribing to other services at the same time. Some people subscribe to both AOL and CompuServe without any problem. The big consideration? You pay two separate charges every month.**

A Quick Tour of Online Resources

In some ways, online services are like a coral reef. They may offer wondrous sights to behold and there may be plenty to explore, but if you're a newcomer, it's difficult to identify where the resources are and what they have to offer. It's all under the surface. You'll want some guidance in the beginning, but once you are immersed, you'll find plenty to keep you busy.

What Access Software Is Best?

Each service provides its own software—free of charge—that lets you connect to that service. The software often comes unsolicited in promotional mailings, with software or hardware purchases (like modems, for example), and with computer magazines—on diskette or CD-ROM. If you haven't gotten a copy through these channels and you don't want to pay for a magazine to get "free" software, call the online service and

request that a copy be sent to you. Remember though, you can't use one service's software to access a competing service.

You should note that the upgrades for online access software is free, so when you see a new version of your service's software, don't hesitate to upgrade. (Older versions of the software may not support faster modem speeds.)

Alert: **Be sure to get the version for your machine type, either Mac or PC.**

Installing the Software

To install the software, follow the instructions provided with the product. There will be a number of questions you'll need to answer, and you should be prompted or prepared to provide the following:

Modem brand The modem brand lets the service know what you are using to communicate so it can communicate with you. Your online service will display a big list of the different modem makes and models, from which you select your modem. Identifying your modem is easier if you have an external modem, since the name and type appear on the front panel of the modem. If you have an internal modem, consult your computer's documentation for specifics.

bps or baud rate Your online service needs to know the speed (sometimes referred to as baud rate) of your modem. If you specify the wrong baud rate, the modem may not work or it may work at a much slower speed than it can attain (like leaving a car in low gear). Sometimes the modem speed is clearly indicated in the name of the modem.

 Alert: **To keep you on your toes(!), some 14.4Kbps modems (U.S. Robotics are among them) require that the baud rate be set to 19.2Kbps.**

Modem port On PC compatibles, these ports are specified as COM1, COM2, COM3, or COM4. Nine times out of ten, the modem is attached to COM1 or COM2. The software for online services usually has a feature to find which port the modem is attached to.

Access number In order to connect with an online service, you need an access number, a phone number that connects you to the service. Online services usually have hundreds of phone numbers all over the country to ensure you don't have to place a long distance or toll call. Some services prompt you for your own phone number (at least the area code and exchange) to help you find the access number in your area.

Faster modems usually have separate access numbers, so when you see the list of local access phone numbers, be sure to select one that corresponds to your modem's speed.

Until you enter this information, you can't go anywhere. Follow the installation instructions that accompany the software.

You may stumble into a number of other opaque sounding features (modem control strings, for example). Don't touch these, since the software selects these based on the kind of modem you select.

Open Sesame

All services let you select a password so other people can't sign on to your account and read your e-mail or run your bill up into the stratosphere. You should change your password regularly and be sure to create a password that you will remember. Make sure the password is not a commonly used word or proper noun since these passwords can be "cracked" by disreputable individuals looking to hijack accounts. Some of the services block the use of names or words by forcing you to use a nonstandard character as part of your password—like a period, hyphen, or pound sign. All of the services provide directions on how to change your password.

Alert: **Change your password on a regular basis to prevent unauthorized access by other people. When coming up with a new password, never use something obvious that people might guess: your [own/spouse's/child's/grandchild's] name, are a few obvious passwords to avoid.**

How to Navigate

The resources of an online service may seem overwhelming (they are!), but everything you'll find online is cross-referenced in numerous ways, so there are many ways to get to where you want to go. Here are the basic elements of an online service and some ways to navigate.

Subjects

When you first enter your online service, a Main Menu appears, a basic road map to let you navigate based on subject matter. Figure 20–1 shows the map for America Online and Figure 20–2 shows the equivalent screen for CompuServe Informational Services (CIS). Travel, Home/Leisure, Fun & Games, Reference, Education, and other avenues of exploration are available by

clicking the associated buttons. If you know which topic you want to investigate, you can click on the appropriate button and go to that area.

Clicking on the Finance button in CompuServe, for example, takes you to the screen shown in Figure 20–3. This screen can change, but you'll always get access to a wide range of options. Each of the buttons at the bottom takes you to another set of options. Publications, for example, gives you access to *Money* and *Fortune* magazines online, among a host of other options.

Some of the main subject areas (Finance, Sports, Entertainment) are more impressive than others—they may have a better inter-

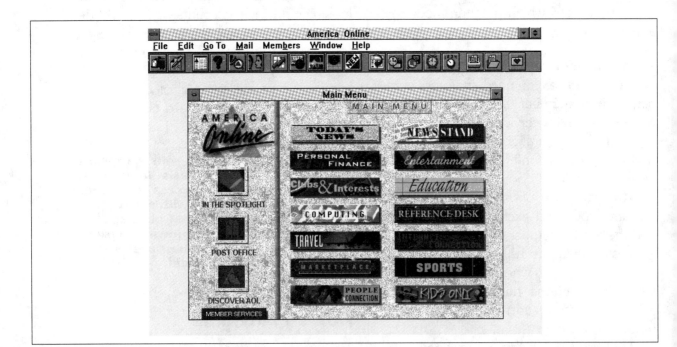

Figure 20–1

America Online's Main Menu gives you multiple areas to select from

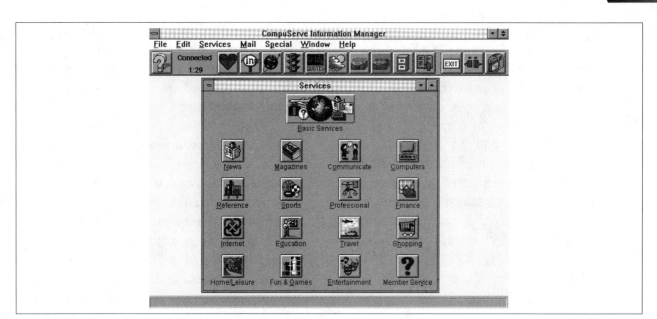

Figure 20–2
CompuServe's Services screen has a very similar menu offering

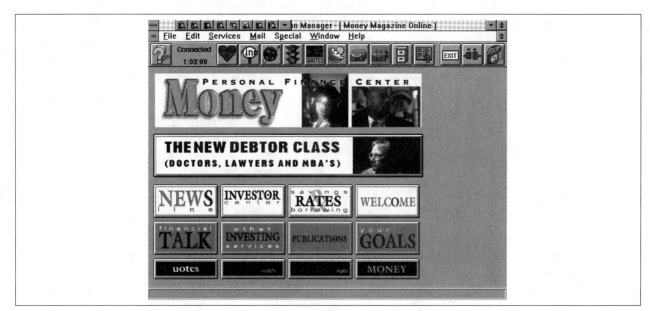

Figure 20–3
The Finance area on CompuServe

face with better graphics, for example. Some of the buttons just provide a list of options—no impressive graphics—and you can click on the one you want to pursue. One area may look better, but appearances don't always mean better content underneath.

Once you enter a subject area, you'll find a variety of additional directions to travel, including forums. A *forum* is an area dedicated to a certain subject and providing its own subset of special services. Here's what you can get in a forum.

Sysops

Sysops (pronounced "sis-ops," and rhymes with "miss-pops"), or "system operators," are people, not destinations. Every forum has at least one sysop. The sysop is part diplomat, moderator, referee, arbitrator, policeman, and den mother—not necessarily in that order. The sysop monitors the forum and makes sure everyone is playing by the rules. The sysop also answers questions regarding the forum (you can send them to "sysop" when you are in the forum you want to inquire about) and can tell you where to direct other inquiries.

Message Boards

With a message board, you can "post" a question (or opinion) about a subject and others can respond in kind. You can also reply to messages or questions that other people post. These messages, and the responses to them, remain online for others to read and respond to, taking on the characteristics of a written town hall meet-

ing. Sometimes referred to as *threads*, they can grow and evolve as more people participate. With an online service, you can respond to any of the messages in the thread at any time.

Forums exist for thousands of topics, and they all have message boards, so if you have a question—or a beef—be sure to navigate to the area where your question or inquiry actually belongs. If you have a question about a Hewlett Packard printer, for example, your question will be answered if you leave it on the HP forum. If you leave that same message in the human sexuality forum, you'll probably just get a gentle message from the sysop indicating you are in the wrong place.

How long before you can expect an answer? That depends on the question, how busy the forum is where your message should be posted, and who happens to see it. Sometimes, a question might be answered in a matter of minutes and sometimes, if your question is particularly hairy, it may be left unanswered. You never know until you try.

Libraries

Libraries can contain all sorts of treasures: software, utilities, shareware programs, free replacement icons, games, demonstration versions of programs, and more. You can browse these libraries and download to your heart's content. If there is a certain type of program you are interested in obtaining, say a painting program, you can find a shareware version online, download it, and experiment with it to see if you really want to buy such a program. If you really like it, you can just pay the registration fee; otherwise, you can delete the program and find a program that better suits your needs.

Conferences, Chat Lines, and CBs

You can also check the live conferences, "CB" lines (named after citizen's band radio, the once-popular form of radio communication) or chat rooms—these are the equivalent of meeting rooms in which you can carry on conversations with everyone in the room as a group or between particular individuals. Again, chat rooms are based on topic, so if you want to talk about gardening, move to conferences or chats in the gardening forum.

Note: **Chat and conference rooms are only really of interest when there are enough people in the room to keep the conversation going. Usually, chat and conference rooms are empty late at night and early in the morning. If the topic you want to chat about is somewhat obscure, look for a schedule (or set one up!) to ensure that enough people will participate.**

E-Mail

E-mail is an electronic messaging service that allows online subscribers to send messages to other online denizens. An e-mail message can be sent to as many people as you wish and it has many advantages over traditional mail, which is commonly referred to by the computer crowd as "snail mail." E-mail is enormously popular, and

for many people, is reason enough to subscribe to an online service. To better understand what e-mail has to offer, read Chapter 21, "A Look at E-Mail."

Getting the Information to Your Computer

Online services are like window shopping; you can see everything, but when you sign off, you still don't have anything. To get the information you want from the online service and onto your own computer, you need to *download* it. When you download a file, the online service sends you a copy of the file. Before sending the file to you, it asks you where on your hard drive you want to store the file—the folder or subdirectory—and what you want to name the file. (The file will already have a name but you should give it a name you'll be able to identify later on.)

Tip: **Always take a look at how big the file is you are expecting to download. You can usually make some judgments about the length of the download based on the size. If you don't want to upgrade that 2,400-baud modem, you should think twice before downloading anything bigger then 250KB. Otherwise, you may find yourself in the middle of a multi-hour download!**

Netiquette

This is a term you'll probably hear a lot, and with good reason. Getting online brings with it all of the basic rules of civility

Wanted: Online Classifieds

Long a revenue generator for newspapers across the country, classified ads are finding a new home online and newspapers are concerned.

Estimates cited by the *New York Times* say that over 30 percent of newspaper revenues come from classified ads and a migration away from newspapers to online services could have serious implications.

One of the big attractions to online classifieds? The *search engine*—the special program that lets a person sort and access only the ads he or she is most interested in. When you enter a keyword search on a classified, you can specify "retired" *and* "Key West," for example, to find any listing that includes these two specifications; a list of only ads that match your search criteria need appear. No more poring over hard to read newsprint to find ads for part-time work or rare collectibles anymore.

Of all the big city newspapers, Boston newspapers have the most to worry about. There, job classifieds are not even sorted by job type, making online ads especially attractive.

and social intercourse you would expect, and then some. In part because of the anonymity that accompanies communicating with people whom you have never seen or spoken to, you should follow some basic rules.

Don't shout Shouting online is signified by typing in all uppercase. THIS IS SHOUTING! It's impolite and shouters typically get an earful from respondents.

Watch the funny stuff Everybody's a comedian, but when communicating with strangers, steer clear. Humor can easily be interpreted as presumptuous and insensitive by the recipient and bawdy humor should be saved for those friends you know won't be offended.

Golden Rule:

Communicate with others online as you would want others to communicate with your mother or grandchild. Don't be rude, don't curse, and don't share the limericks or bawdy humor. Online, you never know whom you may be communicating with.

Don't "flame" Sometimes, when another online person posts an opinion that you think is ignorant, stupid, inane, ridiculous, shallow, or moronic, you might be tempted to respond with excessive outrage.

Try to keep your temper—and your language—temperate. Remember, other people have feelings and your rage or anger can really hurt.

Encountering the Unexpected

Some of the services and options you encounter on some online services (such as CompuServe) have surcharges associated with them. You are provided with ample warning when you are about to encounter such an area, so you can't claim ignorance when the meter starts running. Figure 20–4 shows one such warning.

Where Did My Online Service Go?

On occasion, you may have trouble making an online connection. Sometimes the service may not be available due to maintenance. This is a time when the technicians intentionally bring the system down to straighten things out, add things, or make repairs or improvements, all without fear of disconnecting you or compromising your service.

America Online frequently goes down from 4:00 A.M.–7:00 A.M. EST. Your status in the human aviary—if you're a night owl or early bird—will determine how much

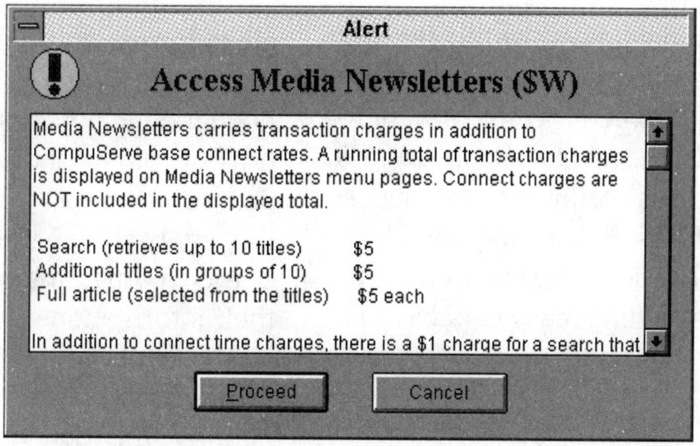

Figure 20–4
Some roads on the Information Superhighway require some stiff tolls

this may ruffle your feathers. If, for example, you try to connect to AOL at very late hours (or the wee hours of the morning, depending on how you look at it), you will be denied access until 7:00 A.M. EST.

> ## Golden Rule:
>
> Dare to explore. Some of the best things you'll find online appear when you let the current carry you. A little serendipity goes a long way—you'll find yourself learning about something you never would have learned about otherwise. If you encounter an area with high surcharges and you aren't interested, find a beach where the swimming is free.

There are other times you may have problems connecting. Many of the services experience "peak usage" hours. These are the times when everybody seems to want to get online and download files. Peak usage is very much like lines forming at the supermarket; certain times of day always find long lines, while at other times the line forms only when you are just getting ready to get in line.

How to Search for Files

Aside from exploring by subject, you may want to find something specific, like a specific file or shareware program, for example.

Online services also allow you to search for particular files. In CompuServe, for example, selecting the Basic Services option leads to the Find a File option, as shown in Figure 20–5.

The Future: The Internet

There's a very good chance that, after reading a few of the thousands of articles written about the Internet, you have Internet fever. All of the online services are [painfully] aware of the intense interest in the Internet and provide some kind of access to it. The Internet is discussed in detail in Chapter 22.

The Internet—the Information Superhighway—has become the communications phenomenon of the 90s. How does the Internet differ from commercial online services? Does it?

The Internet poses both great opportunities for existing online services as well as a formidable challenge. The Internet is a hodgepodge of resources—some utterly useless, others indiscriminately presented, and some—well, great. The resources on the Internet are free, and maintained by outside parties interested in disseminating their information. The number of contributors overshadows anything the commercial online services can provide. So, instead of fighting this juggernaut, online services have instead opened *gateways*—a way for users to access the Internet via their respective service.

Figure 20–5
You can search for files based on a number of different criteria

What's Available

The biggest online services—with the largest subscriber base—are America Online and CompuServe. All of the services start with a basic or flat subscription rate (like $9.95 per month). Your subscription typically includes a set number of "free" hours per month and then an hourly billing rate kicks in after you use up your allotted time. Some online offerings are not covered by the flat rate and demand an additional surcharge. Everyone offers some sort of Internet access.

With new players like Microsoft on the scene—and the emergence of the Internet—rates have been changing fast. To find out what's current, contact the companies listed here for details.

Company	Phone Number
America Online/AOL	1-800-827-6364
CompuServe/CIS (a subsidiary of H&R Block)	1-800-848-8199
e-World (Apple Computer, Inc.)	1-800-776-2333
The Microsoft Network/MSN (The Microsoft Corporation)	1-800-426-9400
Prodigy (Prodigy Services Company)	1-800-PRODIGY

Curiouser and Curiouser

Q: I have a 14.4Kbps modem, but when I dial in to my online service, the connection is always much slower, like 2,400 baud. Is the modem broken?

A: No, the modem is probably fine, but the software you use to connect to your online service may not be properly configured. If the software is set up for a slower modem (the baud rate is probably set to 2,400) then you will send and receive information at the slower rate. Reconfigure your software and things should work just fine.

If that doesn't work, check to make sure you are dialing the correct access number. In some instances, a faster modem needs to use a different phone number than a slower modem. If you are using a slower line, you won't be able to connect at your modem's maximum speed.

Q: I think my online access software is old, but I have no idea what the version number is. Where can I find it?

A: You can find out which program version you are running by accessing the "About" option.

On a *PC compatible*, pull down the Help menu when the program in question is running. The last entry in the pull-down menu will say About...and the name of the program in question. When you select this option, the "About Box" appears, listing all the information you need.

On a *Macintosh compatible*, click on the Apple menu (in the upper-left corner) when the program in question is running. The first entry in the pull-down menu will say About...and the name of the program in question. When you select this option, the "About Box" appears, listing all the information you need.

Q: I'm afraid that if I subscribe to an online service, a virus will come down and destroy my machine. Are my fears warranted?

A: Not really. First, a virus can't download itself to your computer, so you don't have to worry about getting infected when you look away from your computer!

The more things you acquire from outside sources, though—downloading shareware, borrowing diskettes from friends—the higher the likelihood you'll get a virus. Viruses shouldn't deter you from getting online, though. If you plan on spending time online and sharing diskettes with friends and family, get a virus protection program.

Q: I have an account with an online service, but I forgot my password. What can I do?

A: Call the online service's customer support voice line. They'll ask you a question or two to make sure you are who you say you are and they will then reset your password. When they reset the password, be sure to change it to something you'll remember (and that no one else will know!).

Q: What's a BBS?

A: *BBS* is short for bulletin board service. There are thousands of bulletin boards all across the country. Individuals (or companies) will set up a computer as if it were an independent online service. You can call a BBS and get whatever information is available. Many times, a BBS is dedicated to providing information on one particular subject. Stamp collecting? Coin collecting? You can call up and see what's what.

To get on a BBS, you'll need different telecommunications software—like the telecommunications module provided in an integrated software program. The downside of a BBS? If you don't live near the BBS, the calls are almost always toll or long distance calls.

Q: I downloaded all of these images but I can't open them. None of my programs accommodates these formats. What are these file formats and how can I open these files?

A: Some file formats are specific to online services. GIFs, for example, are graphic files that may not be double-clickable (you can't open them with just any old program). To open a GIF, go into your online service software, pull down the File option and select the Open option. You can open GIF files in this way.

A Look
at E-Mail

Postal rates climb, more junk mail comes to your door, and the art and craft of letter writing fades. Have we lost touch with a kinder, gentler time?

What Is E-Mail?

Perhaps those times are fading, but if you have e-mail, you can do more than reminisce about days gone by. You can develop the art of digital correspondence. E-mail—short for electronic mail—is the ability to send a message to another person via computer. E-mail offers so much to so many users that if you aren't already using it, you'll kick yourself for not having learned about it sooner. If you are using it, you'll be happy to hear about features you perhaps were unaware of.

First, the bad news: *Not everyone who has e-mail can contact each other.* You may hear a friend or relative talk about e-mail at work or e-mail at the hospital, but you may not have access to those routes, so you may not be able to reach them at those places. Now, the good news: *Not everyone who has e-mail can contact each other!* Like an unlisted phone number, you may very well cherish your privacy and not want to hear from anybody and everybody. Like an unpublished phone number, your e-mail address is not readily accessible to others (it won't be "published" in your services online directory) unless you want it to be.

Here's some more good news: E-mail doesn't care about what kind of machine you are using. If you use a Macintosh, for example, you can still send messages to your friend in Anchorage who uses a PC compatible. Sending messages from Mac to PC and PC to Mac is not a problem.

Limitations: Rain, Sleet, and Dogs Not a Problem

E-mail correspondence doesn't have the same limitations the postal service has. E-mail doesn't care about the weather, e-mail doesn't care about dogs, and it doesn't care about the physical location of the person you are trying to reach out to. It also doesn't care about holidays—you can send on Christmas right after Midnight Mass, if you'd like. It's especially satisfying that there are no long lines to stand in, and most e-mail systems don't care about postage. Unless you are sending the e-mail by calling a long distance number, you are only paying the standard fees associated with the online service.

Note: **E-mail does have an Achilles heel: your fuse box. If you don't have power, you don't have e-mail!**

How to Send E-Mail

To send e-mail, you must first have online access, as provided by an online service company such as CompuServe, Prodigy, or America Online (AOL). All of these services provide extensive e-mail options. The Internet also provides mail services, described in Chapter 22.

Once you have access, sending e-mail is a breeze. E-mail options are always prominently displayed on the Menu screen and also in their own pull-down menu. To start, you need to open your online service software. To compose mail, which is what you are about to do, you don't even need to connect. From the Mail menu, select the Compose Mail or Create Mail option—something that indicates you are going to create new e-mail. Your first e-mail screen appears. Figure 21–1 shows the e-mail screen from America Online for composing a message.

The easiest way to begin? Send e-mail to...yourself! This is like sending yourself a postcard after moving: You get to see if the service is working the way it should.

To send yourself e-mail, enter your own address in the To field and a title in the Topic field. Type a few words in the large text area at the bottom of the screen. You're now ready to send yourself mail.

If your modem isn't on, turn it on. Click on the Send button on the e-mail screen and (if you aren't connected) you will automatically be connected and your mail will be sent. If you're already connected, your message will be sent instantly. When your message is sent, you'll get some notification that it has been transmitted successfully. Congratulations! You've just sent e-mail.

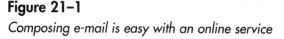

Figure 21-1

Composing e-mail is easy with an online service

Tip: **When you write e-mail, you do a lot better to write and compose "offline" (i.e., write *before* you connect). You don't pay any online charges while you write offline. This is a great option and a real moneysaver. To save more time, write your e-mail messages with your word processor and then cut and paste the message into the mail service.**

Return Address

When sending mail through a commercial online service, your identity is always known. If you send someone a note, they know who sent it—if it came from your account.

Finding People's Addresses

To send mail to other people, you are going to need their e-mail addresses. Typically, people online have nicknames or "handles." Depending on your service, you may have a numerical address. CompuServe subscribers, for example, have a numerical address assigned to them and you can't contact a person on CompuServe without that address.

If you know someone's address, you won't have any problems e-mailing them. You type in the address and it is automatically delivered. But what if you don't know the person's address? Well, you can call

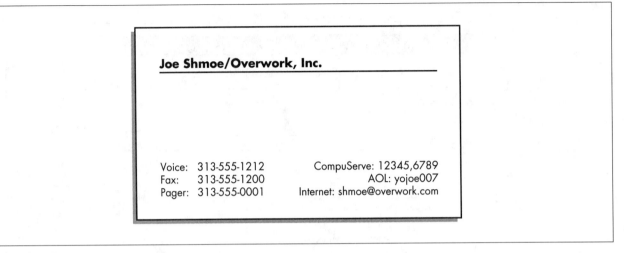

Joe Shmoe/Overwork, Inc.

Voice:	313-555-1212	CompuServe: 12345,6789
Fax:	313-555-1200	AOL: yojoe007
Pager:	313-555-0001	Internet: shmoe@overwork.com

Figure 21–2

Business cards reflect the new channels of communication. With all of the e-mail this person must have to manage, he probably isn't getting enough sun!

them and ask. You may have a business card, which nowadays prominently displays a person's online addresses, as shown in Figure 21–2. You can also write them and ask for their address. Better yet, you can do an online search.

To perform a search, locate the e-mail option for "Directory Search" or "Member Directory" and select it. If you aren't connected, it will automatically connect you (you have to be connected to do a search).

With AOL's directory, you can type in a name, a description—whatever you want—and it searches for members that meet your criteria and lists them for you, as shown in Figure 21–3. This figure's search was based on two key words, "veteran" and "retired."

Is this an invasion of privacy? No. Where did AOL get this information? From you!

AOL lets you "publish" a profile of yourself, a description that you compose. Your profile can include hobbies, age, marital status, favorite foods, whatever you want to tell people about yourself. When someone searches the member directory, they are searching through all of the profiles created by members. If you don't create a profile—and only you can create it and submit it—then your address is effectively "unlisted." No one can reach you unless they already know your address. One example of a profile is shown in Figure 21–4.

Note: **Online searches currently search only the service that you are using. If you perform a search while using CompuServe, only CompuServe's member directory is used.**

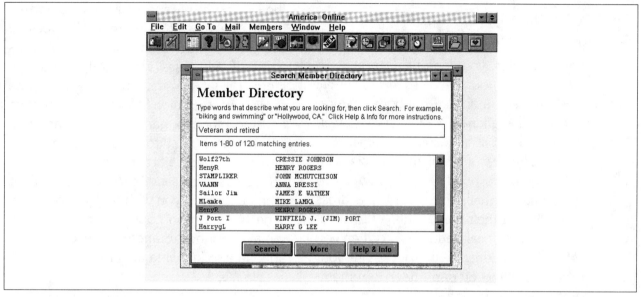

Figure 21–3

AOL can find all AOL members that meet your search criteria. Other online services provide a similar feature.

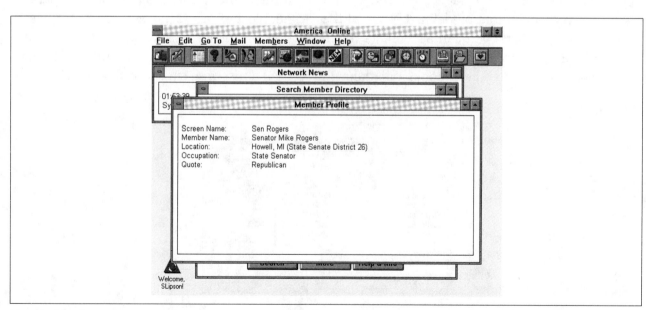

Figure 21–4

This profile is pretty businesslike—understandably—but yours can be as informal—and as revealing—as you wish

Addressing the Envelope

When you do find the addresses of friends and loved ones, you don't want to have to store them in your head, so every e-mail service gives you an address book feature. Your personal address book is always available to you and it contains the names and e-mail addresses of all of the people with whom you correspond. When you want to send someone mail, you open the address book, click on their name, and your "envelope" is automatically addressed. When you find a new address, you put it in your address book so you don't have to remember it or search for it again.

E-mail also offers you the option to create mailing groups. With a mailing group, you can write a message once and send it to everyone in that predefined group at the same time. And you can also create multiple mailing groups. You just select the people from your address book, put them in the list you want, and when you select that group the message automatically goes to everyone in that group. Figure 21-5 shows a list of addresses with groups included. Here, Bill's VFW hall buddies are on one mailing list, the union hall chums on another, and the pinochle gang crowd on another. The number next to the group indicates how many people are included.

You can also send "carbon copies" to as many people as you wish and you can even send blind carbon copies—a copy of your e-mail that goes to another person without anyone else knowing about it.

Acknowledging Mistakes

Mismailing something in cyberspace doesn't result in the return of a message unopened; people typically send e-mail to you based on your name. This means that your e-mail fan letter to Englebert Humperdink may elicit a response similar to this letter:

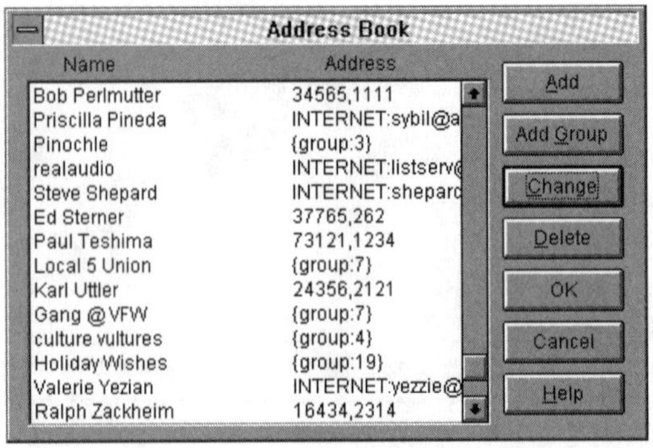

Address Book

Name	Address	
Bob Perlmutter	34565,1111	Add
Priscilla Pineda	INTERNET:sybil@a	Add Group
Pinochle	{group:3}	
realaudio	INTERNET:listserv@	Change
Steve Shepard	INTERNET:shepard	
Ed Sterner	37765,262	Delete
Paul Teshima	73121,1234	
Local 5 Union	{group:7}	OK
Karl Uttler	24356,2121	
Gang @ VFW	{group:7}	Cancel
culture vultures	{group:4}	
Holiday Wishes	{group:19}	Help
Valerie Yezian	INTERNET:yezzie@	
Ralph Zackheim	16434,2314	

Figure 21-5

An address book can include groups of people

Margaret,
Sorry, but you sent this to the wrong Humperdink! I'm living out here in Topeka with my wife, my 2 daughters, and 600 acres. Good luck with your project, though. Sounds interesting.... Bert H.

The only way an e-mail will get to you is if it is addressed to you, so don't feel bad when you open up a heartfelt letter that was mistakenly sent to the wrong "you."

Golden Rule:

When you get a mismailing, it helps the sender if you just drop a reply to let him or her know that their note was misdirected. Replying to a mismailing is a courtesy that everyone hopes everyone else will provide.

Certified and Registered Mail: E-Mail Receipts

When you send a real letter to someone, you don't know for the longest time whether or not they got it. If you need to verify that someone got your letter, you need to spend extra money and time to do so. Not so with e-mail—at least in most instances. With e-mail, depending on who your service provider is, you can get a receipt. When

the receiver opens your piece of mail, you are notified, so you know exactly when that person read your message. With America Online, for example, you get a Status window that tells you all about your messages; which ones have not been opened, which ones have been opened—and when they were opened. An AOL mail Status window is shown in Figure 21–6.

Communicating Between Services

It used to be impossible for an AOL person to communicate with a CompuServe person, but that limitation no longer exists. If you know someone on another online service, you can send a message to them as follows.

If you are from AOL, you send it to the numeric address with a period instead of a comma and the words compuserve.com at the end of it. For example,

12345.6789@compuserve.com

If you are sending from CompuServe to AOL, for example, you send it to:

INTERNET:furlong@aol.com

where *furlong* is the address of the person on AOL you want to contact.

Self to Self

Sending yourself e-mail is more than just an exercise in learning how to e-mail. Self-mailing can come in handy when you need a reminder about an important event. If you

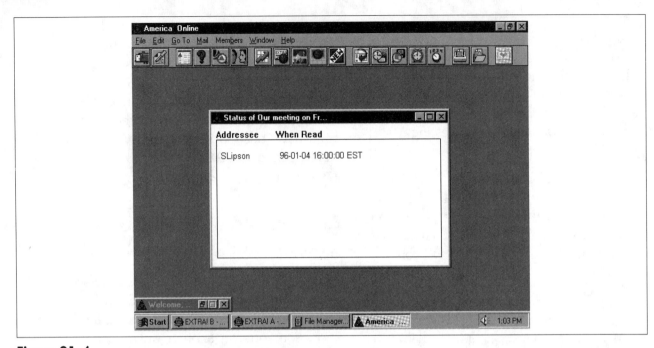

Figure 21–6

AOL gives you a summary listing of who's read what—mail, that is

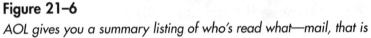

are traveling and you don't want to lose a diskette, you can send the info to yourself and retrieve it when you sit down at your travel destination. If you have an important file and you absolutely don't want to lose it, you can upload a copy to yourself. Even if your machine disappears tomorrow, you can still retrieve that file you uploaded.

E-Mail: Photos Enclosed: Do Not Bend

There *are* limitations to e-mail. For example, your e-mail message itself can't contain any frills. You can't use fancy fonts and you can't use bold, underline, or italics. Your e-mail message is composed of just ASCII text. (When you copy and paste information from your word processor to an e-mail message, only the ASCII text gets pasted.)

There is an easy workaround, though: you can include anything with your e-mail message as an "attachment." You can send digitized pictures, sounds, even big documents with all sorts of formatting.

If you want your pen pal to read your document as you intended it to appear—with all of the formatting intact—select the attachment feature. You will be prompted for the file name to attach and its location on your hard drive. Once you navigate to the file, double-click on it and a copy of it will be sent with your e-mail. The receiver is told that an attachment exists, downloads it, and voilà—pictures, sounds, and long formatted letters with e-mail!

 Alert: **Macintosh and PC users can send e-mail to one another, but attachments that are compressed with programs like *Stuffit* and *WinZip* can't be opened.**

E-Mail Vocabulary

Online communications, whether in e-mail, chat rooms, or bulletin boards, have developed their own vernacular. Here are a few ways to liven up your repartee and speak like a native.

Smiley Faces—a.k.a. Emoticons

Because it is difficult to convey emotion and jest in a few words, a collection of keyboard "faces" has evolved in e-mail. If you turn your head sideways to the left, :-) appears as a smiling face. Emoticons—smileys—typically appear at the end of a sentence to reinforce what was just said. There are hundreds of these little characters. Table 21–1 shows just a few of them.

Abbreviations and Acronyms

The computer industry, in its never-ending quest to keep some things impossible to understand—(:-1) smirk—has produced zil-lions of acronyms to make long, confusing terms into short confusing terms.

In what seems a bit of parody, e-mail writers and online communicators have come up with some very common—and funny—abbreviations for commonly used phrases. Table 21–2 shows some you'll invariably run into, and invariably start using.

Emoticon	Meaning
:-)	Smile
:)	Also a smile
:-D	Laughing
:-}	Grin
:-1	Smirk
:-(	Frown
:'-(	Crying
;-)	Wink
:'-)	Happy and crying
:-@	Screaming
:-&	Tongue-tied
:-\	Undecided
>:-<	Mad
:-o	Oh no!
:-X	Close-mouthed
8-)	Wide-eyed

Table 21–1
Some common emoticons you'll find in e-mail messages

Acronym	Meaning	Acronym	Meaning
AFAIK	As far as I know	BRB	Be right back
BTW	By the way	FAQ	Frequently asked questions
FYI	For your information	FWIW	For what it's worth
GD & R	Grinning, ducking, and running (*after a snide remark*)	GMTA	Great minds think alike
IMHO	In my humble opinion	IANAL	I am not a lawyer, but
IDK	I don't know	LOL	Laughing out loud
OTOH	On the other hand	PMFJI	Pardon me for jumping in
ROTFL	Rolling on the floor laughing	RTFM	Read the f*$&*** manual (*a rude way to tell you that you should look it up yourself*)
SOHF	Sense of humor failure	TIA	Thanks in advance
TPTB	The powers that be	TTFN	Ta ta for now
WRT	With respect to	WYSIWYG	What you see is what you get
YMMV	Your mileage may vary (*you may not have the same luck I did*)		

Table 21–2

Some acronyms and their meanings commonly encountered in e-mail

An Introduction to the Internet

> **"The surging popularity of the Internet is the most important single development in the computer industry since the IBM PC was introduced in 1981."**
>
> —Bill Gates, Founder and CEO, Microsoft Corporation

magine sending electronic mail to your children and grandchildren in Beijing. Or discussing your New Hampshire gardening problem with a landscaper in Australia. Or searching the contents of several university libraries without leaving home. All of this, and more, is possible when you get connected via the Internet.

The Internet is one of the fastest evolving phenomena in the history of computing. This global network of networks links people, countries, and communities together in amazing ways. It is not surprising to see an Internet address on TV (*http://www.fox.sports.com*, for example, during a football game) or a company's Internet address at the bottom of an advertisement in a popular magazine. Even at alumni reunions, as people exchange information, they often exchange Internet addresses. You will soon, if you don't already, have two identities and worlds—the one you keep "in person" and the one you keep in cyberspace. In the cyberspace world, you will be finding friends and colleagues that share common interests. Together or on your own, you can explore the constantly changing features of the online world.

Internet Defined

What exactly is the Internet? Simply put, the Internet is a collection of thousands of computer networks that are networked together. What's a computer network? A computer network occurs when two or more computers are connected to one another to share information.

The Internet is an enormous, constantly expanding, worldwide system of connected networks with literally millions of resources to explore. The rate of its growth is astounding. Sources estimate that the number of people accessing the Internet has doubled every year since 1988, and that 100 million will be online by 1998. As of 1996, half of all Internet users lived in the United States. The rest are in 100 countries. Twenty-two countries joined the Internet in 1995.

A few years ago, you couldn't find a book on the Internet. Now, there are hundreds and hundreds of titles about the Internet. Magazine racks are overflowing with new magazines devoted to the Internet and the online world.

The Internet is here to stay, to grow, and become an increasingly important part of our everyday life. And, as with everything else involving computers, Internet access will become easier and faster as time goes by.

The Internet changes daily, and that means that some sites and resources will evaporate, some will move, and many more new sites will become available. New Internet software is emerging and new technologies for the Internet are becoming available. In short, this chapter is merely a starting place for exploring the Internet. You will need to stay current with the changes in order to benefit fully from this amazing online phenomenon.

Why Would You Care About the Internet?

If you use a telephone, write letters, have hobbies, do research, find it difficult to get out much, or are just interested in what other people have to say, the Internet can and will change your life. People from almost every country on earth, of all ages and viewpoints, freely share their ideas, information, experiences, and opinions over the Internet. You have access to huge databases, whole libraries, museum collections, and esoteric journals. E-mail, certainly the most widely used service, allows you to exchange messages with millions of people around the world.

If you are, for example, particularly interested in the continuing debate over whether or not Shakespeare really wrote all those plays by himself, you can access the Oxford University library for all the latest academic papers. You can sign up for as many newsgroups—like electronic bulletin boards—as you wish on thousands of topics ranging from the seriously scientific to the totally inane. You can read the front page of the *Zambian Post* (one day late), get a detailed map of New Delhi, or read the *Wall Street Journal*. You can send your opinions on domestic and foreign policies directly to the White House. You can download thousands of programs, graphics, sounds, and text files, all for free. You can even create your own "page," a place where people can learn about—you! And last, but not least, you can have lots of fun just exploring.

Exploring the Internet is similar to exploring AOL, MSN, or CompuServe, except it's a whole lot bigger, a lot meatier, and a whole lot more unruly. The Internet is fascinating, stimulating, and thought-provoking. It is also silly, irreverent, and mundane. In short, the Internet is a good portion of the world brought to you electronically.

Internet Origins

In 1969, the Defense Department started a project called ARPANET as an experiment in networking military research contractors, universities, and laboratories. The thinking was that research would go much faster if all the investigators could communicate and share results with each other electronically. In addition, the military was concerned about losing communication in the event of an enemy attack. The Defense Department needed a system that was decentralized—a network that would still remain operative even if an attack rendered part of the network inoperable. The network was not so large at first, but more and more universities got connected. Eventually, the network was divided in two: MILNET, which had the military sites; and ARPANET, for nonmilitary sites. These two networks remained connected by way of the Internet protocol (IP). The IP is the protocol that allows any computer connected to the Internet to communicate with other computers on the Internet.

Today, the Internet (the successor to ARPANET) consists of a federally funded network tied to thousands of subnetworks. No government controls the Internet and there is no central overseer or administrator. The networks on the Internet share a common set of standards for addressing and transmitting messages, but the contents and information are wholly unregulated.

E-Mail on the Net

E-mail, as discussed in the last chapter, is also very popular on the Internet. In fact, it's the Internet mail system that allows you to send mail from AOL to CompuServe to Prodigy; when you send a message between online services, you send it via the Internet.

E-Mail Addresses

Like online services, people on the Internet have e-mail addresses. Every address has several parts. The first part is your personal name, or screen name. How you are identified in the first part of the address depends primarily on how you are connected to the Internet. An Internet address is more complicated than an online service address, but an Internet address can actually tell you something about the sender.

Separating the first part of your address from the second and third parts is the @ symbol, translated and pronounced as "at." The second part is the *domain name*, which is usually the name of the computer your mail is routed through. And the third part is called the *top-level domain*. So, if the address reads: *Furlong@aol.com, aol* is the routing computer and *com*—short for "company"—is the top-level domain. Domain names tell you a lot about a message's origin. Here is a list of Internet top-level domains you are likely to encounter:

Top-Level Domain	Meaning
.com	Business *(largest group on the Internet)*
.org	Nonprofit organization
.net	Network
.gov	Government
.edu	School or university *(second largest group)*
.mil	Military site

An address may also identify geographic location. Countries other than the United States have two-letter top-level domain names, and here are a few of those you might see:

Top-Level Domain	Country
.uk	United Kingdom
.au	Australia
.jp	Japan
.de	Germany (for Deutschland)
.ca	Canada
.fi	Finland (more Finns per capita are online than anywhere in the world)
.il	Israel

Once you're on the Internet, you can obtain a country's two-letter domain name by contacting the Internet Society at isco@isoc.org.

E-Mail, Usenet, and Newsgroups

Usenet is that segment of the Internet populated with newsgroups. There are many thousands of newsgroups on the Internet, which discuss many thousands of topics. Newsgroups are organized into categories, called hierarchies, which help define the content of the newsgroup. The name of each newsgroup is composed of several sections, separated by dots, to indicate the newsgroup's position in a particular hierarchy, as in *rec.sport.football.college*. The first part of the name is the hierarchy to which the newsgroup belongs. Here are the names of the Usenet hierarchies:

Hierarchy	Significance
comp	Topics about computers (the largest and oldest hierarchy)
rec	Recreation, sports, humor, entertainment industry, fun stuff
news	For newsies who even CNN can't satisfy
soc	Topics about social issues (exchange of ideas)
sci	Sciences of all kinds, for everyone from the hobbyist to professional

talk	Discussions or arguments (a great place to vent)
misc	Topics that don't fit in any of the other hierarchies

Starting a new newsgroup requires an application to Usenet and a vote by prospective readers. As a result, some of the more interesting (but unofficial) newsgroups begin with the hierarchy name of *alt* for *alternative*. These are general interest groups that range from staid, moderated groups to the raw, unedited postings of the fringe. Here is a small sample of some official and unofficial Usenet newsgroups:

Newsgroup	Topics
comp.bbs.misc	About BBSs (computer bulletin boards)
rec.boats	Boating
sci.space	Discussions of space programs and research
soc.culture.french	Issues regarding France and the French people
talk.Libertarian	Discussion of the Libertarian Party
misc.invest	Investments and the stock market
alt.peeves	Complaints and pet peeves

Alert: **Newsgroups appear that may have shocking content, shocking titles, or both. Many of the titles are meant to shock, so don't take the bait. If you aren't interested and/or you are easily offended, don't explore them.**

Usenet Abuse

The huge popularity of Usenet and newsgroups has resulted in problems that have frustrated many users. The most well-known abuse of the Usenet is called "spamming," the posting of the same message to hundreds of newsgroups. People post advertisements, illegal pyramid schemes, solicitations, and other annoying messages to lots of different newsgroups, hoping for responses. Most people get very irritated at receiving these messages. Although there is no written law on the Internet against this sort of "advertising"—the Internet doesn't really have any written laws—advertising or soliciting is forbidden and is typically met with a harsh response from other *netizens* (slang for citizens of the Internet).

E-Mail and Mailing Lists

If you like getting mail, then you're really going to love mailing lists. It is possible, with very little effort, to ensure a full mailbox of something like 400-500 messages a day. All you have to do is join a few mailing lists.

A mailing list has an address to which members [of the list] post messages. Each message is delivered to each member of the list. Members can reply to each message, and the reply is delivered to all other members. Thus, you have an ongoing discussion on whatever the topic of the mailing list happens to be. The major distinction between newsgroups and mailing lists is the method in which the messages are retrieved. Newsgroups require the reader to call up the newsgroup and read new messages; mailing list messages come directly to your mailbox.

There are thousands of mailing lists available. Some mailing lists require subscribers to participate beyond just reading messages. For example, one mystery book mailing list requires that each subscriber submit a book review of a recently published mystery in order to get on the list. In contrast, some lists don't allow subscribers to post messages at all. One such mailing list just sends out—on a monthly basis—a list of new chocolate recipes culled from sources on the Internet.

Tip: **When you subscribe to a mailing list, be sure you know how to unsubscribe. Being on an unwanted mailing list can waste a lot of your time if you have to keep sorting through unnecessary messages delivered to your e-mail address.**

Internet Infamy: Lawyers Abuse the System

Laurence Canter and Martha Siegel are two Phoenix lawyers who have carved out an unenviable niche for themselves in Internet history; they were effectively banned from the Internet for *spamming*—posting an advertisement to thousands of newsgroups to drum up business for their Immigration Law practice.

Internet natives were mortified; the act was online blasphemy, yet Canter and Siegel were unrepentant. They felt it was their constitutional right to send the messages they sent. They even claimed their messages generated over $100,000 in new business.

Netizens responded swiftly and with considerable ferocity: All messages originating from Canter and Seigel were intercepted and destroyed. Their fax machine was swamped by a flood of dummy calls, effectively disabling their machine. Their service provider was also deluged, and cut off Canter and Seigel's service. Canter and Seigel were outraged. They went to another service provider who offered them the same [dis]courtesy.

Aside from being *persona non grata* on the Internet, Canter and Siegel have published a (terrible) get-rich-quick book that describes the merits of "advertising" on the Internet. Robert Metcalfe, the founder of 3COM and the inventor of EtherNet, termed the book "evil" and suggested in his *PC Week* magazine column that readers "shouldn't even buy it to burn it."

The trick with mailing lists is to sample a mailing list before you subscribe. If you are too indiscriminate in picking lists, you will be inundated with mail you have no interest in reading, and you'll spend lots of time deleting messages from your mailbox. Aside from that caveat, mailing lists are a wonderful means of exchanging ideas and information with people. Whatever your interests, you are certain to find mailing lists and people on them that will intrigue you.

> ### Golden Rule:
>
> Obey the rules of netiquette on the Internet. Although you may feel at times like you've stumbled into some sort of space alien saloon with no rules of order, your contribution to civility helps set the tone.

Getting to the Internet

There are basically two ways to connect to the Internet. By far the easiest method is via an online service like AOL, CompuServe, MSN, or Prodigy. An established service can provide you with an attractive, graphical interface, suggest interesting sites, manage your e-mail, simplify your travels, and give you easy access to newsgroups and mailing lists. In return, you pay them for all the time you spend connected to the service. It's the easiest way to go, but it can be very

hard on your credit card, since one hour a day on such a service can end up costing you [easily] $75 a month in service charges.

Tip: **Using an online service is the way to go if you are new to the Internet or if you spend only limited time connected to the Internet. Online services provide free technical support, so if you are having problems accessing the Internet or are confused by the process, help is always available.**

Internet Via an Online Service: The Easy Way

Connecting to the Internet through an online service is easy. Services such as CompuServe and AOL offer Internet access as just another option on their Main menus. For example, clicking on the Internet Connection button on the AOL main menu provides you with the Internet menu, as shown in Figure 22–1.

Basic Internet Options

The options displayed here—Gopher, WAIS, and the World Wide Web—are search options that help you find things on the Internet. FTP stands for file transfer protocol, and is the program necessary to download files from the Internet. AOL and other services make access and navigation of the Internet easier because they give you fast access to the basic tools you need to get around on the Internet. Here's a look at some of those tools.

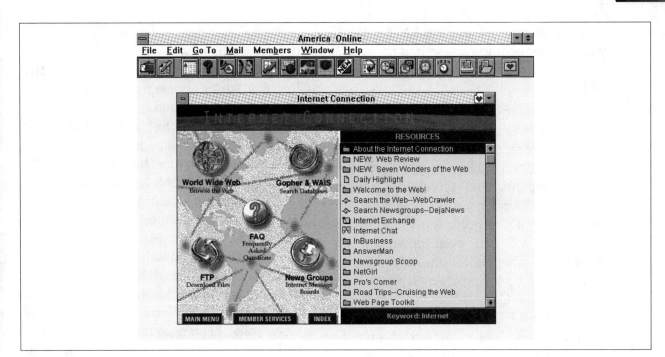

Figure 22-1

Access to the Internet is easy when you do it via an established online service

Gopher

Gopher is a search engine—a tool to help you search for and retrieve files from the Internet. Gopher searches by looking from menu to menu, from computer to computer. The original Gopher was developed at the University of Minnesota in 1991. It is probably not a coincidence that the mascot of the university is a gopher. Nevertheless, Gopher "tunnels" from one computer to the next, and from one menu to the next.

Although gopher has been somewhat eclipsed by the World Wide Web, it is still the most efficient way to search large databases such as the U.S. Census Bureau.

WAIS

WAIS (pronounced to rhyme with "raise") stands for Wide Area Information Service. WAIS can be more effective than Gopher because it is able to locate a file based on its contents, not just its title. WAIS is actually a database of keywords based on file contents. You don't need to know the name of the file you want, you just need to be able to describe it well enough for WAIS to locate it. Most of the time, when you call up a Gopher server, you'll see a WAIS option. However, WAIS is not very user friendly, and all the information accessible by WAIS is also available to Gopher and the World Wide Web, so it's likely you will only want to use WAIS when a more complex search is required.

FTP

The file transfer protocol is an Internet utility that lets you collect files from the Internet and place them on your hard drive. There are thousands of files, graphics, games, fonts, programs, and sounds out on the Internet waiting for you to download and use. In fact, if you go to the White House FTP site, you can even download the President's schedule for the day. Impress your friends by telling them who's having lunch with the Commander in Chief today.

If you use FTP, you will find that many archives are mirrored, which means the files are stored on both the original server—an information repository—and on one or more additional server sites. This allows more people to access the file at the same time. If you want to download files and there are several mirrors for the server, choose the less active one. Chances are it will take less time to transmit the file.

On Your Own: A Direct Connection to the Internet

Exploring the Internet can be an expensive proposition if you do your exploring via one of the commercial online services. It isn't difficult to spend 20 or more hours a month just having fun poking around or accessing newsgroups and mailing lists. Getting your own direct connection is the best remedy for this situation. There is a growing number of Internet service providers (ISPs) who can provide you with a local phone number to access the Internet. An ISP is like a regular online service except much smaller, usually local, and intended only for Internet access. Most charge a flat fee per month (between $15 and $30). Some are big, national ISPs, while others serve only a limited area.

A direct connection is often harder to set up. A direct connection requires additional software and a lot more perseverance. There are canned solutions—like the various Internet kits that provide all the software you need plus instructions on how to set things up. Some starter kits have CDs, some have diskettes; they each may include different versions of the same software or entirely different software. If you're new to this world, though, it all seems like so much mumbo jumbo.

Alert: **Some starter kits claim to provide software for "instant access" to the Internet. Unfortunately, they don't say how much that particular service will cost you, or if access will require a toll call. Unless you have already done research and know the per month cost of the service provided, be careful of buying a starter kit that ties you into one service provider.**

Finding an Internet Service Provider (ISP)

If you aren't going to use an online service like AOL or CompuServe, you'll need to find an Internet service provider (ISP). How do you find a good service provider? A recommendation from a friend is always good, but failing that, you'll have to do some research. Talk to folks at the local user groups, talk to someone at your nearby computer store, and look through Internet-specific magazines.

 Alert: **Don't go with any service until you have communicated with at least one person who uses that service. If you're already on AOL, MSN, or some other provider, get on the appropriate message board and ask others for their experiences. From there, make a list of possible providers, then get on the phone and start the screening process. Tell the provider what kind of computer and modem you have, and then ask these questions:**

- **Do you provide software? What software do you recommend?**

- **What are the monthly fees? Are there additional fees? Activation fees?**

- **Is there a set number of "free" hours of access that my monthly fee covers?**

- **Can you give me a local phone number? What is that phone number?**

- **Will you help me configure my software once I have installed it?**

- **What are the cancellation rules? Are there penalties?**

By the time you finish asking these questions, you should have a fairly good idea of how helpful each of the providers might be. Cross out the ones who seem too impatient to answer your questions. Circle those that answer your questions and are helpful with their suggestions.

 Alert: **A "local" access number may still be a toll call that will generate colossal phone bills. To guarantee that the call is "free," dial the operator and ask if the number is toll free when called from your exchange. If you can't get a toll-free number with a particular provider, seek another service provider.**

The World Wide Web (WWW or 3W)

Every time you open the newspaper or turn on the TV, you see something like, "Find us on the World Wide Web at http://www.toocool.com" or "Come visit our web site at http://www.evencooler.com." Thanks to its ease of use, interactivity, and commercial potential, the Web has been hailed by some as the single most important computer publishing advance since the development of online publishing. Others feel it's the greatest time-waster since the advent of video games. A more reasoned assessment? It's a measure of both.

What is the Web?

The WWW is another system for accessing information on the Internet. It started in 1989 at the European Center of Particle Physics in Geneva (known by its French acronym, CERN) as a way for scientists to publish documents over the Internet. The Web links one Internet site to another with *hypertext links*. With hypertext links, you click on words in a passage and jump to a new location where more information on that topic is provided. On the Web, hypertext is better defined as hypermedia; you can click on an image as well as a word and make a similar jump.

Eventually, Web publishers began creating their documents using something called *Hypertext Markup Language* (HTML), the lingua franca of the Web. HTML allows publishers to design documents using text, graphics, audio, and video.

The Web continued to slowly expand until 1993, when programmers at the University of Illinois' National Center for Supercomputing Applications released *Mosaic*, a free software program that let people access the Web without knowing much about computers. This was the defining moment for the Web (and the Internet), since it made the vast array of resources available to a largely nontechnical audience. You no longer needed strong technical skills or a computer background to take advantage of what the Web offered.

What is UNIX?

As you become more familiar with the Internet, you'll invariably hear the term UNIX—a technical term that is pronounced the same as Cleopatra's "neutered" servants (you have to wonder about computer professionals).

UNIX is a network operating system that is used by universities and research facilities. Developed in the 1960s at the legendary Bell Laboratories, it was designed for "multitasking"—doing several different things (for multiple users) simultaneously. As the preeminent operating systems for large networks, it is used by many companies, universities, and organizations—and the Internet.

There are versions of UNIX available for desktop computers, but it is not intended for typical home users; UNIX is oriented for technical people and is not graphically based.

Browsing the Web

Hand in hand with the growth of the Web has been the growth in the number of *browsers* for Web travelers. A browser is the interface you use to access and navigate the Web.

Mosaic was the original browser, and that has been met with a number of other similar—and competing—products, most notably *Netscape Navigator* from Netscape Communications. Like any piece of software, these products differ in the features they offer, their ease of use, and their price.

Note: **NCSA's *Mosaic* is available free on the Internet, but you have to already have access to the Internet and have enough Internet savvy to know how to download it. If you want a free browser to get started, call your user group; you can bet they will have free software and utilities available for navigating the Internet.**

The major national online services all provide browsers. The America Online browser is called WebCrawler, Compu-Serve calls its browser NetLauncher (which is actually a version of *Mosaic*), and MSN offers the Internet Explorer.

What is a URL?

To successfully navigate the Web, you need to know about URLs. The string of punctuation and letters is the universal resource locator (URL). A URL (pronounced "You Are Ell") is an address used to locate a site or document on the Web. If you know a site's URL, you can go directly to it by entering the URL in the address field and pressing RETURN. For instance, if you want to access the White House, enter **http:// www.whitehouse.gov/**. The URL for CNN is http://www.cnn.com/, and the URL for the Vatican Museum is http://www.chris-tusrex.org/wwwl/vaticano/O-Musei.html/. Sure, you have to type a lot, but did you ever think you would be able to view the art at the Vatican on your own computer?

Browser Features

A good browser should make navigating the Internet easy. Browsers vary in quality and in the number of features they offer. Most have "What's New" and "Explore the Web" sections that will point you to easy-to-use resources. They also provide search engines, some better and faster than others.

Netscape: Wall Street Darlings

James Clark, founder of Silicon Graphics and also Netscape Communications, had a vision: he saw what the Internet could be. Leaving Silicon Graphics, he hired five of the six designers of NCSA's *Mosaic* and has led the revolution in providing access to the Internet.

Clark wasn't the only one with vision: Wall Street was watching too. When Netscape Communications went public, the stock soared from $22 to over $70 on the first day. While many were sure the stock was artificially high and predicted it would plummet, it has since soared past the $150 mark, making James Clark an overnight billionaire.

Documents on the World Wide Web are commonly referred to as "pages." Traveling from Web page to Web page rarely follows any logical pathway—you can bounce from a university to a food company to an art museum—and the addresses are often difficult to remember. To make things easier, a good browser creates a list of all of the places you have visited during a session, so if you want to return to a particular site, you can look at the list, find the name of the place you wish to return to, and click on it.

You'll jump there instantly without having to retrace your steps through the labyrinth.

You can also save addresses for use in later sessions. When you find a place you know you'll want to return to, the browser lets you "mark" the location for access at any time—not just during the current session. You can "save your place" on the Web and create a list of your own favorite sites. The list of personal favorites is usually referred to in the software as the Hot List, Favorite Places, Personal Favorites, or Bookmarks section.

Tip: **Speed—or a lack of it—may prove frustrating when trying to explore the Web. If you want to speed things up (with or without a fast modem), your browser lets you filter out graphics, a major cause of slow transmissions. The display won't look nearly as inviting, but your speed increase will let you poke around in a lot more places.**

Up Close and Personal with a Browser

Figure 22–2 shows what a browser looks like. The buttons at the top of the page allow you to go back to the previous page, reload a page, go forward a page, see your file of favorite places, set preferences such as "no graphics," go to the home page (the equivalent of a table of contents or starting page), get help, and stop loading a page.

Searching the Web

If you are interested in a specific topic and are tired of double-clicking around hoping

you'll find it, there are some efficient ways of finding things on the Internet. All browsers have a search capability, some faster and better than others.

There are also some good search engines available on the Web that are more powerful than most browsers. Although they all have different features, the basics are the same. When you call up one of these search engines, you see a search form. Enter one or more keywords that describe your topic of interest and submit the search as instructed. Selecting the best keywords is the critical aspect of an efficient search. You need to select a keyword or keywords broad enough to get most of the information you want, but narrow enough to exclude unnecessary information. Remember to conduct separate searches for synonyms, as in "cat" and "feline." You will probably get additional sites to choose from if you do.

The search engine then looks for items that match your keyword and returns a list of sites to you. If you are not satisfied with the results, try another search engine. Every search engine searches in a different manner, and efficient searching may require some practice. If you have difficulty narrowing the search for exactly what you want, try reading the "Helpful Hints" that accompany the search engines. They can save you lots of time.

A Web Page of Your Own

A web page is your opportunity to publish on the Web. Who makes web pages? These days, just about everybody. Artists, photog-

Figure 22–2

Netscape Communications offers the most popular—and most powerful—browser out there

raphers, and writers create home pages to gain a wider audience for their work. Businesses, both large and small, create web pages to generate P.R., and organizations, from the Sierra Club to the American Cancer Society, set up web pages to spread their messages and to disseminate information. Governments, from a small-town city council to the executive branch, create web pages to inform and encourage business and tourism. Even individuals with nothing to sell and no cause to espouse create web pages just for fun.

If you think you might like to set up your own web page, the first thing to do is look at a lot of web pages. Look at how they are

put together and make note of what you like and don't like about each one. Next, work out the design and content of your page on paper. Think about what graphics you want to include and what other sites you might want to link to your page.

Now, the hard part (or fun part, depending on your interests)—translating your page into HTML. If you are interested in seeing what HTML looks like, some browsers have a feature called "Source," which will show you the page in HTML format.

The easiest way to translate your page is pay someone to do it for you. However, some online services, like Prodigy and America Online, will help you to publish your own page and do the translating for you. Failing that, there are plenty of services out there who will create your page, find or provide a server on which to park it, and maintain your page if you want changes. Naturally, costs vary widely. Your best bet, though, is to start with a freebie: If you subscribe to AOL or Prodigy, they will let you do a web page for free. Free is good, especially when you're just experimenting.

The harder way is to create the home page yourself, although it is not as difficult as you may think. There are several very good "authoring tools" (also known as editors) available as shareware that are reasonably easy to use. There are even plug-in authoring tools for Microsoft Word and Novell's WordPerfect. If you enjoy tinkering at your computer, you'll want to create a web page.

As with any other part of the Internet, publishing on the Internet is undergoing rapid changes. If you are interested in publishing on the Web, you'll need to stay informed. Fortunately, all the information is out there—in magazines, in books, and on the Web itself. All you have to do is look.

The Future of Online Services

We know the Internet is growing rapidly, but growing into what? The Internet is fast becoming the global electronic marketplace and the resources available are dizzying. E-mail will continue to expand and be part of daily life for more and more people. Corporations will become increasingly dependent upon it for conducting business.

There is one clear trend, however. The commercial online services recognize their real competition is not with each other, but with the Internet. Since competition has historically meant good news for the consumer, we can only assume that the Internet's influence will benefit us all. The successful commercial services will provide better reliability, more speed, and lower costs.

Regardless of whether or not the Internet becomes a massive global marketplace, it will certainly continue to grow and serve as an amazing vehicle for communication between people throughout the world.

Taking in the Sites: A Tour of the Web

You'll certainly come up with your own favorite list of Web sites, but to get you started, here's a quick tour of some very interesting—and popular—sites.

The White House

No introduction needed here. You can send your message directly to the White House— and keep up-to-date on Executive news of the day—from your desktop. Figure 22–3 shows the White House Web Page (http://www.whitehouse.gov/).

The Smithsonian Institute

If you visited the White House Web Page, why not [virtually] do some sightseeing at The Smithsonian? The Smithsonian Home

Page, shown in Figure 22–4, gives you access to several different branches of the organization (http://www.si.edu/).

Aside from the National Museum of History (that boasts the Hope diamond as one of its exhibits), The Smithsonian also includes the Arthur M. Sackler Gallery, and The Air and Space Museum.

San Jose Mercury News

It should come as no surprise that Silicon Valley's best newspaper should also offer an impressive presence on the Internet. Figure 22–5 shows the *Merc*'s Web site (http://www.sjmercury.com/main.html).

 Tip: **If you have kids who are interested in getting a computer-related job in Silicon Valley, point them to the *San Jose Mercury News* online classifieds. There are tons of job listings and searching is easy.**

Alzheimer's

If you are living with or know anyone affected by Alzheimer's disease, check out the Institute for Brain Aging and Dementia Web site, as shown in Figure 22–6 (http://teri.bio.uci.edu/dement.html).

SeniorNet

SeniorNet has an ever-growing presence on the Web. Figure 22–7 shows Senior-Net's Web site (http://seniornet.org/).

MIT Media Lab

The Massachusetts Institute of Technology Media Lab is considered the foremost research facility into all things, well, Media. The Media Lab's Web site, shown in Figure 22–8, always has something interesting to offer (http://www.1010.org/).

Project Gutenberg

There's a movement afoot to get all of the great literary works—those in the public domain, anyway—online. Project Gutenberg is that "library." Figure 22–9 shows the Project's Web site (http://cso.uiuc.edu/PG/welcome.html/).

The MIT Postcard Post Office

Nobody ever said the Internet wasn't fun. With MIT's postcard post office (Figure 22–10) you can send an e-mail postcard to a friend. There are many cards to choose from.

When you send a card to someone, they get a receipt, and proceed to the MIT Post Office window (online). They present their mail receipt and the "clerk" gives them your card (http://postcards.www.media@mit.edu/postcards/).

Progressive Networks— RealAudio

Want to listen to National Public Radio via your modem? How about ABC News? Progressive Networks makes this possible, and several companies are offering

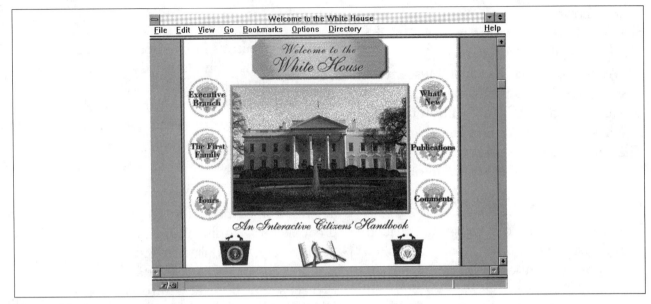

Figure 22-3

Whatever your political views, the White House Web Page gives you access to the big house from your own house

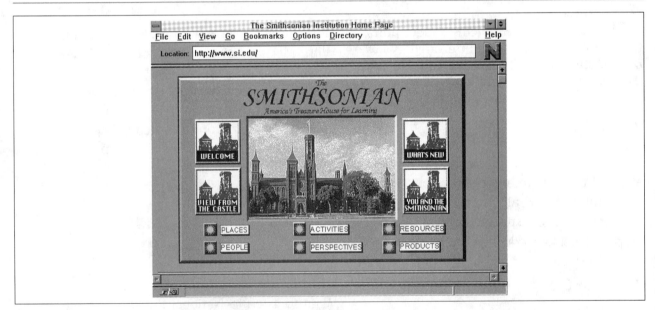

Figure 22-4

The Smithsonian offers access to several different museums, including the National Museum of History and the Air and Space Museum

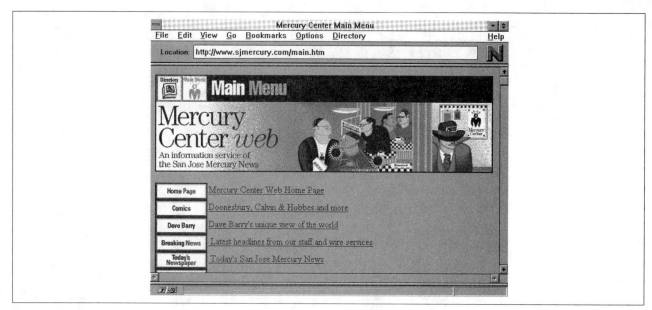

Figure 22–5

The San Jose Mercury News*: A great paper and a great Web site*

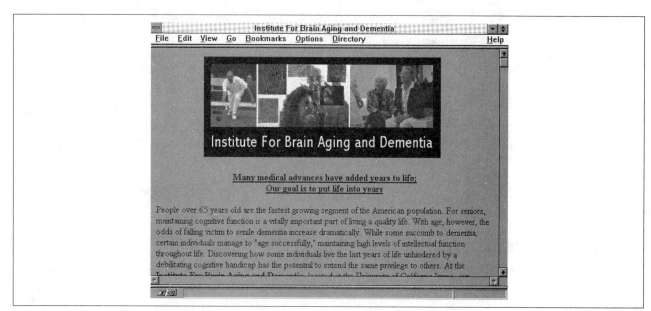

Figure 22–6

There is a wealth of information—and a good support system—for families who are affected by Alzheimer's

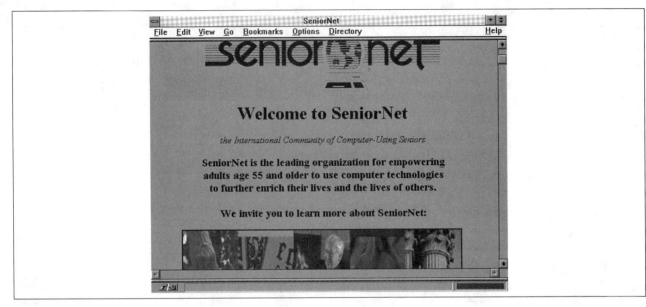

Figure 22-7

SeniorNet's Web Page is your gateway to resources and information of interest to older adults

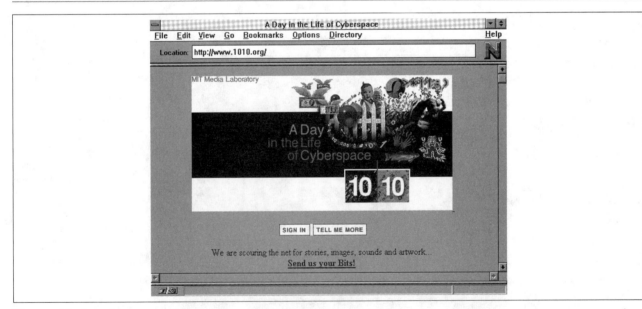

Figure 22-8

MIT's Media Lab is the academic version of the Bauhaus—always reaching for new ways to express and communicate

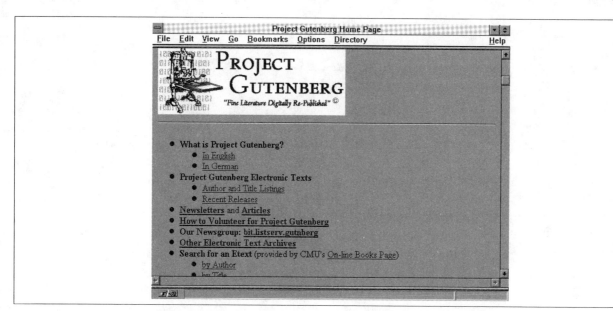

Figure 22–9

The Project Gutenberg expects to have hundreds of great books online in the coming years

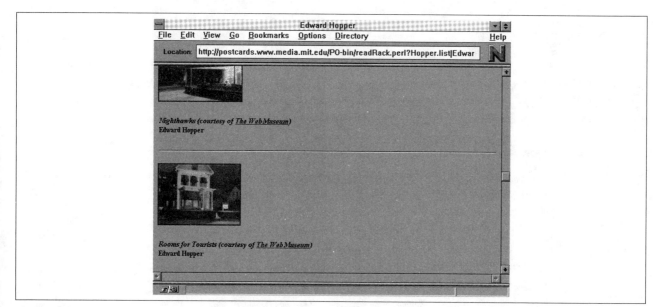

Figure 22–10

Send a nice postcard to a friend: "Greetings from the Net—wish you were here!"

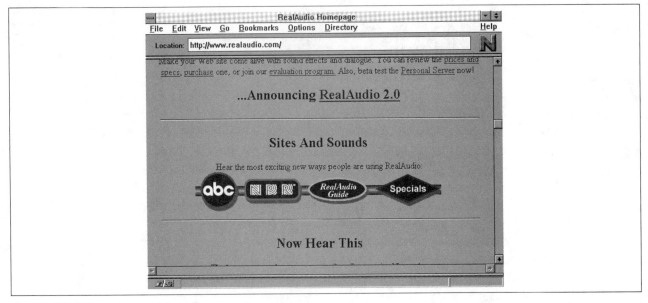

Figure 22–11

With RealAudio, you can call up NPR's "Morning Edition," "Talk of The Nation" or other shows and select whatever segment you wish to listen to—when you want to listen to it

Figure 22–12

You can visit the Exploratorium—San Francisco's premier science museum—on the Web.

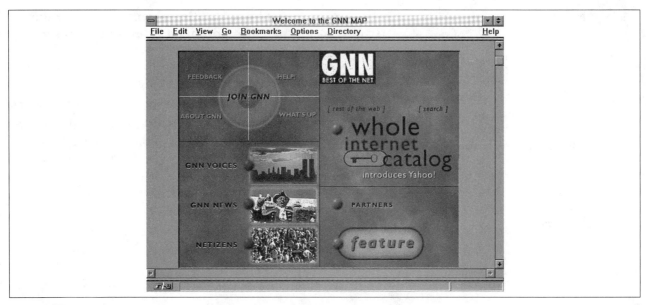

Figure 22-13
Global Network Navigator *offers a wide array of features and interesting content*

Figure 22-14
SGI, the company founded by James Clark before he left to start Netscape Communications, has an excellent Web Page—even if some of the material may be a bit heady

"Internet broadcasts." Figure 22–11 shows the Progressive Networks Web site (http://www.realaudio.com/).

 Alert: **RealAudio currently has some pretty hefty hardware requirements—including a minimum of a 14.4Kbps modem. If you can't get any audio results, it's probably because you need a faster computer.**

The Exploratorium

Here's one of the best science museums anywhere in the world—and with a great Web Page, too. Figure 22–12 shows the

Censorship on the Net

Of course, with any revolutionary (or evolutionary) step in communications, you can't be surprised by the accompanying clamor regarding what exactly is communicated. Led by Senator James Exon, a bill is being proposed to "crack down" on those communications deemed "inappropriate."

Much of the bill hopes to put the service providers in the role of network cops, ensuring that what is sent through their systems is not pornographic or illegal. In many ways, this is like making your postman or postal worker responsible for what individuals send through the mail. Not surprisingly, many who best understand the world of online communications are against this sort of regulation, while politicians with little or no experience are anxious to gain favor by casting the Internet as something it is not. Aside from a seriously flawed—and now widely discredited—*Newsweek* article about the availability of pornography on the Internet, the fears are largely unfounded. Many parents cite the violent nature of broadcast television and the wide sponsorship and acceptance of same as reason to be at least a little accepting of a medium that is far more democratic in its design than broadcast TV.

Of course, censorship, applied with such a wide brush, has a profound impact on the community.

Computers—and the Internet—open a new channel of communication that governments neither understand nor control—even with censorship.

Exploratorium's site (http://www.exploratorium.edu/default.html/).

GNN—*Global Network Navigator*

A product of O'Reilly & Associates, the *Global Network Navigator* should be on your "best of" list. Figure 22–13 shows the *Global Network Navigator's* Home Page. It is an excellent source for all things Internet (http:/gnn.com/).

Silicon Graphics

The final step on our quick tour of interesting sites on the World Wide Web is Silicon Graphics, the company that makes the computers used to create all of those special effects in movies produced or directed by George Lucas and Steven Spielberg. Their site, shown in Figure 22–14, is worth visiting, even if just to see how the other half (maybe the other .5 percent) live (http://sgi.com/).

The World
of SeniorNet

> "We don't stop playing because we grow old. We grow old because we stop playing."
>
> —Mary Furlong

Online services and the Internet have proven to be an excellent tool for the exchange and dissemination of information. With a computer, a modem, and a phone line, you have access to the knowledge base of hundreds of universities and research facilities around the world.

The SeniorNet "Connection"

Online services—and the channels of communication that they provide—serve an even more important purpose; they enable communities to form, not based on race or geography or socioeconomic standing, but on the emotional, moral, and personal needs of individuals. Online communities, like SeniorNet, allow members to enjoy and embrace a sense of common being and mutual understanding. By connecting electronically, in a way never before possible, members of SeniorNet and other online communities transcend physical and geographic limitations.

What is SeniorNet?

SeniorNet really started in San Francisco in 1983 as a small research endeavor. The study was intended to show whether older adults were interested in or could benefit from the use of computer technology. Not surprisingly—*at least not to seniors*—the research showed that older adults were *very* interested in this new technology and could benefit greatly from it.

The Voice Of SeniorNet

SeniorNet was founded in 1984, but its charter and mission can't convey the organization's heart and soul the way its members can:

"I have been pretty much stuck at home since my disabilities became too severe to do otherwise. I was beginning to feel ostracized or out of the world as if everyone considered me dead already. SeniorNet is not just a 'playpen,' it is a serious place of social interaction that allows one to climb out of the well of self-pity and share your views and feelings with others. You can help others and get help yourself. Yes! I am also having fun! It's like getting out of jail."

"I'm a gardener and a fisherman. I treasure the ability to connect to people who have been struggling with my questions about earwigs, squash rot, bottom rigs, etc. What a font of wisdom, all nicely collected in one place in Cyberville. It's like the electronic barber shop or tavern."

"How it pleases me to be able to talk 'computerese' with my grandson. Computers run this world and I felt like the world was leaving me behind. That's what got me into computers, but it's the way my computer has expanded my world that keeps me at it. I really can't imagine living without a computer again."

Today, SeniorNet is a thriving nonprofit organization with over 17,000 members. SeniorNet publishes a quarterly newsletter, and has established over 75 Learning Centers throughout the United States. Thousands of seniors participate in SeniorNet online via America Online, the Microsoft Network, and the World Wide Web. The continuing mission of SeniorNet is to help older adults gain access to and learn about computer technologies so that they can share their knowledge and wisdom with society and with each other.

What SeniorNet Provides

SeniorNet is a facilitator. The organization provides information and instruction on how to access and use computer technology, but it also provides people. These people help answer questions such as "How do I go online?" or "Why would I use a computer?" They help those seniors who think computer technology may not be for them.

They help you get over any technical hurdles so you can take advantage of what computing really offers. As soon as you send that first e-mail message to your grandchildren, produce that first desktop-published piece, or write the President of the United States a letter and get a response, your life changes. As a result, society changes too. It now can tap your talents, experience, and wisdom.

A Sense of Community

SeniorNet rose out of the desire to focus on the concept of "community" rather than on the concept of technology. In other words, how could technology help to create the sense of belonging to a community? The modern world does not always allow for the kind of connectedness that used to exist for people. We often don't know our neighbors, much less spend our evenings visiting with them on the front porch. Families live far apart and have overly busy lives. Friends move away. It's very easy to become isolated from others, often difficult to make new friends, and tempting to retreat into the television and a solitary lifestyle.

SeniorNet's experience has been that while people may go online initially for information, they *stay* online because of the friendships they develop and the support they receive from other members. We look to a community to define mores and traditions, to provide us with substantive information, and to create the kind of world we want to see. SeniorNet provides older adults with greater access to the tools and knowledge they need for community building and "world making." One SeniorNet member, Phil Bernheim, said it best, "Communities used to be geographic. Now they are communities of the mind, and we all have something to share."

The Evolution of SeniorNet

As mentioned earlier, SeniorNet had its origins in an informal research project begun in

From Research Study to SeniorNet

SeniorNet—as an online community—began in 1986 by connecting 20 people together on a small online service called Delphi. The idea was to create an online community connecting older adults from around the country and the world and allow them to share their interests and knowledge. That small electronic community was so successful that sponsors began to give the fledgling nonprofit group more and more grants, allowing it to bring in more and more seniors. Then, in 1990, SeniorNet teamed with America Online, opened the SeniorNet Forum on America Online, and reached many more thousands of older adults. Today, tens of thousands of seniors use SeniorNet for information, entertainment, support, exploration, and social interaction.

the summer of 1983. Researchers saw that a large component of the population (namely seniors) was getting no attention from the computer world. This raised a number of questions: Were seniors interested in computers? In what kinds of programs would they be interested? Did they have special needs in terms of hardware or software?

Communication Is Good for You

Who says expressing your feelings—electronically—is good for you? The experts, that's who.

In 1993, West Chester University, near Philadelphia, provided 14 nursing home residents between the ages 59 and 89 with computer training and access to the online service Prodigy. They used it to send e-mail, play games, and follow the stock market. After six months online, researchers found the group had become significantly less depressed and had actually gained in cognitive ability. "I had no idea there was such a wide, wide world out there," marveled one 76-year-old participant. "I was able to share my recipes and find out what the cheapest VCR was without leaving the building. This is the first time in six years that I have felt really useful."

The Best and the Brightest

To answer these questions, the University of San Francisco researchers began to give computer workshops in places like church basements and senior citizen centers, using inexpensive home computers. Within a short period of time, they had their answers. The students, ages 55–90, were everything an educator dreams of: bright, engaged, motivated, and hungry to learn. The researchers found that older adults brought an enormous amount of experience and knowledge to computing, along with a great deal of enthusiasm. After all, computers are simply tools of the mind—they help to create, calculate, write, organize, and (most importantly) to communicate.

The Benefits of SeniorNet Membership

SeniorNet can serve you better—and you are better served—with a membership. Here are some of the advantages you'll receive by joining this non-profit organization.

SeniorNet Offline

When you join SeniorNet, you receive the quarterly newsletter *Newsline*. *Newsline* is an outstanding source of member-contributed computing ideas, information about software and hardware, profiles of members, and updates on SeniorNet activities. It is also the place you can find out about all your SeniorNet benefits. It regularly publicizes member discounts, offers SeniorNet products, announces new Learning Center locations, and informs members about upcoming events.

SeniorNet Learning Centers

If you are fortunate enough to live near a SeniorNet Learning Center, your membership makes you eligible for free or low-cost courses in computer skills. There are currently 75 Learning Centers in the United States. There is also one in New Zealand. Small classes (usually no more than ten students) assemble for an eight-week course to learn about computer applications. The centers usually offer the following hands-on computer classes: Introduction to Computers, Word Processing, Going Online with SeniorNet, Spreadsheets, and Databases. Instruction is given by knowledgeable senior volunteers, who enjoy introducing others to the joys of computing.

Classes are *always* affordable. A six-week course on Microsoft Works at the San Jose Learning Center, for example, costs just $15!

The volunteer instructors are no longer surprised by the ardor their students exhibit. "They're more enthusiastic than youngsters I've taught," says senior volunteer Jack McKenchie.

Volunteers and the Learning Centers

The Learning Centers could not accomplish what they do without the dedication of volunteers. One such volunteer is Pete Petrides from Groton, Connecticut. Known online as MysticPete, Pete was a systems engineer for a company that built submarines. Pete worked for two years to find the local funding and support for the Learning Center at the Groton Senior Center. As of now, over 200 students have taken classes there. SNET of Connecticut is the local sponsor, Apple Computer donated Macintoshes and modems, and the Microsoft Corporation has donated copies of software. SeniorNet provides the *SeniorWorks* tutorials for the members to use. Pete says, "By the time the students graduate, there is not much that they can't tackle."

Another member, Mabel McConnel, took the idea of SeniorNet to Hawaii when she was 85 years old. Thanks to Mabel, there are centers on Maui, in Honolulu, and one at the Kokua Outpost. Mabel dedicated nine years of her life to volunteering at the SeniorNet centers. She specialized in teaching others how to do electronic advocacy—accessing bills from the State legislature and sending electronic mail to the White House and Congress.

The Learning Centers often sponsor other activities. These may include outreach programs where volunteers tutor at local elementary schools, as do the centers at the University of San Francisco and the Essex Community School in Vermont. Other centers, such as the Peoria program, offer outreach to homebound elderly. There, SeniorNet members install modems in the homes of frail, elderly people and provide personalized instruction on the process of getting online.

Publications

If you don't live anywhere near a Learning Center, SeniorNet publishes some excellent books to inspire and educate you, and they are available to members at discounted prices. The following list summarizes them.

- *The SeniorNet Source Book*—This book is a collection of creative ways in which SeniorNet members are using their computers. It is great for discovering how other seniors are enhancing their lives with their computers.

- *Portraits of Computer-Using Seniors*—This is another inspiring collection of senior profiles and their computer-based projects.

- *SeniorWorks*—This is a collection of step-by-step tutorials on Microsoft Works, an integrated software package that includes word processing, database and spreadsheet applications.

- *SeniorNet Guides*—This is a series of pamphlets that provide practical advice and specific details (like price and product names) about what to buy and how to get started in the computing world.

- *Going Online with SeniorNet*—This is a self-paced tutorial to help you learn to use SeniorNet Online and guide you through the Internet.

SeniorNet Online

You can reach SeniorNet online through a few different channels. Each access route offers different advantages. Here's where you can find SeniorNet.

SeniorNet Via America Online

SeniorNet has been online with America Online since 1990 and has enjoyed the same explosive growth on AOL that AOL itself has enjoyed. AOL currently has about 4.5 million members and projects that it will reach the 7 million mark by the end of 1997. That's a lot of people, and many of them are older adults. SeniorNet expects to continue to grow with AOL.

SeniorNet via the Microsoft Network (MSN)

In August 1995, SeniorNet joined with the Microsoft Network at its launch in conjunction with the release of Windows '95. SeniorNet has a different look on MSN than it has on AOL, but shares many similar features. There are, of course, forums on many subjects. One section, called Pathways to Learning, provides tutorials on using computers and software. In another section, Living Archives, members share memories of World War II, holiday traditions, and the like. MSN expects to cultivate a larger international user community and SeniorNet is looking forward to incorporating various cross-cultural aspects into its community.

On the Internet/World Wide Web

SeniorNet is always evolving and is in the process of establishing a dynamic presence on the World Wide Web (http://seniornet.org). As this Web site develops, SeniorNet will profile members and Learning Centers. It will introduce a multimedia magazine in which it will share member-generated articles and stories as well as information and trends about technology and aging. The SeniorNet Multimedia Showcase will focus on members and their computer projects. Seniors will be able to find out about software applications useful to older adults and review descriptions posted by other members on how these products are being used.

SeniorNet plans to link its home page on the World Wide Web with many other sites of interest to seniors, such as the Senior Computer Information Project (http://www.crm.mb.ca/scip), which is a Canadian site with dozens of relevant links. Other sites of interest, like the Social Security Home Page (http://www.ssa.gov), will also be linked to SeniorNet.

SeniorNet Forums

Figure 23–1 shows the screen you'll see when you type in the keyword **SeniorNet** on America Online. You can see that there are four main areas within SeniorNet, as well as various SeniorNet-sponsored projects and announcements. SeniorNet Forums is by far the largest part of SeniorNet, and it's where you'll find hundreds of member-initiated message boards on almost any topic imaginable. Here is a very small sample of SeniorNet forum topics:

Arts & Entertainment

Investments/Finance

Food, Drink & Recipes

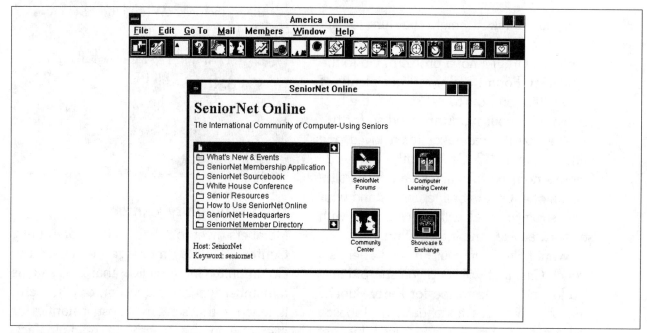

Figure 23–1

Welcome to SeniorNet on America Online

U.S. Military

Gardening

Books, Discussions, and Reviews

Widows and Widowers

Divorced Pals

Genealogy Research

Bridge Players

Alzheimer's/Dementia Support

Collecting

Language Clubs

Animal Friends

Politics

Senior Entrepreneurs

Travel

Writing

If you think it might be fun to put together a family tree, but don't quite know where to start, it's not a problem. Go to the Genealogy Forum and you'll get plenty of good advice on how to get started, the best software for your hardware, and so forth.

Are you the caretaker for a loved one with Alzheimer's? Or recently widowed? There's no need to deal with a difficult situation alone. Others online understand your daily struggles and will provide you with support, advice, and information.

Want to keep up your French? There's a French Club that will keep you sharp. Have you lost a favorite recipe for Party Punch? The one that calls for a dash of Tabasco and a quarter-cup of lemon juice? Just get into the Recipe Forum and you'll probably have the recipe before the day is out.

One very popular forum for beginners as well as advanced users is the Getting into Computers Forum. It is here that members ask questions about their hardware and software configurations or discuss topics such as "virtual reality" or scanners for digitizing photos. SeniorNet provides knowledgeable volunteer members who are well versed in computers to answer questions posed on the message board.

> ## Golden Rule:
>
> Try not to ask global questions like "How do I get started in genealogical research?" or "I think I want to start taking pictures. What kind of camera should I buy?" First, locate the applicable forum and read through the past postings. If you still have questions, they are much more likely to be informed questions, and therefore much more likely to get a quick response.

The Community Center

Members meet to "chat" in the Community Center. Unlike message boards, the Community Center is live; that is to say, as a member types in a question or comment, it reaches the screen almost instantly for everyone in the "room" to read. In fact, there is a "cocktail hour" every evening where members can engage in small talk, arrange to chat in a private room, and find other members with similar interests. It may seem a little disjointed at first, sort of like trying to follow four conversations at once. But with a little practice, you soon learn to filter out the other conversations and concentrate on your own. If you are shy about joining in, that's okay. "Lurkers" are welcome to just listen in.

"Chat rooms are a godsend for someone who's an invalid or otherwise shut in," says one member, "You can make friends here, friends that will look out for you." That is not just idle talk. Recently, online friends noticed that one of their members had not signed on for a few days. Concerned, they called the police in the town where she lived and asked that they investigate. The police found her, ill and disoriented, and got her to medical help.

There are regularly scheduled social and educational events in the Community Center. For example, on Saturdays at 11:00 A.M., the Diet Club meets, hosted by a SeniorNet member.

SeniorNet often invites a guest to the Community Center who will answer questions on issues of interest to seniors. Recently, members were able to "talk" to Senator Edward Kennedy about his view of the future of Medicare.

The Computer Learning Center

In the Computer Learning Center, SeniorNet publishes online tutorials that members can print and study. Articles might include a discussion of financial software, how to send e-mail to a subscriber of another online service, or information on computer viruses and software to protect against them. This area also has a Computer Tools section, in which you will find hundreds of programs, utilities, and text files to download—for free!

Showcase & Exchange

As the icon indicates, this area is an uploading and downloading area. Members can upload sounds, graphics they have created, recipes, transcripts of political speeches, copies of articles—anything they think others should know about or might be interested in. For example, one of SeniorNet's longtime members, Mike Moldeven, has uploaded a couple of well-written and idea-filled guides to communicating with one's grandchildren who live far away. Called *Too Far Away Grandma* and *A Grampa's Notebook,* they have been downloaded by many members who have used them to help establish and maintain online relationships with their children and grandchildren.

Joining SeniorNet

If you are interested in more information on SeniorNet but you aren't online yet, write to SeniorNet at

SeniorNet
One Kearny Street
San Francisco, CA 94108

or call

1-800-747-6848

or FAX

415-352-1260

If you are on America Online already, enter the keyword **SeniorNet** and find the membership application on the opening screen. There is also a membership application in the SeniorNet area of the Microsoft Network and one on the facing page.

Fees

The membership application at the end of this chapter describes the costs of membership. SeniorNet has a special arrangement with America Online in which new members pay a low monthly fee and get unlimited use of SeniorNet plus one hour per month of other America Online services.

In most urban and suburban areas in the United States there is a local telephone number for network access. However, members in Alaska, Hawaii, Puerto Rico, and Canada must also pay a 20¢ per minute surcharge at all times, unless they use an access number located in the continental United States (then long distance charges kick in).

In Closing...

The world is changing very fast, and it is one of SeniorNet's goals to become a resource for seniors in Cyberspace. But SeniorNet will never lose sight of the primary reason it exists—to be a true community of people. As in any good community, the residents share knowledge, give support, and help each other to stay involved. As one member said, "I never would have thought that you could actually download caring and empathy. But you can. I've seen it happen over and over again online."

When asked to respond to "What does SeniorNet mean to you?" in one of the forums, the answers were illuminating:

"I have been given the pleasure of another family—always ready to listen and help in any way," posted Sally B.

"Captured my heart, my time, my interest—and given this old guy some things to talk about," wrote PapaJohn.

"My three sons are computer engineers, and one of them insisted I buy a Mac to type the Garden Club's Cookbook. I didn't want the Mac and I didn't want the modem and I didn't want the subscription to SeniorNet he gave me for Christmas—but now I am really and truly hooked."

"Just because you retire, life isn't over. You can always learn new things and do new things."

"I'm an old lady, except when I'm online. Then I'm 37, blonde, and ready to roll!"

SeniorNet Membership Application

YES, I want to join SeniorNet, the nonprofit organization that empowers adults 55 and over to use computer technologies to benefit themselves and share their wisdom and knowledge with others. SeniorNet has over 16,000 members, publishes a variety of instructional materials, offers discounts on software and other computer-related products, and has 75 Learning Centers throughout the U.S. where senior volunteers teach other seniors. **PLEASE TYPE OR PRINT CLEARLY**

Type of Membership

Individual
- ❏ 1-year $35.00
- ❏ 2-years $50.00

Couple
- ❏ 1-year $40.00
- ❏ 2-years $65.00

With your membership you will receive the SeniorNet publication:

- ❏ *The SeniorNet Sourcebook*
  Describes creative computer projects undertaken by SeniorNet members to provide you with ideas on new ways to use computers.

SeniorNet Online

- ❏ I have a computer and a modem, and I want to join SeniorNet Online. Please send me the **FREE** software and information kit.

I own (a): ❏ Mac ❏ Windows ❏ DOS

- ❏ 3.5" disk ❏ 5.25" disk (only in DOS)

- ❏ I already have an America Online account.
  - ❏ My e-mail address is _____
- ❏ Please send me more detailed information.

For new accounts, the first month subscription to SeniorNet Online is **FREE** and includes 10 hours of access to other America Online (AOL) areas. The rate for SeniorNet Online is $9.95/month and includes unlimited access to the SeniorNet area plus 1 hour of other AOL services. Additional time online is billed at $2.95/hour.

senior❂net

Membership Information

Name: _____

Address: _____

City: _____

State: _____ Zip: _____

Phone: _____ Year of Birth: _____

Computer skills:
- ❏ Non-user   ❏ Intermediate
- ❏ Beginner   ❏ Advanced

Type of computer you own:
- ❏ Windows
- ❏ DOS
- ❏ Macintosh
- ❏ Other

Do you have CD-ROM?   ❏ Yes   ❏ No
Do you have a modem?   ❏ Yes   ❏ No

Payment Information

- ❏ *Check enclosed.*

Please make checks payable to SeniorNet.

- ❏ *Bill my credit card.*
- ❏ Visa   ❏ Mastercard   ❏ AMEX   ❏ Discover

Card #: _____ Exp. _____

Name on card: _____

Signature: _____

For fastest service, call: 800-747-6848
Or fax your order to: 415-352-1260

Or mail your application to:

SeniorNet
1 Kearny Street, 3rd Floor , San Francisco, CA 94108
415-352-1210

INDEX

The Books to Use When There's No Time to Lose

Computer Fundamentals for Complicated Lives

Whether you set aside an *evening*, a *lunch hour*, or reach for a **Busy People** guide as you need it, you're guaranteed to save time with Windows 95 and its associated productivity applications. Organized for a quick orientation to Windows 95, Word, Excel, Access, and the Internet, each **Busy People** title offers exceptional time-saving features and has the right blend of vital skills and handy shortcuts that you must know to get a job done quickly and accurately. Full-color text make the going easy and fun.

Written by a busy person (like you!) with a skeptic's view of computing, these opinionated, well-organized, and authoritative books are all you'll need to master the important ins and outs of Windows 95 and other best-selling software releases—without wasting your precious hours!

**Windows 95
for Busy People**
by Ron Mansfield
$22.95 USA
ISBN: 0-07-882110-X
Available Now

**Word for Windows 95
for Busy People**
by Christian Crumlish
$22.95 USA
ISBN: 0-07-882109-6
Available Now

**Excel for Windows 95
for Busy People**
by Ron Mansfield
$22.95 USA
ISBN: 0-07-882111-8
Available Now

**The Internet
for Busy People**
by Christian Crumlish
$22.95 USA
ISBN: 0-07-882108-8
Available Now

**Access for Windows
95 for Busy People**
by Alan Neibauer
$22.95 USA
ISBN: 0-07-882112-6
Available Now

To Order, Call 1-800-822-8158

OSBORNE

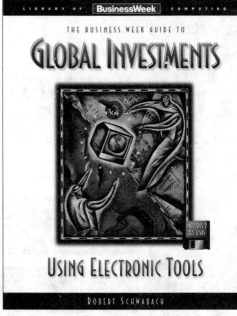

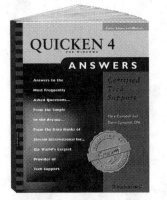
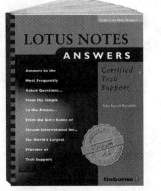
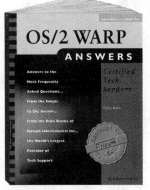

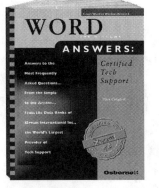
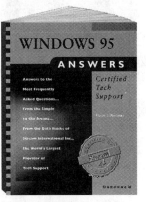

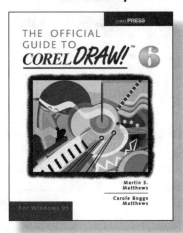